Pratinav ~~~

Islam in Histor

Most of the essays included in this volume were originally published in the South Asian Studies Association of Australia (SASA) journal, *South Asia*, special issue, vol. XXII, 1999. The publishers thank SASA for allowing them to reprint these essays.

Islam in History and Politics
Perspectives from South Asia

Edited by

ASIM ROY

OXFORD
UNIVERSITY PRESS

OXFORD
UNIVERSITY PRESS

Oxford University Press is a department of the University of Oxford.
It furthers the University's objective of excellence in research, scholarship,
and education by publishing worldwide. Oxford is a registered trademark of
Oxford University Press in the UK and in certain other countries

Published in India by
Oxford University Press
2/11 Ground Floor, Ansari Road, Daryagnj, New Delhi 11 002, India

Öxford University Press 2006

The moral rights of the author have been asserted

First published 2006
Oxford India Paperbacks 2008

ISBN-13: 978-0-19-569836-7
ISBN-10: 0-19-569836-3

Typeset in Naurang 10/12
by Excellent Laser Typesetters, Pitampura, Delhi 110 034
Printed in India by Replika Press Pvt. Ltd.

Contents

Preface and Acknowledgements

I

For all kinds of reasons, studies in Islam have always been a delicate and contentious matter. This is especially true for those that raise issues in the nature and meanings of the faith in space and time, whether internally from the perspectives of the believers, individually and collectively, or externally from that of the non-believers or outsiders. In the current state of a phenomenal global preoccupation and continual engagement with Islam, there is a resultant feeling of a 'siege mentality' shared by almost all over-a-billion strong votaries of the Islamic faith. This makes Islamic studies even more hazardous or perhaps this task may even be set aside as another run-of-the-mill product.

We feel, nonetheless, keen about waving our flag with some justifications. Much of this intellectual exercise associated with the fierce debates and discussions on contemporary Islam, raging for quite some time on a global scale, has been at a level that appears largely uninformed, superficial, and often prejudiced—spawning out sweeping, cavalier, and judgmental opinions. Such interventions confuse and incite people more than they make them informed and understand the issues better, looking at them from alternative perspectives. It has become abundantly clear now even for the most optimists that no amount of bloody hunting and killing of the 'terrorists',[1] or forcible 'regime changes', or shoving down 'democracy' down the throats of distrustful and angry millions by its champions holding guns in their other hands is either going to stop suicide-bombings or make democratic citizens out of those millions any time soon. How many of us are really convinced about the logic and strategy of a 'final solution' by killing those who are ready anyway to die and are dying with a smile on their faces? There must be something frightfully missing, in our understanding of such minds as well as in our perception of this desperate and tragic, mother of all crises of modern times. We cannot indeed even begin to get to grips with the problem until we gain a better understanding of its roots. While these conflicts are glibly presented as rooted in historical memory of the Crusades, it is conveniently overlooked that so much of this problem is of modern, and even of recent origins traceable to colonial and postcolonial politics as also social-economic and religious-cultural dislocations, wrongs and discontent. Again, as people turn the focus on the shibboleth of an apocalyptic clash between the Islamic and Western civilizations, popular today as 'anti-Western *jihad*', they seem blissfully oblivious of the fact that since the second wave of Islamism and Islamic revivalist and violent movements in the post-Second World War decades, the thrust of militant anger and resistance was not directed at the West, but at the authoritarian, self-serving, and elitist Muslim nationalist leaders of Egypt, Syria, and Iraq.

Informed knowledge and distancing oneself from the half-truths and untruths cooked and dished out from the citadels of power and wealth are the pre-conditions for getting to grips with truth in history. The importance of alternative perspectives seeking to rise above distortions of historical truth is precisely what we have generally brought to bear on, and canvassed for our task in this volume, relative to the complexities of our specific issues and circumstances of Islamic history and politics in the domain of South Asia.

There is a second even more significant consideration underlying our claim in behalf of this volume on South Asian Islam. Facing the most threatening crisis of our time, with real potentials for its indefinite continuation into the future, we strongly feel that the need of the moment is to understand that the problem—almost universally perceived as revolving around Islam and Muslim militancy is really not one between 'us' and 'them'—it is a common problem not just facing us all, we all bear responsibility for it. An understanding of this nature presupposes one's preparedness to listen to the other as well as its concomitant value of tolerance. This applies not only to the non-Muslim world vis-à-vis the Muslim, but also to Muslims among themselves.

Had there ever been a reason for re-emphasizing and seeking to recover the genius of Islamic tolerance, adaptability, and creative dynamism in bringing an incredibly diverse Muslim world together—a capacity that is a common knowledge to any student of historical Islam—unquestionably the need for it is far greater now. The general predisposition in the non-Muslim world to see Islam as a monolithic religious culture ruled by the scripture, combined with the present hegemonic challenge of the Islamists, fundamentalists, and *jihadi*s, seeking the rule of 'sharia' over all aspects of modern Muslim life have witnessed a very significant heightening of a highly unitary perception of Islam. This development is hardly likely to be helpful for today's Muslim world that would have a desperate need to come out of it's siege mentality and meet others for constructive dialogues on an even ground.

The impact of this refurbishing of the notions of unitary Islam has been particularly hard, deleterious, and regressive for the Muslim communities with rich and diverse regional cultural traditions. In the changed circumstances of the Muslim world today, liberal Islam would rather be seeking re-affirmation of its freedom to define Muslims in the way they have understood and accepted Islam. Given the need and the challenge to forge a consensual understanding of the unity and dynamism of Islam within the variety, plurality, and creativity of the Muslim civilization, the relevance, importance, and potential of the Islamic model, as it evolved in history in South Asia, cannot be overestimated. Studies in the general, and more importantly, in the regional settings of South Asia, such as in Bengal, clearly reveal the tradition of tolerance, and creative adaptability of Muslims in South Asia, 'living together separately' in the Indic world of unity in diversity.[2] It is about this spirit and tradition of Islamic tolerance and the story of legions of Muslim living for over a millennium in a proverbially diverse plural world of South Asia that the troubled Muslim world of our time, as also the rest of the world, would find strength and hope to hear. While the entire Muslim world has been groping for an answer from their own tradition that the rest of the world is willing to listen, the historic opportunity has been presented to South Asia to step out in front and remind themselves, along with all others, of the glorious tradition of tolerance and accommodation enshrined in the history and politics of the region. The present volume is a symbolic and humble effort on our part to raise South Asia's consciousness as a paradigmatic example to rise up to this global crisis and challenge. The volume does not necessarily or directly ask or answer all the raging questions about today's Islam and Muslim. For the discerning readers, however, there are innumerable and invaluable insights into the minds and works of Muslims in South Asia for mapping, probing, and grasping the backdrop of seminal issues and developments through the colonial to postcolonial centuries. Over all, these sources clearly reveal a pattern characteristic of people living together for ages generally peacefully in a plural world with their differences as well as commonalities. These essays together also bring into sharp relief the changing and static meanings of being Muslim in a world that kept changing around them in many areas, but remained unchanged in other respects through a complex process of transition from pre-colonial through colonial to the contemporary states.

II

The essays included in this volume have, with some exception, been the outcome of the first major international symposium on South Asian Islam held in Australia, presented at the forum of the South Asia section of the Asian Studies Association of Australia Biennial Conference, 1996. Organized primarily with the assistance of the professional human and other resources of the South Asian Studies Association of Australia (SASA), it attracted generous sponsorship from the Australia-India Council, the National Centre for South Asian Studies, Melbourne, and the Asian Studies Association of Australia (ASAA). It also attracted a number of leading international scholars in the field— including, in alphabetical order, Javeed Alam, Paul Brass, Mushirul Hasan, Zoya Hasan, Barbara Metcalf, Thomas R. Metcalf, Gyan Pandey, and Francis Robinson, together with a large local contingent of Australian and New Zealand-based scholars. Over fifteen panels and fifty papers were altogether presented at the symposium, all of which were not included, for various reasons, in their later publication in a Special Issue of the SASA Journal,[3] in accordance with the terms and conditions of the SASA-initiated conferences and symposia.

The far too limited international accessibility of the journal version of a major contribution of its kind led to extensive queries, internationally, from scholars and researchers in the matter of its publication in a book form. I am most thankful to the relevant SASA official, Associate Professor Ian Copland, Editor of *South Asia*, for having extended his fullest cooperation in this matter and giving me a free hand to find and negotiate with any likely publisher, subject to due acknowledgment of its earlier publication in *South Asia*. I am also pleased and obliged to the Oxford University Press, New Delhi, for this publication, in particular to Manzar Khan, for his initial interest in the proposal. My deepest and warmest appreciation goes to Shashank Sinha for his infinite patience and understanding of various problems—personal and otherwise—cropping up at various stages in the preparation of the revamped manuscript and slowing me down. For showing similar patience and consideration at a later stage, Somodatta Roy deserves my highest appreciation. Over all, Oxford University Press has, for me, set up a model of fast-tracking a major publication since the submission of the proposal.

At a very personal level, I do need to express my deepest feelings for my family whom I always found closer as the going got tougher. I should particularly mention my two daughters, Konya and Tanaya, both most brilliant professionals, whose intellectual company and the power of critiquing my research and writing have been as much a source of pride for me as it may easily become a source of envy for any comparable academic parents.

Endnotes

1. This highly confusing and inappropriate label has since been changed, as mentioned below in the Introduction, by the US and other Western governments to 'extremists', 'radicals', or 'militants', the most popular substitute now being 'jihadis'.
2. See, Mushirul Hasan and Asim Roy (eds), *Living Together Separately. Cultural India in History and Politic*s (New Delhi, 2005). The issues of partition (1947) and communal violence in the colonial and post-colonial times may, understandably enough, cast long and dark shadows in the minds of some of our readers, in relation to the matters of 'tolerance' and 'adaptability', and so on. Leaving aside the question that these issues are the most complex, multi-dimensional, and contentious ones in the historiography of Modern South Asia, our particular concern has been that of an 'historical tradition' of tolerance as well as the question of its 'recovery', the implications of the latter is there for all to comprehend.
3. Asim Roy and Howard Brasted (eds), *Islam in History and Politics. A South Asian Perspective*, *South Asia* (Journal of South Asian Studies), vol. XXII, Special Issue, 1999.

Introduction

Asim Roy

I

One may easily be excused, in the present ambience of global politics, for wanting to turn away from even a mere hint of another intellectual exercise on Islamic history and politics. The world has been deluged in recent times with all kinds of material on Islam and Muslim, churned out relentlessly by the print and visual media, leaving aside the relatively smaller output of authentic academic contributions and an infinite variety and volume of interventions from the so-called 'experts' on Islam and Muslims.[1] Islam has indeed never been so ubiquitous as it has become in recent years. Its presence is easily found today in every nook and corner of contemporary life—globally, nationally, and locally—dominating the media, academia, polity, economy, and society, including the discourses and deliberations in public places, parks and pubs, and even within individual households around the lounge and dining table.

What is behind this current obsessive preoccupation with Islam? The answers are given and found in legions, but the commonest and the most popular explanation would surely embrace the nine-letter word— 'Terrorism'—a word that creates more confusion than offer real meaning and understanding. Given the unprecedented and kaleidoscopic rise of Islam to the focus of global attention, raising some central issues about Islam in the process, especially since the stunning and tragic event of 11 September 2001 (henceforward 'the 9/11'), no serious academic intervention in any field of Islamic history and politics— global, regional, or national—can ill-afford to escape these questions. Never before in history has the world cast Islam totally in this manner into a cauldron, heedless of its distinctive features and attributes

historically evolved through centuries in its regional settings and formulations. Today's world would need to be persuaded hard to recognize
Islam in South Asia, and for that matter in any other non-Western Asian
region, as any more than a geographical extension of the so-called
Islamic heartland of West Asia.[2] Historiography of Islam seems to have
turned a full cycle. Scholars on South Asian Islam urging an inductive-
regional approach have fought tenaciously over a long period to wrest
and secure its distinctive form and place from the stranglehold of the
Islamists and the champions of monolithic Islam.[3] The Islamic radicals
and their recent western opponents together have knocked off the
national boundaries of South Asian Islam by reinforcing the foundation
of Islamic monolith. The South Asianists in the Islamic contexts are,
therefore, confronted with the same basic questions as their counterparts everywhere in the Muslim world, and called upon to find their own
answers for those. More importantly, South Asia has not been immune
from this Islamic upsurge, rather parts of it emerged as an epicentre of
militant Islamic movements, as discussed below.

At the core of the popular perceptions, across the world, of this
intriguing and explosive situation in recent years there is a strong sense
of Islam being a source as well as an object of challenge and crisis. Such
perceptions however, are not new about Islam in history. Muslims in
history may perhaps have had more than their rightful share of crises
and challenges since the dawn of their history, as Prophet Muhammad
was forced to take his incipient group of faithfuls to safety (1 A.H [ijira]/
AD 622) from Mecca to Medina, and defend later the growing but
fledgling community from the destructive challenges of the non-Muslim. That the rise of Islam was perceived as a threat by medieval
Christianity is recorded well in history, and is clearly evidenced by the
'scurrilities of medieval polemic and lampoon' and Muhammad's
demonization as a 'false god', a 'false prophet', and a 'cunning and self-
seeking impostor'. One widespread medieval legend even presented
him as 'an ambitious and frustrated Roman Cardinal', who 'sought an
alternative career as a false prophet.'[4]

One of the two greatest crises and challenges to confront the Muslim
in history has been the non-Muslim Mongol invasion and conquest of
a very large part of the Muslim world, extending over central, west, and
south Asia, as well as its heartlands, resulting in the fall of Baghdad
and the Abbasid Caliphate (AD 1258). This particular threat, potentially
very serious, was fortuitously averted, with the wholesale conversion
of those conquerors to Islam. The second one, far more powerful and
comprehensive than the Mongol invasion, came with the colonial might
of the modern west. This challenge was not resolved that easily by

conversion and hence remained effectively the first incidence of real subjugation of the Muslim world by the non-Muslim. It is not surprising, therefore, that this encounter has forced Muslim into the myriad experiences of colonial domination and exploitation in the nineteenth and twentieth centuries, and has since continued to encircle and impinge on their lives and culture in various forms.

In recent times, the debacle of the USSR and the consequent elimination of the communist 'threat' to the hegemony of western capitalism, saw the steady emergence of the most serious external challenge to Islam in the resurrection of its old perceived 'threat'. Slowly but steadily, the 'evil' communist Soviet imperial system and ideology found its replacement in an equally 'evil threat' to western values and institutions of democracy, free will, human rights, and so on. It came in the form of an Islamic ideology and movement variously branded, in the western media and political parlance, as Islamic 'fundamentalism', 'radicalism', 'militancy', 'extremism', 'resurgence', 'Islamism', and 'political Islam'. The spectre of a 'fanatical' and warring Islam sweeping across the world, directly challenging the western political and cultural dominance, often posed as an apocalyptic civilizational conflict, has emerged as a central concern in the post-Soviet west. In the few years immediately following the Soviet disintegration, Khomenian Iran, Palestinian Al-Hamas, Lebanese Hizbullah, Islamic Brotherhood of Egypt, Islamic Salvation Front in Algeria, National Islamic Front of Sudan, Taliban in Afghanistan, Mujahideen of Jama'at-i Islam in Pakistan, India, and Bangladesh and Jumma Islamiyah of Indonesia, Moros of the Philippines, together with the religiously concerned and sensitive Muslims in many other western and Asian countries, altogether came to create a massive source of 'hype' in the global media and politics. Then came in quick succession, in the new millennium, the daring aggressions of the Islamic militants spearheaded by Al-Q'aida and other Islamic Jihadis, mounting a series of assaults on western and Asian countries—attacks on the World Trade Centre and rather significantly, on the Pentagon (11 September 2001), the Madrid bombing (March 2004), Bali bombings (October 2002 and September 2004), the successive bomb explosions targeting the London transport system (July 2005)—all these pulverizing experiences brutally challenged the icon of western power and dominance. With the end of the Cold War, if Francis Fukuyama saw history buried under the rubble of the Berlin Wall and asked us to 'witness' not just the passing of a particular period of post-war history, but 'the end of history' as such, 'the endpoint of mankind's ideological evolution', he is squarely proved short-sighted and wrong within a mere decade or so.

In the wake of this militant aggression, the stereotyping of Islam and Muslims at the global level, together with the unprecedented pressure and indignities brought to bear on this community as a whole under the specious, dubious, and ill-defined label of 'terrorism' have brought about a crisis for the votaries of Islam, the like of which is not found in the past history of Islam. Almost all Western European countries have, it is reported, an 'increasingly popular anti-Muslim platform in their societies,' and Germany, France, Holland, Britain, and Italy have all seen 'a rise in anti-Muslim feeling and incidents in society, as well as in strongly anti-Muslim and anti-immigrant statements by politicians'. For lots of Europeans, who 'associate Muslims with poor, violent ethnic neighborhoods', 'Islam is the cause of the problem', and 'they blame the religion and its adherents not only for social problems at home, but global trends like terrorism.'[5]

It is generally unknown and often overlooked that, prior to the 9/11, the general intolerance towards Muslims in the US had reached such a proportion as to call for some Senators as well as Members of the House of Representative to move a Senate as well as a separate House Resolution in 1999 (Senate Resolution 133: 'A Resolution Supporting Religious Tolerance Towards Muslims'). Both Resolutions were referred to their respective Committee on Judiciary. Senate Resolution was passed unanimously in late July 2000. The House Resolution came up to the Subcommittee on the Constitution, but regrettably, it was rejected at the Committee level. A columnist of the Pioneer Planet reported:

> ...several Jewish and Christian groups have been protesting the passage of this resolution. These groups did much behind-the-scene lobbying asking that the resolution be rewritten or removed from the Congressional docket altogether.'[6]

It may be more than a coincidence in measuring the depth and spread of the growing anti-Muslim mentalities in the post-Soviet decades that India saw, in 1992, the stunning destruction of the historic Babri Mosque by the Hindu fanatics, followed, in 2002, by the Gujarat massacre leading to a mass killing of Muslims by fanatical Hindus, the two most brutal aggressions ever perpetrated on the Muslim minority in India by the saffron-robed champions of militant Hinduism with clear evidence of criminal connivance at the governmental level.

II

If the issue of polarity between the 'secular west' and the 'religion-centred Muslim states and societies' has been simmering for centuries,

Bin Laden's stunning intervention on the 9/11 in the name of 'sacred duty' not only gave a violent turn to this debate but sealed as well the question for many. Here was the final proof of a religiously inspired community in action, if any further substantiation was at all required. This position has ready appeal as impeccable for many, and seems right as far as it goes. It puts a rather different gloss to this position to know that the demands or grievances couched in terms of the 'sacred' are patently 'political' for many others. Bin Laden's first telecast of 7 October 2001, after the event of 11 September gave three reasons for the attacks—presence of the US soldiers on the sacred land of Muslims in Arabia, Jewish occupation of Palestinian land, and suppression of the Palestinians, with perceived connivance of the US Government, and finally, the Iraq War.

There is an extraordinary degree of vagueness and confusion about what constitutes the core of Islamism, or Islamic radicalism, or political Islam. Opinions are distinctly polarized between the normative, or essentialist view of religiously inspired action and the 'instrumentalist' perception of socio-politically motivated secular source of apparently religious action. The nature of the problem is clearly underscored by a recent and rather significant shift in the US official attitude in favour not only of replacing the meaningless term 'terrorism', which means all things to all men, but also rejecting identification between the so-called 'terrorism' and 'fundamentalism'. The informed academia has always been dismissive of this facile popular identification of the two. Religious fundamentalism in its accepted sense of a return to and affirmation of the final authority and inerrancy of the scripture or fundamentals of a religion as well as claiming a monopoly over truth, has rarely been a significant component of the radical and militant agenda of political Islam. It is quite suggestive that this equation is now considered inappropriate even in the ranks of US Defence Academy and the CIA, being replaced by terms such as religious 'extremists' and 'radicals'. One wonders as to what extent has the rapidly growing profile of Christian fundamentalism across the US religious-political spectrum been a determinant in this changing attitude.

The current wave of Islamic radicalism defies any simple answer. It is clearly rooted in both religious and secular grounds and is an outcome of both internal and external factors, that is, reasons originating from within the Islamic community and those imposed from outside it. It is important to bear in mind that the dissociation between 'fundamentalism' and 'extremism'/'militancy' made by the US and later adopted by other western governments, is not based on their recognition that the extremist agenda precludes religious purpose and motivation. Both the

US and UK governments, on the contrary, have lost no opportunity of condemning the attacks on the western religious, cultural, and political systems and the values informing them. Discerning observers of the so-called 'war on terrorism' since the 9/11 could not have overlooked a general disregard on the part of the governments and media to turn the focus on the clearly articulated 'political' demands consistently put forward by the *Mujahideen* or Jihadis. We have already raised the relevant issue of Bin Laden's telecast after the event of the 9/11, making clear political demands with a religious overtone. This is a fine example indeed of Muslim political demands intersecting with religious concerns. Others however, continue to raise questions. In a strikingly evocative style, Oliver McTernan affirms that none of the responses and reactions to the 9/11 and its fall out 'do justice to the complexity of the growing phenomenon of faith-based violence' and asks:

> Who can claim to understand fully the minds and motives of those young, educated and talented men, all of whom spent the last months of their lives meticulously planning the destruction of themselves and thousands of others? Who can claim with certainty that it was grievance, real or imagined, and not their profoundly held religious beliefs that motivated their use of commercial aircraft to commit mass murder....[7]

Drawing together the examples of Mohamed Atta, one of the principal architects of the 9/11, and Richard Reid, the British 'shoe bomber', McTernan drives home his central concern:

> These two young men, who came from completely different ethnic & social backgrounds, were united in their readiness to sacrifice their own lives, evidently believing themselves to be on a sacred mission and acting on God's authority.... Given this mindset, I doubt if the world will ever succeed in completely eliminating the threat of the faith-inspired terrorist.[8]

He moves on further to take a position, which appears to contradict his initial guarded stance, as he strongly urges clear recognition that 'religion can be an actor in its own right and should not be dismissed as a surrogate for grievance, protest, greed, or political ambition.'[9] One can use his own words against his position, 'who can claim with certainty'?

Most people would be naturally inclined, understandably enough, to seek religious meaning and significance in all multi-faceted developments in the Muslim countries, and this has precisely been the case with radical Islamism, which to them is what it says to be—religious in its origins, inspirations, and expressions. It is not for us so much a question of rejecting this popular perception as revealing its inadequacies and simplistic nature. What appears strikingly religious in both form and meaning may not necessarily be essentially religious in inspiration. It is now widely known throughout the Muslim world that Islam is being systematically pressed into secular use by not only Muslim governments, but also people and groups who are opposed to those governments. Many people described as 'fundamentalists' are very far from the actual fundamentals of the religion that they claim to espouse, as noted above. Islam has proved itself a powerful political tool. Religion in South Asia, as perhaps elsewhere, has often been found to conceal secular concerns: transcendental symbols were often, in reality, nothing more than convenient covers for not so elevated mundane interests. One could so easily be misled by the religious symbolism of political Islam. People on the opposite side of the spectrum in this debate, seeking to read exclusively or essentially 'secular' meanings into actions carrying 'Islamic' labels and attributes, are often found to miss out or misread the hidden religious core or the subtle religious implications of a Muslim 'political' action. [10]

Further, there is very little awareness of the inner divergences and complexities in the religious contents of Islamism. The Islamic contents of their agenda are substantially divergent and dissimilar. It is possible to see in all this a broad revivalistic spirit and urge, but no agreement about what is to be revived. The understandings of the pristine 'purity' and 'simplicity' of Islam are not one and the same. There are many different versions of the 'golden age' in Islam. With different groups and interests in Islam, different models and degrees of Islamization have been canvassed, and each ultimately was designed to suit their particular purpose and interest. Hence, the process is often rather 'selective'. Particular matters of *shari'a* are picked up or ignored to justify matters of specific concerns and interests.

III

We need to go no farther than South Asia to identify the cross-purposes to which the call of 'Islamic fundamentalism' is pressed into service by people in government and outside it. Here there is no dearth of examples of Islam being deployed to foster national unity and integration, as well as to suppress, where necessary, legitimate assertions and demands of ethnic nationalism. Islam is also found in this region to legitimize authoritarian regime, and suppress democratic aspirations and movements of the people. Conversely, Muslims in opposition to an undemocratic regime, resort to the Islamic ideology in defence of their objectives. There is on the other hand, clear evidence of the instrumental use of Islam in either maintaining or acquiring political power as is the case, by either winning the confidence or neutralizing and weakening the

Muslim clergy, the *ulama*. Above all, the recent surge of Muslim government-sponsored Islamism is often induced by the lure of petro-dollar as well as that of augmenting foreign reserve through a massive export of skilled and unskilled labour to the rich and expanding job markets of West Asia. The social-psychological appeal of a puritanical form of Islam, at a time of socio-economic stresses and strains, has been underlined in various sociological micro-studies. A massive dislocation of life inherent in the process of a profound social and economic change in the developing countries came, on one hand, to accentuate the role of religion as a psychological anchorage for the destitute, deprived and marginalized, and project, on the other, religious authenticity as a bond of unity and a badge of identity in a strange, harsh, and hostile social environment. Idealistic youth often turns to the pure and simple faith as a reaction against the materialistic life style of the comfortable and privileged classes and against all-round corruption and erosion of values. The forces and circumstances casting Islamic radicalism to its present fiercely controversial mould are indeed as complex as these are diverse and multi-faceted.

A recent probe into the minds of Muslims living in Europe, the results of which appeared in the New York Times, offers some fresh insights into their makings and workings. The findings, barring specif-ics, are not generally dissimilar from the realities obtained globally where Muslims are placed in a minority situation, as in India. The reference is here to those young Muslims in Europe who have come to be known as 'home-grown jihadis'. A Nixon Center study of 373 mujahideen in Western Europe and North America between 1993 and 2004 found more than twice as many Frenchmen as Saudis and more Britons than Sudanese, Yemenites, Emiratis, Lebanese, or Libyans. Fully a quarter of the jihadis it listed were western European nationals.[11] The *New York Times* report identifies several groups of Muslims in major European countries, with varying perceptions of and attitudes toward their integration into the countries they live in, corresponding to their respective social, economic, and cultural standing. There is the first generation of Muslim, postcolonial migrants from former Euro-pean colonies, like Indians and Pakistanis in Britain, of largely working-class background, who came to rebuild Europe after World War II. They lived 'on the margins of European society in territorial, cultural, and symbolic ghettos' and stayed poor. They didn't make it in the new society, and kept a 'myth of return to the home country'.

The European-born children of the first generation immigrants have been educated in European schools, speak Western languages fluently and are 'more assertive than their parents.' The vast number of these generally young Muslims does not share the same upbringing and hence common views and attitudes. There is, among them, a small percentage of socially successful 'Muslim yuppies', generally well known and projected as 'those who made it'. They are largely secularized and assimilated. Once Muslims move out of their working-class neighbourhoods and into the ranks of the middle-class, they tend to favour assimilation. They are 'not perceived as Muslim any more', and 'not interested in using their religion as a social and political marker.'

The less accomplished segment of the second generation has experienced barriers to acceptance by European society, including widespread discrimination at every level of society, from housing to education to cultural practices. They feel there is no way for them to fully integrate into society, so they want to 'carve out their own identity'. The 'perceived moral permissiveness of Western culture' strengthens in them the urge 'to assert Muslim culture aggressively and maintain the boundaries around Islam.' Facing challenges of this nature, Islam everywhere is fast becoming a 'protest identity', urging even the non-devout Muslim to observe conformity to orthodox and conservative Islamic practices such as the *halal* (religiously sanctioned) food in public venues to show their separation from the non-Muslim societies, and wearing the *hijab* (the head covering). Practices such as these have come to be infused in the Muslim mind with multi-symbolic meaning—an icon of distinct identity, a form of 'protest', and a way to 'resist'. A very large group of young descendants of European Muslim immigrants have thus remained generally aloof from the wider society and 'quiet' adherents to ancestral religious and cultural tradition.

All the young Muslim groups mentioned above stand in sharp contrast with a potentially radical young group, who 'keep western society at arm's length', and keep to the 'food, culture, music, and television of their home countries'. Moreover, they incline towards a fundamentalist form of Islam over the traditional Islam of their ancestors. It is tantamount to a 'reinvention of the religion, a typically born-again phenomenon' that 'gives a value to their uprootedness.' All this, however, can detract nothing from the stark socio-economic and the consequent psychological dimensions of the growth of radicalism among these young Muslims, who are 'poor' and live in 'crime-prone' and 'segregated neighbourhoods like the British council estates or the French banlieues.' The issue is largely linked to the problems of 'destitute neighbourhoods'. Some of the suburbs, or banlieues, outside Paris with sizeable Muslim populations have a 17 per cent unemployment rate, compared to a 9.4 per cent national rate. These are the neighbourhoods, where young Muslims are increasingly becoming radicalized. The critically important attribute of this section of the Muslim population has been that they grow alienated from both their parents' culture and the culture of Europe. A growing and strong sense of alienation of this nature together with the perceived anti-Islamic and neo-colonial policies of the western governments, spearheaded by the USA, created the siege mentality and rebellious response of this group. A number of radical Muslim suicide-bombers in Europe as elsewhere in the Muslim world are known to share their respective unhappy social-economic and cultural-political experiences.[12]

Naturally enough, with its highest proportion of Muslims in the world, South Asia reverberated with the global impact of this Islamic challenge. Pakistan's involvement with the ideological and military training of the Taliban cadres, initially with massive US support against the 'Evil Soviet Empire', continuing in the later period after the Soviet defeat as an anti-US and anti-west movement, is a well-trodden field. Despite Pakistani President Musharraf offering an olive branch to the US and the western allies and committing himself to the elimination of Al-Qa'ida, Taliban, and other Islamic radicals from his country, the remote and highly inaccessible mountainous region between Pakistan and Afghanistan has continued to remain a stronghold of the extremists. From this vantage point these outfits have continually managed, until very recently, to organize violent activities against their enemies in the neighbouring regions such as Afghanistan and India, and also set up militant cells to unleash violence in countries like Bangladesh.

One country that has not, until recently, been actively associated with militant extremism is Bangladesh, which is now on the fast track of becoming a major outpost of militant Islam linked to some of the key centres of Islamic militancy in South, Southeast, and West Asia.[13] This is a country, which has the third highest Muslim population after Indonesia and Pakistan, is half the population of the United States, but only about the size of the state of Iowa or Illinois. The 'radical' transformation and growing strength of the forces of Islamization in this country had not been as sudden as it is often assumed. The anti-secularists had shown their hands almost as early as the euphoria of the nation born in blood (in 1971), died down.[14] The early dream of the nation and its founding father and President, Shaikh Mujibur Rahman, for a 'secular, democratic, and socialist people's republic' was shattered by bullets from a cohort of cowardly army officers operating under the cover of night that almost wiped out his entire family, including him (1975). The event ushered in a period of coups and counter-coups, military dictatorship as well as its civilianized disguise, and weak and squabbling democratic governments that saw a steady rise of both conservative and Islamist forces, culminating in the formation of the present government in a compromising situation.

In recent times the nation has turned into a haven for Islamic radicals. It is important to bear in mind that Bangladesh is covered by jungles which allow radical Islamists to hide their training and operations from sophisticated surveillance and helps to protect them from the threat of capture—elaborate escape and evasion plans are in place. The violence perpetrated by the extremists has become endemic in the country, being responsible for scores of bombings and killings targeting the democratic, secular, progressive, enlightened forces, patriots, freedom fighters, free thinkers, writers, cinema halls, cultural organizations, theatre, drama, circus, minorities, and indigenous people of Bangladesh; Ahmadiya Muslims & their mosques, temples, churches, popular shrines of Muslims saints resorted by both Muslims and non-Muslims. Major victims in public rallies include Shah A.M.S. Kibria, a freedom fighter, diplomat, under-secretary general of the UN and the finance minister in the previous Awami League government, whose assassination followed a similar attempt on the life of the ex-Prime Minister, Shaikh Hasina Wazed, of the Awami League and daughter of Shaikh Mujib, resulting in twenty-two deaths. The spate of bombings culminated in the 'Operation Purple' of 17 August 2005, which saw massive and coordinated bomb blasts exploding 459 bombs in half an hour, covering 63 of 64 districts of Bangladesh. It is estimated that there were more bombings in Bangladesh in 2004, an average of one per month, than in the previous five years combined. The new tactic of suicide bombing has come shortly after reports that Bangladeshi police believed that up to 2000 suicide bombers were ready to go operational. South Asian analysts have long noted that the country would be ripe for Al-Qa'ida but little effort has been made to stop their development and penetration of the country. *Time* magazine has been banned from reporting in the country since 2002. Alex Perry, its South Asia bureau chief, ran a piece exposing the government's lack of response to the build up of Islamist militants with links to Al-Qa'ida. It is estimated that 172 Islamist militant camps are currently operating in Bangladesh, some of these camps are believed to house activists from Jemaah Islamiyah, the Indonesian militant group responsible for the Bali bombings, and other activities in the region. Pakistani groups such as Lashkar-i Taiba and Jaish-i Muhammad, both with links to Al-Qa'ida, are also believed to be operating in the country.

Al-Qa'ida's link with Bangladesh has been detected as early as 1998. The most threatening group is the Harakat ul-Jihad al-Islami (HuJI), an Islamic extremist organization, who call themselves 'Bangladeshi

Taliban' and whose membership largely overlaps with one of the allies in the ruling coalition of Khalida Zia's government. A Bangladeshi militant leader, Abdul Salam Muhammad also known as Fazlur Rahman, with suspected connexion with HuJI, was one of just five men to sign bin Laden's fatwa, in February 1998, declaring war against America and Israel, and thus making HuJI an official member of bin Laden's International Islamic Front for Jihad Against the Jews and Crusaders.[15] Soon after, Indian police arrested two Indians and a Sudanese national who reportedly admitted planning to bomb American embassies in New Delhi and Dhaka, under instructions from bin Laden. True to its motto, HuJI assisted 150 al-Qa'ida-Taliban combatants from Afghanistan to escape, in 2001, when the ship docked at Bangladesh's main port of Chittagong. Closer to home HuJI provides training and support to Islamic recruits from southern Thailand at more than a dozen camps located in the south Chittagong Hills near the Burmese border known as the 'Bin Laden trail'—support that has no doubt contributed to the continuing violence in southern Thailand. The group recruits heavily from the 250,000 Burmese Muslim refugees who have settled in the area, dispatching them to jihad in Bosnia and Chechnya. HuJI also allegedly shelters key members of Jemaah Islamiyah, the radical group responsible for the Bali bombings.

International network and financiers of the global militants very substantially bolster Bangladesh militancy. The annual income drawn from these international sources by the votaries of political Islam in Bangladesh is estimated over a staggering figure of 120 billion in Bangladesh currency. The government has no control over the Islamic NGOs' misappropriation of money in the name of religious and charitable activities that commonly facilitates the cause of militant Islam. Religious education has made an astonishing progress since discarding the secular constitution. In 84,000 villages of Bangladesh the number of *madrasah*s is 74,000. While students in the primary schools have doubled in the last decade, the number has multiplied by thirteen times in madrasahs. In the state schools at the secondary level, the government spends Tk 3000 per capita, while in government madrasahs it is Tk 5000 per capita in 20,000 madrasahs with 5,000,000 students, though the government virtually lacks control over the syllabus, curriculum, or financial transactions of the madrasahs.

The appraisal above reveals that the current government has been unable to fight Islamic militancy effectively because its coalition partners are a major part of the problem. While it leaves no shred of doubt that Islamic militancy in this fledgling nation has been nourished internally by the government connivance and indulgence, externally it is also found to be boosted by the ideological and material help of other global Muslim organizations and states. Nor is there a speck of doubt that such disconcerting and dangerous trends in Bangladesh society and politics, if not impeded or thwarted soon enough, will continue to be a source of disruptive development and that, in its turn, is likely to destabilize not only one of the world's poorest democracies but the region as a whole.

IV

Critical interpretation of developments bearing religious labels, as in Islam, which does not quite readily differentiate between the religious and non-religious domains, is a daunting task. Possible secular components of explanations of religious actions are as important, as these are often so problematic. Scholars inclined towards secular interpretations tend to carry their zeal often too far to the point of reducing a religious phenomenon to anything but religious, just as a mirror-image to the efforts of those who see and seek nothing but religious explanations. The real challenge here is to explore and remain watchful of the nuanced and delicate balance of an historical complex in which the religious is integrated with non-religious considerations in a symbiosis.

Given the complex interaction and enmeshing of forces and factors of so diverse a nature, it is foolhardy indeed to hazard an exclusive and mono-causal explanation for the global emergence of the so-called Muslim 'terrorism',' 'extremism', 'radicalism', or 'militancy' since the turning point of petro-dollar crisis in the early seventies flowing into the millennial tragedy of the 9/11. Admittedly, no student of this gradually unfolding story of an epic proportion can afford to overlook or underplay the religious concerns underlying the process of Islamic reassertion, especially since the last three decades. Yet, to reduce the phenomenon of political Islam to Islamic fundamentalism is only to pick up no more than a piece, perhaps a major piece, of a broken mirror. 'Political' Islam is what it really means to be saying that it is not all about the religion. Probing the secular and mundane concerns underpinning resurgent Islam is not to devalue its religious import, it is rather about exploring and explaining how a believer in Islam seeks his/her faith to illuminate, inform, and answer life's problems, challenges, and threats—spiritual or mundane, religious or secular. The greater challenge for its students is to set the role and relevance of the religion within a holistic framework. Much of the discontent, disaffection, bitterness, frustration, fury, and iconoclasm of the Muslim world today would seem to have been rooted in Islamic history, and an adequate understanding of that history needs to focus on a remarkable nexus in Islam of faith, community, power, and history. This raises the most vital issue which concerns not only Islam as a faith and ideology but also Islamic history, and to that extent, today's Muslim concerns as yesterday's.

The close identity of religion and politics in Islam is a very common assumption. 'From the beginning' Islam has been, in the words of H. A. R. Gibb, 'both a religious and a political community.'[16] Lately, some Muslim scholars have questioned its validity, primarily on two grounds. First, the links are no different, as they point out, from that in other religions like Judaism, Christianity, Hinduism, Buddhism, and Sikhism. Secondly, except in the early years of Islamic history, the religious and political life of Muslims remained effectively separate. One is prepared to accept the partial validity of this position. However, it is difficult to adopt this position fully. It bears reiteration that a total identity of the faith, its social ideal, and the community is a special genius of Islam. The centrality of the community and the social ideal in Islam is as crucial as it is well known. In Islamic religious mythology, disappointed and dejected Allah, at the repeated failures of his message revealed to mankind before Islam, was persuaded to entrust the Muslim with the final chance, care, and responsibility for the propagation of His final revelation. As Muslim accepted this onerous responsibility, it must be acted upon; it is both an individual and a collective responsibility. Peace, order, and harmony can only be maintained by the individual and collective discharge of responsibilities and right living, in accordance with God's commands. The historicity of the mission, as well as its gravity and urgency as the last warning and the last chance for the humanity constituted additional imperatives. The Islamic mission, to the believers, is mankind's last opportunity to redeem themselves not merely through individual piety but through actualization of the social ideal in history.[17]

In addition, there are some vital historical explanations for the inter-twining of the temporal and the spiritual in Islam. Because of the absence, in Islam, of the 'church', which represented the organized community in Christianity, the religious struggle for Muslims has not been 'between the church and the state, but for the state'.[18] Hence, we have this identity of faith and power, religion and state, as well as the very strong appeal of an Islamic State among Muslims. Further, and more importantly, the 'state and religion' issue was not really faced by Muslims. Mecca was the most likely place for confrontation between the believers and their temporal and religious opponents, but Muhammad left Mecca for Medina, where the temporal and the spiritual were united in his person, thus avoiding a potential discord between the two orders.

Later, history witnessed sweeping success for Islam and Muslims at both temporal and spiritual levels. Islam steadily emerged as a strident and leading civilization. Islamic scholarship, science and art has, for over a millennium, dazzled the world, especially in the core area stretching from the Guadalquivir in Spain through the Arab lands and Turkey to Iran and on to India. The success was, perfectly understandably, seen by the earlier generations of believers in religious terms. History seemed to have vindicated the faith, especially for those who cherished to believe it. The obvious gap between the ideal and the actual, or faith and history was either overlooked or glossed over, because of this ultimate vindication of the faith, together with the comforting thought and reality that Muslims ruled Muslims.

The first serious crisis and challenge to Islam in history, as already mentioned above, in the form of the infidel Mongol conquest of the heartland of Muslim world was fortuitously averted, with the conversion of those conquerors to Islam. The later crisis, stemming from the challenge of modernity and Western colonial dominance, was not to be resolved so easily in the Mongol way. One after another, the Muslim lands fell like a pack of cards before the onslaughts of Western imperialism. This was not to be brushed aside as a mere political crisis; rather many saw it as a profound spiritual crisis, 'an appalling gap between the religion of God and the historical development that He controls.'[19] The twin motifs of modern Muslim response to the new challenge have been, on one hand, strong resistance and defence against the external aggression and encroachment, as well as scathing attack on internal decadence, corrosion, and corruption, on the other. Muslim countries, in the post-World War II period, have been able, by and large, to throw off the foreign yoke, but the problems of the Muslim world persist in new shapes and forms—economic imperialism persists in new shapes and forms; Muslim collaborators thrive; creation of Israel at the heartland of the Muslim world and the pathetic Muslim helplessness against it burns; the rage against the exclusive American dominance of a sole superpower, derisively called in the developing world as 'coca-colonialism', continues unabated; squabbles, conflicts, and even wars among Muslim states prompted by petty and greedy nationalistic self-interests undermine the vitality of the ideal of Islamic unity and solidarity; and finally, the despotic and corrupt Muslim rulers of both secular and religious variety and the exploitative Muslim classes have been making a mockery of the Islamic ideal of social justice. The issue of social and economic justice has indeed been a powerful and consistent driving force for many major and minor Islamic revivalist and millenarian movements in Muslim history across time. In the South Asian context, two major

Islamic movements in the earlier part of the nineteenth century under the British colonial rule—the Fara'izi and Tariqah-i Muhammadiyah—both driven by the faith as well as the peasants' demands for socio-economic justice are significant exemplars of this phenomenon.[20]

A reason for widespread unrest in the Muslim world is, in Edward Said's view, a tragic betrayal of the Muslim masses by their elites. Committed to their faith and perplexed by the inadequacy of their community and history in the contemporary world, eager to act, yet not knowing what to do, the Muslim masses are often easy prey to every cold and cruel tricks of a skilful manipulator of the secular or religious variety. The cries of suffering, anguish, and anger, arising from this greatest and continuing tragedy in the history of this community, remain drowned under the roaring blasts of the kalashnikovs, grenades, and sam missiles on one side, and the world's most advanced and sophisticated 'weapons of mass destruction', on the other.

V

These are some of the most basic and critical concerns about Islam and Muslims that South Asia has come to share in a very large measure, particularly in recent times, with the rest of the Muslim world in ferment. It is abundantly clear from our exposition above that the all-consuming challenge today, facing Muslims individually and collectively, the like of which has not been recorded in history, is to hold Islam together, and by doing so, hold themselves, against their own house dangerously divided, confronting a world largely confused, frightened, furious, and disturbingly alienated. With so much passion and prejudice all around, objective analysis and understanding of the burning issues are a desideratum, one blaming the other and all having the 'right' answers of their own.

The basic need of the hour would seem to be inducing oneself to understand that the present crisis is not one between 'us' and 'them'. Judging by its nature, growing escalation, and the frightful potentials for the future one cannot but see this as a common and real crisis facing us all. The basic assumptions underlying a sense of understanding of this nature are one's preparedness to listen to the other as well as its concomitant value of tolerance. This applies not only to the non-Muslim world vis-à-vis the Muslim, but also to Muslims among themselves. The issue of tolerance has been at the centre of this debate for obvious reasons. Apart from the primary importance of tolerance as a general principle in dealing with this raging problem, the recent crisis has considerably aggravated the un-informed popular image of 'intolerant Islam' or 'fanatical Muslim'. Admittedly, sections of the Muslim community have not helped this matter either. Tolerance is at a premium in the Muslim in-house dissensions and conflicts. Most important of all, the question of tolerance has drawn the focus of another pre-existing and continuing academic consideration, emphasizing the relevance and importance of South Asian Islam as well as the concerns of this particular volume.

The interminable debates, discussions and speculations on Islam, in recent years, within and between the non-Muslim and Muslim worlds, especially in relation to Islamic fundamentalism, radicalism, and militancy, have had the consequence of reinforcing the stereotypical non-Muslim image and notion of a centralized, unified, and monolithic Islam. The Islamic fundamentalists, Islamists, and sections of Muslim orthodoxy have already been predisposed to this centrist position. This exclusive focus on a largely imaginary, fictional, and unhistorical Islamic monolith has a critical bearing on Islamic studies in a regional perspective, like in South Asia, as we have briefly raised the question at the very outset of our Introduction. This is likely to prove incalculably significant for the future development of Islam, as well as for its studies. Sharply opposed to the idea of a unified and homogenized Islam underpinning the current debates, the historical Islam, as revealed in the intensive research-based studies in regional settings such as in the Bengali-speaking region, remains a very rich and dynamic social-cultural process.[21] The disproportionate emphasis placed on the theme of unity, to the total exclusion of the role and place of variety in Islam has, as shown in a number of contributions in this publication, not only caused a gross distortion of a remarkably protean historical process, but also reduced the complex process of Islamization to one of simple and linear development. Islam and Islamic studies have only been poorer for this. A great civilization was not made within the narrow and rigid frame of a belief and social system, but by the breadth, elasticity, tolerance, and creativity in the process of its historical development in space and time. It is this infinitely complex and creative form of interactions between the ideal and the actual that made Islam a rich, vital, living, and great civilization. The absence of substantive studies in Islam, globally speaking, in diverse regional settings helped to conceal a reality, widely experienced by Muslim believers in many parts of the Muslim world namely, its distinctive regional and local formulations and geniuses. Underlying the undoubted creedal, doctrinal, and some ritualistic unity in Islam, the Muslim world, at the micro level, presents a much more complex reality of pluralism and diversity.

We may have a special reason now for re-emphasizing and seeking to recover the genius of Islamic tolerance, adaptability, and creative dynamism in bringing an incredibly diverse Muslim world together into a whole of unity in diversity, as clearly evident in the development of Islam in history—a glorious and shining history that began to be distorted and clouded largely since the advent of the colonial and modern centuries. The rising tendency in the non-Muslim world to perceive and project Islam as a monolithic culture ruled by the scripture and the scripturalists, combined with the in-house discord in the Muslim world largely caused by the growing hegemonic challenge of the fundamentalists and the Islamists seeking the rule of Sharia over all aspects of modern Muslim life have created a situation incalculably confusing and damaging for the entire Muslim world today. Threatened and haunted by the spectre of fundamentalism, militancy, and a unitary perception of Islam that is rigid, intolerant, and inconceivably unworkable in today's real world, the culturally rich and diverse Muslim communities in the world today have been desperately seeking re-affirmation of their freedom to define themselves as Muslims in the way they have understood and accepted Islam. Hence, the claim for a single monolithic universal perspective on Islam is not only unhistorical and untenable, but also fraught with grave danger in this global environment. The need and the challenge to establish a consensual understanding of the unity and dynamism of Islam within the variety, plurality, and creativity of the Muslim world has never been greater and so critical, and it is precisely in this context, the importance and potential of the Islamic model, as it evolved in history in South Asia, cannot be exaggerated. There has been a considerable body of research and studies in the general and more importantly, in the regional settings of South Asia, such as in Bengal, as mentioned above, to bring out the tradition of tolerance, adaptability, plurality, and creative dynamism that Islam brought to bear on its task of bringing in and holding together the extremely diverse Islamic people of South Asia, 'living together separately' in the Indic world of unity in diversity. It is about this spirit and tradition of Islamic tolerance and of legions of Muslim living for over a millennium in a proverbially diverse plural world of South Asia that the troubled Muslim world, as also the rest of the world, would badly need to hear. The present volume within the usual limitations of a collective work, lacking in a single theme, should offer substantive insights into the workings of this people in history and politics of South Asia.

Many amongst us would have legitimate doubts and questions about this part of the world today and tomorrow. History cannot cover and answer everything; far less it is about telling the future, and no historian should dabble in what lies in the womb of the future. Islam in South Asia has a brilliant track record of creative adaptation and accommodation to its social and cultural environment, as made abundantly evident by many a finding in this volume. In history as in life, success and failure are not eternally defined attributes. Today's success is tomorrow's failure and vice versa.

Endnotes

1. In reference to Europe in very recent times, we are told: 'The continent has been deluged with hundreds of documentaries, news stories, films, and editorials about Islam in the last few years, part of a lively debate about the religion's influence.' 'Islam and Europe', *New York Times* (14 July 2005).

2. This pro-West-Asian bias has been persisting for long, despite the great majority of world Muslims living in South Asia.

3. Asim Roy, 'Islam in the Environment of Medieval Bengal, with special reference to the Bengali sources' (Ph.D thesis, Canberra, 1970); ibid. 'The social factors in the making of Bengali Islam', *South Asia*, old series, annual no. 3 (1973), pp. 23–35; ibid., *The Islamic Syncretistic Tradition in Bengal* (Princeton, 1983); also its South Asian edition (New Delhi, 1987); ibid., *Islam in South Asia: A Regional Perspective* (New Delhi, 1996); ibid., 'Thinking over "Popular Islam" in South Asia: Search for a Paradigm', in Mushirul Hasan and Asim Roy (eds), *Living Together Separately: Cultural India in History and Politics* (New Delhi, 2005), pp. 29–61; T.N. Madan (ed.), *Muslim Communities of South Asia. Culture, Society and Power*, 3rd enlarged edn (New Delhi, 2001); Imtiaz Ahmed (ed.), *Ritual and Religion among Muslims in India* (New Delhi, 1981).

4. Bernard Lewis, *The Arabs in History*, 4th edn (London, 1966), pp. 47–8. Cf also: 'Beginning as a kind of demon or false god worshipped with Apollyon and Termagant in an unholy trinity, the medieval Mahound developed in the West into an arch-heretic whom Dante consigned to...Hell' (ibid. p. 48).

5. Esther Pan (Staff writer), 'Islam and Europe', *New York Times* (14 July 2005).

6. Raeed Tayeb, 'US Muslims deserve measure of goodwill', *Pioneer Planet* (15 December 1999); see also http://www.pioneerplanet.com.80/seven-days/1/.

7. Oliver McTernan, *Violence in God's Name, Religion in an Age of Conflict* (London, 2003), x.

8. Ibid.

9. Ibid.

10. The complexities underlying the interpretive process of Islamic or Muslim social and political actions and movements have been especially focused in Chapter 3: Asim Roy, 'Impact of Islamic Revival and Reform in Colonial Bengal and Bengal Muslim Identity: A Revisit', and Chapter 11: Asim Roy, 'Salience of Islam in South Asian Politics: Pakistan and Bangladesh'.

Relevant material with bearings on this problem are also found in Chapter 9: Adeel Khan,' 'Ethnicity, Islam and National Identity in Pakistan' and in Chapter 10: Samina Yasmeen, 'Islamization and Democratization in Pakistan. Implications for Women and Religious Minorities'.

11. Robert S. Leiken, *Foreign Affairs* (19 July 2005).

12. Esther Pan, 'Islam and Europe'.

13. Given that Bangladesh is relatively under-represented in this volume, the Bangladesh situation has received greater space here than Pakistan. The analytical review of the Bangladesh situation here is largely based on the following recent reports and commentaries:

'Bin Laden has "tentacles" in Bangladesh', *Pacific Rim Bureau* (*http://www.CNSNews.com*). CNSNews.com are Copyright © 2000 by the Cybercast News Service.News Wire Powered by CustomScoop Copyright 1991–1999; Dane Chamorro, 'Bangladesh a terrorist hotbed', *Hong Kong Standard* (15 April 2005); Francois Hauter, 'Dacca threatened by fascists of the Koran', *Le Figaro* (21 September 2005); Muhammad Kamal Uddin, 'Bangladesh cries for peace', *SAN-Feature Service* (22 September 2005); Mahmuduzzaman Babu et al., 'Bangladesh under attack', *SAN-Feature Service* (7 December 2005); Elizabeth Griswold, 'Terrorism. Bangladesh for beginners', *SAN-Feature Service* (31 December 2005); Chris Blackburn, 'Terrorism: Crisis in South Asia', *SAN-Feature Service* (5 January 2006).

14. See Chapter 11: Asim Roy, 'Salience of Islam in South Asian Politics: Pakistan and Bangladesh'.

15. The four other signatories have been bin Laden himself, Zawahiri, Rifai Ahmed Taha of the Egyptian Islamic Group, and Mir Hamzah of Pakistan's Jami'at-ul-Ulema.

16. Gibb, H. A. R., *Mohammedanism* (New York, 1962), Chapters 2 and 3.

17. W.C. Smith, *Islam in History* (Princeton, 1957), pp. 10ff, 211.

18. Ibid. p. 10ff.

19. Ibid.

20. For a detailed exposition of this issue in particular reference to these two Islamic movements, see below Chapter 3: Asim Roy, 'Impact of Islamic Revival and Reform in Colonial Bengal and Bengal Muslim Identity: A Revisit'. It is important to recall here that the early Chishti *sufis* in India were known to believe and preach that helping the needy and those in suffering was the highest form of prayer.

21. See above, Introduction, pp. 1–2. For a fuller and very recent critique of the problem, see Asim Roy, 'Thinking over "Popular Islam" in South Asia: Search for a Paradigm', in Mushirul Hasan and Asim Roy (eds), *Living Together Separately. Cultural India in History and Politics* (New Delhi, 2005), pp. 29–61.

1

Religious Change and the Self in Muslim South Asia since 1800*

on the birth of Muslim agency

FRANCIS ROBINSON

In the nineteenth and twentieth centuries South Asian Muslims, along with Muslims elsewhere in the world, began to experience religious change of revolutionary significance. The change involved a shift in the focus of Muslim piety from the next world to this one. It meant the devaluing of a faith of contemplation on God's mysteries and of belief in His capacity to intercede for men on earth. It meant the valuing instead of a faith in which Muslims were increasingly aware that it was they, and only they, who could act to create a just society on earth. The balance which had long existed between the other-worldly and the this-worldly aspects of Islam was moved firmly in favour of the latter.

This process of change has had many expressions—the movements of the Mujahidin, the Faraizis, Deoband, the Ahl-i Hadiths, and Aligarh in the nineteenth century; and those of the Nadwat ul Ulama, the Tablighi Jamaat, the Jamaat-i-Islami, and the Muslim modernists in the twentieth. It has also been expressed in many subtle shifts in behaviour at saints' shrines and in the pious practice of many Muslims. Associated with this process of change was a shift in traditional Islamic knowledge away from the rational towards the revealed sciences, and a more general shift in the sources of inspiration away from the Iranian lands towards the Arab lands. There was also the adoption of print and the translations of authoritative texts into Indian languages with all their

* This paper was first delivered as a keynote lecture at the Biennial Conference of the Asian Studies Association of Australia in July 1996, and published in *South Asia*, vol. XX, no. 1 (1997), pp. 1–15.

subsequent ramifications—among them the emergence of a reflective reading of the scriptures and the development of an increasingly rich inner landscape. Operating at the heart of this process was the increasing assumption by individual Muslims of responsibility for creating Muslim society on earth—a great and heavy responsibility. Moreover, in the context of British India, where foreign power had colonized much public space, this was a burden of which Muslim women were asked to take a particularly heavy share.

In the scholarship devoted to the Christian West the shift from otherworldly to this-worldly religion, which brought man to stand before the unfettered sovereignty of God, is regarded as a development of momentous importance. Among its many outcomes was helping to shape the modern Western senses of the self, of identity. There is an assumption here, of course, which is that the 'self' is historically defined, that is that the late Roman self might be differently constituted as compared with the twentieth-century Western self. Let us consider some of the shaping processes at work. The new willed religion, which man entered into only of his choice, gave him a sense of his instrumentality in the world, of his capacity to shape it. The new and heavy weight of this responsibility to an all-powerful God led to what has been termed the 'inward turn'—this started with the emergence of spiritual diaries in the Reformation and has continued with an ever deeper exploration of the psyche. Then, this new sense of human instrumentality, aligned to a deepening sense of self, helped to foster senses of individual personal autonomy. All this tended to affirm the worth of ordinary life, the value of ordinary human experience. There was value in productive work, in marriage, family life, love, sex; there was growing distress at human suffering and a growing sense that good consisted of human activities for the benefit of human welfare.[1]

It is not suggested for one moment that we can look at the impact of the shift to this-worldly religion and somehow read off a series of developments or potential developments among South Asian Muslims. Nothing could be so crass. The particular circumstances of nineteenth- and twentieth-century India, not to mention the ideas and values inculcated by Islam, are different from those of Reformation Europe. Nevertheless, what is worth doing is noting the significance of the shift from other-worldly to this-worldly religion for shaping modern senses of the self in the West. And this should prompt us at least to consider the extent to which a similar change might have helped to shape Muslim senses of the self in South Asia.

Before embarking on this exercise, there are other factors contributing to the shaping of the self which need to be acknowledged. There

is the growing influence of Western civilization with its ideas of individualism, personal fulfilment, and the rights of man—with its endorse-
ment of earthly existence and earthly pleasures, and its celebration of
individual lives, great and small. Such ideas and values were instinct
in much Western literature and in many institutions; they were, of
course, embodied by many of the colonial British. There is also growing
exposure to other forces which helped to fashion the more autonomous
self. There is the spread of capitalist modes of production with their
capacity to break down old communal loyalties and empower individuals; there is the emergence of the modern state with its concern to reach
down through the thickets of the social order to make contact with each
individual; there are the changes in the technology of communication—
I think particularly of print and the shift it helped to bring from orality
to literacy—which enabled individuals to command knowledge as never
before and assisted them in the process of exploring their inner selves.[2]
There are, of course, many forces at work in shaping the changing
Muslim senses of the self. Our concern is to suggest that the shift from
other-worldly to this-worldly religion is worthy of exploration.

Before embarking on our exploration it is necessary to outline the
nature and impact of the shift to this-worldly Islam. The nineteenth and
twentieth centuries in South Asia saw a growing attack on intercessionary
sufism, indeed, at times on all forms of sufism itself. The reformists
were determined to rid the world of its enchanted places, that is of
anything that might diminish the believers' sense of responsibility.
They were determined to assert the principle of *tawhid*, of the oneness
of God. This theme ran through all the movements of the age from the
Mujahidin of Saiyid Ahmad of Rai Bareli to the Jamaat-i-Islami of
Maulana Maududi. Not all movements gave quite the same emphasis
to this theme. If the Ahl-i Hadiths and Ahl-i Quran were opposed to all
forms of institutionalized sufism, the Deobandis on the other hand
confined themselves to attacking practices at saints' shrines which
presupposed the capacity of the saint to intercede for man with God.
There were ironies, too. Maududi, while abhorring the tendency of
sufism to compromise the oneness of God, nevertheless found an
excellent organizational model in the sufi order which he used for his
Jamaat. (His vision of the role of the Amir of the Jamaat was similar
to that of the sufi master to whom all his disciples gave unquestioning
submission). This said, we should be aware that there was enormous
sensitivity to behaviour at saints' shrines among almost all Muslims.
It affected non-reformers as well as reformers. It was an important
concern for the ulama of the Firangi Mahal family of Lucknow. The
research of Claudia Liebeskind on three Awadhi shrines in this period,

moreover, has illustrated how behaviour at them changed in order to accommodate some reformist preferences at least.[3] What we need to be aware of is that in the nineteenth and twentieth centuries increasing numbers of India's Muslims from the upper and middle classes were finding the credibility of the friends of God, who had long provided them with comfort, undermined. There could be no intercession for them. They were directly answerable to the Lord, and to Him alone.[4]

There can be no doubt that Reformist Muslims felt the weight of this new responsibility and were meant to feel it. They knew that it was their choice to will the good and forbid the evil. It was their choice as to whether a Muslim society which followed God's wishes existed on earth or not. Moreover, they knew that they were answerable to Him for their actions. Husain Ahmad Madani, principal of Deoband in the mid-twentieth century, often wept at the thought of his shortcomings.[5] Rashid Ahmad Gangohi, one of the founders of the school, when reading the Quran alone at night, would weep and shake and appear terrified at those chapters dealing with God's wrath.[6] The Reformist God was certainly compassionate and merciful, as God always had been, but he was also to be feared. Indeed, 'Fear God' was the very first practice sentence that women in the reformist tradition, who were learning how to read, had to confront.[7] There was a constant sense of guilt that the believer was not doing enough to meet the high standards of this most demanding God. 'Oh God! What am I to do? I am good for nothing', Maulana Muhammad Ilyas, the founder of the Tablighi Jamaat, would exclaim as he paced at night. And when his wife told him to come to bed, he said that if she knew what he knew she would be doing the same. 'I find no comparison between my anxiety, my effort and my voice,' he wrote, 'and the responsibility of *Tabligh* God has placed upon my shoulders. If He shows mercy, He is forgiving, merciful, and if He does justice, there is no escape for me from the consequences of my guilt'.[8]

Nothing brings home more the weight of responsibility with which Reformist Muslims were faced than their visions of Judgement. Consider the picture in Ashraf Ali Thanvi's *Bihishti Zewar*, which has been so ably translated and introduced for us by Barbara Metcalf. Thanvi draws on a vision initially generated by Shah Rafi al-Din, one of the four sons of Shah Wali Allah, and therefore at the heart of the Reformist tradition. *Bihishti Zewar* is one of the most influential books of twentieth-century Muslim South Asia.

The believer is first of all reminded of the Prophet's emotion at the thought of heaven and hell. 'He wept greatly until his blessed beard was wet with tears. Then he declared: 'I swear by that Being in whose power is my life that if you know what I know about the afterlife, you would flee to the wilderness and place dust upon your head."'

Then the believer is told the signs of the coming of Judgement. The proper order of the sharia will be reversed; people will think the wealth owed to God is their property. They will seek knowledge of religion not for its own sake but for worldly gain. The natural order will be reversed, stones will rain down from the sky; people will turn into pigs and dogs. The Imam Mahdi will appear to lead the Muslims into battle against the Nazarenes. The one-eyed Dajjal will appear claiming to be the Messiah. Hasrat Isa will descend from the sky with his hands on the shoulders of two angels to kill the Dajjal. The sun will rise in the west. A balmy breeze from the south will produce a fatal growth in the armpits of the believers. Then, on a Friday, the tenth Muharrum, in the morning when all people are engaged in their respective work, a trumpet will suddenly be sounded. At first, it will be very, very soft. Then it will grow so much louder that all will die from terror. The heaven and earth will be rent. The world will be extinguished.

Then comes the Day of Judgement. After forty years God will order the trumpet to be blown again. Heaven and earth will again be established. The dead will emerge alive from their graves and will be gathered on the Plain of Judgement. The sun will be very close, and peoples' very brains will begin to cook in its heat. People will sweat in proportion to their sins. Only the Prophet Muhammad's intercession will persuade Almighty God to intervene.

Angels in great number will descend from the heavens and surround everyone on every side. The throne of Almighty God, on which will be the Illumination of Almighty God, will descend. The accounting will begin, and the Book of Deeds will be opened. Of their own accord, the believers will come on the right hand and the unbelievers on the left. The scales for weighing deeds will be set up, and from it everyone's good and bad deeds will be known. Thereupon everyone will be ordered to cross the Bridge of the Way. Anyone whose good deeds weigh more in the balance will cross the bridge and enter into paradise. Anyone whose sins weigh more, unless forgiven by God, will fall into hell.... When all the inhabitants of heaven and hell are settled in their places, Almighty God will bring forth Death in the shape of a Ram, in between heaven and hell. He will display Death to everyone and have it slaughtered. He will declare: 'Now death will come neither to the dwellers in heaven nor to the dwellers in hell. All must dwell for ever in their respective places.' There will be no end to the rejoicing of the inhabitants of heaven and no end to the anguish and grief of the inhabitants of hell.[9]

The awfulness of this eschatological vision, the powerlessness of the believer to achieve salvation except through the preponderance of his good deeds on earth, gives real insight into how individual senses of responsibility were likely to be deepened. The penetration of this sense into the individual's inner self, its approach towards the quiddity of the human being, helps to explain the high levels of emotion it generated. It also helps to explain the growth of sectarianism–the many Muslim groups fashioned in nineteenth- and twentieth-century India that exist to this day–as Muslims in different social and intellectual locations strove with great sincerity to find the right way towards salvation. It helps to explain the world of *manazara*s, *fatwa* wars and high combativeness that typifies these groups. This was the price to be paid for the huge release of religious energy generated by what could be called a process of personal religious empowerment.

This sense of responsibility was not just felt among ulama of the reformist tradition, and those who followed them, it was felt no less by Muslim modernists, those who wished to build bridges between Western science and Islamic understandings. Listen to that very great man Saiyid Ahmad Khan:

> But since I have been the pioneer of Modern Education which, as I have said, is to some extent opposed to Islam, I regard it as my duty to do all I can, right or wrong, to defend my religion and show the people, the true, shining countenance of Islam. This is what my conscience dictates and, unless I do its bidding, I am a sinner before God.[10]

A similar spirit illuminated those other great modernists, Muhammad Iqbal and Fazlur Rahman, in their endeavours to show the people the shining countenance of Islam.

We should also note that this sense of responsibility has come to be spread more and more widely through the Muslim society of South Asia as the reforming movement has continued to develop, and as it has come to interact with a society where books were more widely available, and literacy was slowly but surely growing. It is one of the ironies of this process that much of this activity was set going by ulama who, by translating key works of the Islamic tradition into Indian languages and by printing them large-scale, aimed to give Muslim society strength to cope with colonial rule, but in the process they helped to destroy their own monopoly over religious knowledge. If in the nineteenth century the effort was concentrated on a literate élite, the aristocracy which was attracted to the Ahl-i Hadiths and the Ahl-i Quran, the *sharif* classes which tended to go to Aligarh and the lesser bourgeois of the *qasba*s which tended to go to Deoband, in the twentieth century the effort was taken more widely into society, in part through the publications of the Jamaat-i-Islami, which, though élitist itself, spoke to a whole new generation of Western-educated Muslims, but for the most part through the Tablighi Jamaat, or Preaching Society, which aimed, and aims, to involve ordinary Muslims in taking a basic understanding of reformist Islam to the masses. The loss of the ulama's monopoly, this process implied, was a necessary sacrifice in striving to deepen the sense of personal responsibility in society as a whole. This democratization of the possession of religious knowledge and its interpretation, which went hand in hand with the emergence of the concept of the caliphate or vice-regency of man in Muslim thought, is a development of enormous potential and importance for the future of Muslim societies.[11]

There is one final point which needs to be made about the shift towards this-worldly religion and the spread of a new sense of responsibility—it seems to have fallen rather more heavily on women than on men. It is now a commonplace of the literature devoted to gender and identity in South Asia since 1800 that with non-Muslim occupancy of public space women move from their earlier position of being threats to the proper conduct of Muslim society to being the mistresses of private Islamic space, the central transmitters of Islamic values, the symbols of Muslim identity, the guardians of millions of domestic Islamic shrines. Women come, in fact, to bear an awesome responsibility. Thus they had a central role to play in the reformist project. Their education, to the extent, as Ashraf Ali Thanvi declared, of acquiring the learning of a *maulvi*, was crucial to waging war on all those customs which threatened the unity of God and to maintaining fully in place the power of Muslim conscience in fashioning Islamic society. Thanvi also admitted that women would have to struggle harder than men to achieve this outcome.[12]

For Maududi and the Islamists women are expected to acquire knowledge of Islam, just as men do, and to examine their consciences in the same way. On the other hand, they were biologically and psychologically different from men and their place was in *purdah* and in the home. They were to be the rulers of domestic space, sealed off from all those elements of *kufr* which polluted public space. 'The harim', he declared, 'is the strongest fortress of Islamic civilization, which was built for the reasons that, if it [that civilization] ever suffered a reverse, it [that civilization] may then take refuge in it'.[13] Muslim modernists sent out conflicting messages, on the one hand emphasizing the spiritual and moral superiority of women, which might militate against their education, while on the other increasingly coming to see their education in Western learning and through the medium of English as the measure of the health and development of society. Wherever women found themselves, a heavy weight of responsibility rested upon them.

This weight is borne down to the present, although the extra burden of political pressures have come to join those of patriarchy and willed religion. Much of the discourse, both about Pakistani identity and about Muslim identity in India, has come to take place around the position and behaviour of women. If there is a correlation between burdens of responsibility and growing senses of the self, there is room for there to be increasingly stressful tension between women's expectations and those of the wider society in which they more.

We now move from the shift towards this-wordly Islam and the new sense of responsibility it fosters to the impact of this responsibility on Muslim senses of the self. There are four themes which should be noted. They are—self-instrumentality, the idea of the individual human being as the active, creative agent on earth; self-affirmation, the autonomy of the individual; to which is connected the affirmation of the ordinary things of the self, the affirmation of ordinary life; and finally, the emphasis on self-consciousness, the reflective self, which in the Western experience is referred to as the 'inward turn'.

Self-instrumentality

The first outcome of responsibility was that each individual Muslim had to take action to achieve salvation. The theme of individual instrumentality in this world runs through all the manifestations of this-worldly Islam. The life of Saiyid Ahmad Khan was a testament to his belief in self-help, and the need for the individual to take action for the good of his community and of Islam. Ashraf Ali Thanvi, in considering the process of character formation, insists that knowledge of what one should do is itself not enough: 'knowledge is not true knowledge unless it is acted upon', only thus is the inner self shaped.[14] For his contemporary, Muhammad Ilyas, Tabligh was the concrete manifestation of 'knowing meaning doing' in the light of the Quran's exhortation to Muslims both to acquire and to transmit knowledge.[15] Maududi makes perfectly clear the duty of Muslims to act on their knowledge of God's commandments if they wish to be saved. This world is the ground on which men prepare for the next. But the clearest statement and vision of man's instrumentality comes in the thought of Iqbal who makes the role of human self, or ego, in the creative activity of shaping and reshaping the world the focus of much of his work. For him the reality of the individual is demonstrated not just in thought but in action in this world—not *cogito ergo sum* but *ago ergo sum*. 'The final act', he declares in his *Reconstruction of Religious Thought in Islam*, 'is not an intellectual act, but a vital act which deepens the whole being of the ego and sharpens his will with the creative assurance that the world is not just something to be seen and known through concepts, but to be made and remade by continuous action.'[16] Man must not only act but must be the prime mover in God's creation. The new Muslim self is a doing self. Hence the bursts of creative energy released by Indian Muslims during the past two centuries.

SELF-AFFIRMATION

Individuals who will their religion on the basis of their own knowledge have the capacity to be increasingly autonomous and self-affirmative. They make their own choices. Ashraf Ali Thanvi, for instance, aims to give this capacity to women by giving them the learning of a maulvi and much practical knowledge as well. Iqbal's moral and religious ideal is of the man who achieves self-affirmation by being more and more individual and more and more unique. In both cases unrestrained individualism is constrained by the godly purposes these authors have in mind for their subjects. There is, however, an essential tension between this-worldly Islam's desire to empower humankind on earth and on the other hand to continue to focus their attention on godly ends. Once the genie of individualism has been let out of the bottle, there is no guarantee that it will continue to submit to Islam.

AFFIRMATION OF ORDINARY LIFE

With the affirmation of self there also come the affirmation of the ordinary things of the self, the ordinary things of daily life, which the philosopher, Charles Taylor, terms 'one of the most powerful ideas in modern civilization'.[17] We can see this process at work in the new trends which emerge in the *sirat* literature, in the biographies of the Prophet, whose number increase greatly in the twentieth century. Increasingly Muhammad is depicted not as the 'perfect man' of the sufi tradition but as the perfect person. He is said to have been 'beloved, charitable, frugal, generous, gently, honest, lenient, a lover of children, modest, pure, steadfast and successful'. Less attention, as Cantwell Smith has pointed out, is given to his intelligence, political sagacity, and capacity to harness the new social forces in his society and more to his qualities as a good middle-class family man—his sense of duty and his loving nature, and his qualities as a good citizen, his consideration for others and in particular those who are less fortunate.[18] This transition is also mirrored in changes which take place in biographical writing more generally; the concern is less with what the individual might have contributed to Islamic civilization and the transmission of knowledge and more on his life in his time and his human qualities. Even in the writings of the ulama it is possible to see them responding to the humanistic preferences of their times and depicting much more rounded lives to support their didactic purpose.[19] Another dimension of this process is the growing discussion of family and domestic issues, and particularly women, in public space. This discourse is begun by men such as Nazir Ahmad, Hali, and Mumtaz Ali in the nineteenth century but in the twentieth century it is increasingly taken up by women and not least by the tens of women who aired their views in the pages of those remarkable journals *Ismat* and *Tehzib un Niswan.* All matters are discussed in public from education, diet and dress to love marriages, divorce, and the sources of women's inferiority. The writing is often assertive in style, demanding that women and their lives be given respect.[20] Finally, the rise of the short story and the novel is, of course, an indication of the new value given to understanding human character and the many ways of being human. The themes, often shocking in their day, which were taken up by leading practitioners such as Manto and Ismat Chughtai—family life, relationships, feelings, sex—indicate the new arenas of life in which Muslims are finding meaning. Such is the new importance of these profoundly human matters that religious thinkers cannot afford to ignore them. 'The Islamic pattern of inner life,' declares the religious philosopher Syed Vahiduddin, 'finds expression in religious and moral acts, in prayer, in love, in forgiveness, in seemingly mundane activities such as sex and domestic life, which should be radiated by the glow of the world beyond...'.[21]

THE INWARD TURN: THE GROWTH OF SELF-CONSCIOUSNESS AND REFLECTION

The final theme is the growth of self-consciousness and reflective habit. A major element of this-worldly Islam in almost all its forms is the requirement for self-examination—a willed Islam had to be a self-conscious one. Muslims had to ask themselves regularly whether they had done all in their power to submit to God and carry out His will in the world. In book seven of *Bihishti Zewar* Ashraf Ali Thanvi has a rather charming way of illustrating the process of regular self-examination to ensure purity of intentions and avoidance of wrongdoing. He suggests to the believer that she set aside a little time in the morning and in the evening to speak to her lower-self [*nafs*] as follows:

> O Self, you must recognize that in this world you are like a trader, Your stock-in-trade is your life. Its profit is to acquire well-being forever, that is, salvation in the afterlife. This is indeed a profit! If you waste your life and do not gain your salvation, you suffer losses that reach to your stock-in-trade. That stock-in-trade is so precious that each hour—indeed, each breath—is valuable beyond limit.
> O Self, recognize God's kindness that Death has not yet come.
> O Self, do not fall into the deception that Almighty God will surely forgive you. [Don't bank on his mercy]
> Say to yourself, 'O Self, you are like a sick person. A sick person must follow good regimen. Sinning is a bad regimen...
> Say to the Self, 'O Self, the world is a place of journeying, and on a journey complete comfort is never available. You must endure all kinds of trouble. Travellers put up with these troubless because they know that when they reach home they will have all comfort.... In the same way, you must endure hard work and distress as long as you dwell in this world. There is work in acts of worship; there is distress in giving up sin; there are all kinds of other troubles. The afterlife is our home. When we arrive there, all trouble will be ended.[22]

This theme of self-consciousness and self-examination is to be found in many religious thinkers of the late nineteenth and twentieth centuries, whether we look at Muhammad Ilyas, Maududi and Vahiduddin, or Saiyid Ahmad Khan and Iqbal. In seventeenth-century Europe, as we have noted, this process was accompanied by the emergence of the spiritual diary.[23] Some similar, although not directly comparable, materials exist for twentieth-century Muslim India. There is, for instance, Maulana Mohamed Ali's semi-spiritual *My Life: A Fragment*, which was written while he was interned in the First World War. There is also Dr Syed Mahmud's record of his spiritual reflections while in jail after the non-cooperation movement.[24] Beyond such works there is a great deal of correspondence with sufis which often does contain processes of self-examination. With such evidence for the reflective habit, alongside the widespread exhortation to examine the self, it is arguable that the development of this-worldly religion helped to open up an interior landscape. Whereas in the past the reflective believer, the mystic, might have meditated upon the signs of God, the new type of reflective believer meditated increasingly on the self and the shortcomings of the self. Now the inner landscape became a crucial site where the battle of the pious for the good took place. Doubtless, there had been Muslims in the past—in particular times and in particular contexts—for whom this had been so. The importance of the shift towards this-worldly Islam, however, was that self-consciousness and self-examination were encouraged to become widespread.

The role of reformism in helping to throw open a window on the inner landscape does not end with the end of belief. Once the original purpose has been lost the window may still remain open for purely secular purposes. The exploration of the inner territory may equally be the quest of one who is purely Muslim by culture. How far the exploration may be a consequence of early religious upbringing, or of values in society widely shared, or of exposure to Western culture will always be hard to judge, even on a case by case basis. That the process of exploration was taking place is evident in books as varied as Ismat Chughtai's remarkable novel of psychological insight *Terhi Lakir* (The Crooked Line) published in 1944 through to K.A. Abbas's *I Am Not An Island: An Experiment in Autobiography* published in 1974.[25]

Arguably the shift towards this-worldly Islam has emphasized new strands in Muslim selves. There is the sense of empowerment that comes with the knowledge that it is humanity that fashions the world. There is the sense of personal autonomy and individual possibility that comes with the knowledge that the individual makes choices. There is the transfer of the symbols and centres of meaning in life from the signs of God and the friends of God to the mundane things of ordinary life. And there is the development of that extra dimension to the self, the interior space. Arguably the individual has become more complex and the possibilities for human fulfilment have become greater.

We have noted the central role of the human self for the thinkers of this-worldly Islam. The fashioning of a new human self was the central activity of the reformist project. The unlimited capacity of man to create and shape the external world is a central feature of Iqbal's thought and is exemplified in this challenge he makes man hurl at God:

> You created the night—I lit the lamp.
> You created the clay—I moulded the cup.
> You made the wilderness, mountains and forests
> I cultivated the flowerbeds, parks and gardens.[26]

We should note, too, that these manifestations of this-worldly Islam empower man but do not give him unlimited freedom. His power is in the service of God's word (Thanvi). His power is to be within the limits set by Him (Maududi). His power, his human potential, can only be fully realized within the framework of the community created by Him (Iqbal).

There remain a few reflections. First, there is an essential tension between the forces of individualism, potential and actual, set loose by this-worldly religion, and the continuity of the Muslim community as the community of all Muslims. We have noted that a central feature of this-worldly Islam is the empowerment of individuals, indeed the requirement placed on individuals to act on earth. What makes sure, for most Muslim thinkers, that these actions are designed to promote Islamic ends is fear of Judgement and faith, or just faith. But, willed Islam would appear to be a two-edged sword. It can release great religious energy and creativity, as it has done in South Asia and elsewhere. But, on the other hand, it opens the door to unbelief. Muslims, who can choose to believe, can also choose not to believe, and become Muslims merely by culture. Once belief goes, those mundane areas of life which reformist Muslims cherish in the name of God— work, home, family, relationship, sex—now could become prime theatres of meaning in themselves. With the shift towards this-worldly Islam, and the increasing disenchantment of the world, I wonder, has Islam turned onto a track that, as in the West, leads down a secularizing path? Certainly, here is a package of ideas ready to be powered forward in society by the growth of capitalism and the individual freedoms the modern state can fashion.

Secondly, we have noted how the responsibilities for this-worldly Islam came to bear with especial weight on women. I am not equipped to assess the outcomes of this especial burden, although it seems a subject worthy of investigation. Nevertheless, there is no doubting the tension which exists between ideas of family and community on the one hand and individualism on the other. 'There was a sense of a collective in the lifestyle of this house', declares Gaythi, the heroine of Altaf Fatima's *Dastak Na Do* [The one who did not ask], 'the selfish god of individualism had not yet crossed its threshold.'[27] And I wonder if the strident tone of many of the contributions to *Ismat* and *Tehzib un Niswan* in the 1940s was a reflection of the pressure that women were expected to endure. And I wonder, too, if this might not explain the desire of some to test the boundaries of what was acceptable. I think of the erotic novels of Rashid Jahan, of the treatment of sex by Ismat Chughtai which led to her being put on trial in the 1940s, or more recently of Taslima Nasreen's stubborn jousting at the boundaries of the permissible.

Thirdly, willed Islam, self-conscious Islam, leads to a powerful concern to assert and to police the boundaries of difference; it surely also leads to a deepening of community affiliation in the psyche. By the same token, it may also form part of the groundwork for the development of a Muslim political identity and responsiveness to Islamic symbols in politics. This said, we should note that leaders of this-worldly Islam have gone in very different directions in the political sphere from Muhammad Ilyas and Abul Hasan Nadvi, who have insisted that Islam is all about fashioning individuals and has nothing to do with the political sphere, to Maulana Maududi, who insisted that mastery of the political sphere is essential to achieve right guidance for society.[28]

More thought needs to be given to the implications of the deep cultural transformation brought about by the shift in Muslim piety firmly towards this-worldly religion. It is important to get a stronger grasp on its role in shaping modern Muslim selves. Among other things it would be useful to heave a sense of its contribution, as compared with global processes, to fashioning the greater individualism of some twentieth-century Muslim selves. But we also need a sense of how it may be leading to abrasive interactions between the search for individual fulfilment and the obligations of community, an abrasiveness often felt most particularly by women.[29] Doubtless, as the different paths trodden by Nadvi and Maududi suggest, those travelling down the high road of this-worldly Islam can branch off in different directions. Among them may be that of a well-developed ethical self and a largely private faith.

Endnotes

1. Charles Taylor, *Sources of the Self: The Making of Modern Identity* (Cambridge, 1989), pp. 1–24.
2. For the significance of the role of print and the shift from orality to literacy, see Francis Robinson, 'Islam and the Impact of Print in South Asia' in Nigel Crook (ed.), *The Transmission of Knowledge in South Asia: Essays in Education, Religion, History and Politics* (New Delhi, 1996), pp. 62–97.
3. The shrines concerned were those of Takiya Sharif, Kakori, Khanqah Karimiya, Salon, Haji Waris Ali Ahah, and Deva. Claudia Liebeskind, 'Sufism, Sufi Leadership and "Modernisation" in South Asia since c. 1800' (Ph.D dissertation, University of London, 1995).
4. For the general process see Barbara D. Metcalf, *Islamic Revival in British India: Deoband, 1860–1900* (Princeton, NJ, 1982).
5. Ibid., p. 163.
6. Ibid., p. 166.
7. Barbara D. Metcalf, *Perfecting Women: Maulana Ashraf 'Ali Thanawi's Bihishti Zewar: a Partial Translation with Commentary* (Berkeley, 1990), p. 63.
8. S. Abul Hasan Ali Nadwi, *Life and Mission of Maulana Muhammad Ilyas*, trans. by Mohammad Asif Kidwai (Lucknow, 1979), p. 108.
9. Metcalf, *Perfecting Women*, pp. 222–30.
10. Speech of Saiyid Ahmad Khan quoted in *Altaf Husain Hali*, trans. by K.H. Qadiri and David J. Matthews (New Delhi, 1979), p. 172.

11. For these developments see Robinson, 'Islam and the Impact of Print'; Barbara D. Metcalf, 'Meandering Madrasas: Knowledge and Short-term Itinerancy in the Tablighi Jama'at', in Crook (ed.), *Transmission*, pp. 49–61; and Christian W. Troll, 'Five Letters of Maulana Ilyas (1885–1944), the Founder of the Tablighi Jama'at', translated, annotated, and introduced in C.W. Troll (ed.), *Islam in India: Studies and Commentaries 2: Religion and Religious Education* (Delhi, 1985), pp. 138–76.

12. Metcalf, *Perfecting Women*, pp. 1–38.

13. Cited in Faisal Fatehali Devji, 'Gender and the Politics of Space: the movement for women's reform, 1857–1900' in Z. Hasan (ed.), *Forging Identities: Gender, Communities and the State* (New Delhi, 1994), pp. 35–6. The whole point is summed up in a classic text: Abul A'la Maududi, *Purdah and the Status of Women in Islam* (New Delhi, 1974).

14. Metcalf, *Perfecting Women*, p. 107.

15. Troll, 'Five Letters', p. 143.

16. M. Iqbal, *The Reconstruction of Religious Thought in Islam* (Lahore, 1954), p. 198.

17. Taylor, *Sources*, p. 14.

18. Wilfred Cantwell Smith, *Modern Islam in India: A Social Analysis* (London, 1946), pp. 64–7.

19. Robinson, 'Islam and the impact of print,' in Crook (ed.), *Transmission*, n. 80, pp. 96–7.

20. See, Gail Minault, *Secluded Scholars* (New Delhi, 1998) and Azra Asghar Ali, 'The Emergence of Feminism Among Indian Muslim Women, 1920–47' (Ph.D dissertation, University of London, 1996), especially pp. 319–81.

21. Christian W. Troll (ed.), *Islam in India: Studies and Commentaries, 3: The Islamic Experience in Contemporary Thought* (New Delhi, 1986), p. 153.

22. Metcalf, *Perfecting Women*, pp. 235–6.

23. See, for instance, Tom Webster, 'Writing to Redundancy: Approaches to Spiritual Journals and Early Modern Spirituality', *The Historical Journal*, vol. 31, no. 1 (1996), pp. 35–56. But, it remains important to realize that the rise of self-consciousness was not restricted to one time or one culture. Peter Burke, 'Representations of the Self from Petrarch to Descartes', in Roy Porter (ed.), *Rewriting the Self: Histories from the Renaissance to the Present* (London, 1997), pp. 17–28.

24. Mahomed Ali and Afzal Iqbal (ed.), *My Life: A Fragment: An Autobiographical Sketch* (Lahore, 1942). Syed Mahmud's spiritual reflections may be found in the Firangi Mahal Papers, Karachi.

25. Abbas's father was known for his strict reforming principles. K.A. Abbas, *I Am Not An Island: An Experiment in Autobiography* (New Delhi, 1977), p. 35 and K.H. Ansari. *The Emergence of Socialist Thought Among North Indian Muslims (1917–1947)* (Lahore, 1990), pp. 288–9. Ismat Chughtai's background was notably liberal but in her early religious background she was exposed to a strict maulvi, ibid., pp. 316–17.

26. Translation of part of Iqbal's poem 'God's Talk with Man' in N.P. Ankiyev, 'The Doctrine of Personality', H. Malik (ed.), *Iqbal: Poet-Philosopher of Pakistan* (New York, 1971), p. 274.

27. Altaf Fatima, *The one who did not ask*, trans. by Ruksana Ahmad (London, 1993), pp. 62–4.

28. The point is well made in Ahmed Mukarram, 'Some Aspects of Contemporary Islamic Thought: Guidance and Governance in the World of Maulana Abul Hasan Ali Nadwi and Maulana Abul Aala Mawdudi' (D.Phil. dissertation, University of Oxford, 1993).

29. Precisely the kind of study to elucidate this issue, even though it is on a Hindu rather than a Muslim community, has recently been completed by Mines in the context of Madras city. Mattison Mines, *Public Faces, Private Voices: Community and Individuality in South India* (Berkeley, 1994).

2

The Composite Culture
and its Historiography

JAVEED ALAM

A considerable body of literature both in History and the Social Sciences,[1] has grown over the last fifty years or so which has argued that the unique genius of India worked to evolve, over the centuries since the coming of Muslims into the Indian sub-continent, modes of thinking and living which are a subtle intermixing or synthesis of the world-views and living habits of Muslims and Hindus. In fact there is a further thesis, where it has been repeatedly said that it has been a chief characteristic of Indian civilization ever since antiquity to take over or assimilate or synthesize attributes from diverse cultures which came in contact with it.

I will not, in the following discussion, go into this at all. I will only look at the nature of the synthesis which came about after the encounter with Islam from the eleventh century onwards. It is this particular synthesis that is now generally referred to as the 'Composite Culture'. Contemporary historiography, both liberal and Marxist in contradistinction to the conservative-reactionary, has treated it as a powerful resource in our society to combat communalism and other forms of sectarian strife. I want to look at this a little more closely, focusing chiefly on the inner changes in the cultural composition of Indian society and secondarily on the idea of whether the mere existence of composite culture in itself can be a basis of communal harmony. The precise scope of this enquiry will become clear as we go on.

In the words of Tara Chand a co-mingling and a 'sense of larger allegiance',[2] and according to Humayun Kabir a 'fusion of mentalities',[3] did come about in the encounter of Hinduism and Islam or in the carefully weighed argument of Nurul Hasan, there was 'the development of a composite culture tradition....'[4] Nehru's *The Discovery of India* written on the eve of India's independence is in fact a major source of this trend of thought. Later on a large number of people from diverse disciplines and with varying intellectual perspectives have been imparting to this kind of thinking a fresh impetus.[5] Even if we look at the terrain of secular cultural practice today it seems evident that the presence of composite culture is taken for granted, a kind of a cultural given.

Let us look at the philosophical basis and historical character of what has come to be known as the composite culture. It is not the intention here to deny the existence of a composite culture; I do believe that something in the nature of a composite or a common ground did evolve, affecting life at the key points and that some of it still survives influencing our social life at many intersections. Having taken note of this I do not any more want to go into the specific features of what constitutes or constituted composite culture.[6] I would rather examine its foundations and try to see what were its infirmities. Its decline and loss are what immediately concern me.

Given both its historical availability and contemporary decline, what however seems to me to be questionable is the non-disaggregated manner in which the thesis has been advanced and the way it is assumed to be a living force in our social life. From the plane of philosophical thought, architectural styles, musical composition to modes of thinking, styles of living, moral outlook, etc. everything has been advanced, to suit the needs of the argument, as evidence of the composite culture. Let us begin by first ignoring the impersonal level of architectural style or musical composition or even the philosophical thought because some features within these can survive even after people belonging to different traditions come into hostile relationships. If instead we were to think of each other or the day-to-day sharing in life activities then one can go into both the strengths and weaknesses of what has been emerging as the cultural synthesis. The moral worldviews of, let us say, the *Bauls*[7] in Bengal or the *Bhakti* saints, and the trends they gave rise to in day-to-day living, do suggest to us a very high degree over large areas of coming together or 'co-mingling' or 'fusion' of thought and living. In many other ways, independent of these, in their day-to-day interactions and dealings people did develop common themes and interests and meaning systems in their social life and they did share in religious festivals and ceremonies and auspicious occasions and derived meaning and satisfaction from these.

But the curious feature of syntheses and coming together was that these survived for as long as they were left alone; in other words, as long as there was no intervention from above. Once the intervention began—either by spokesmen of dominant versions of the orthodoxy or by the élite or by the state as such—the common features or compositeness begin to dissolve into the existing or parallel neo-orthodoxies propounded by these spokesmen, or with modification get reassimilated into prevailing modes of life sanctioned by the orthodoxy. The frail nature of the composite culture or syntheses was precisely in their inability to withstand the interventions from above.

It is here that we find the slippery ground on which the historiography of this genre stands. Historians, as political partisans, only asked the question in terms of either/or; whether there was and is a composite culture or not.[8] When the question is posed this way, there can only be interminable debate because evidence can be garnered for whatever way one may wish to argue. The historians never asked what was the foundational basis of our composite culture and the kind of terrain on which it was standing.

Now the problem has been that at these folk levels what came about as an intermingling or fusion or synthesis has been of a pre-reflective kind, that is, it was not thought out and consciously appropriated by the people belonging to different religious traditions or by the bearers of culture within them. Or, even at the pre-reflective levels, the compositeness that has been here was not aligned with contending orthodoxies in a way as to be taken as necessarily acceptable when consciously thought about. Once the orthodoxy felt the danger and began intervening, by whatever modalities from above, they more or less succeeded, and are succeeding, in pushing back or defeating most of these trends.

These interventions, starting roughly from the first half of the nine-teenth century, did not have a uniform character to them. From the angle of the Muslims in India, some of these represented a retreat into traditional or fundamentalist Islam of rather primitive varieties. Shah Waliullah or Saiyid Ahmad of Bareilly and their lesser known followers like *Haji* Shariatullah of the Faraizis in Bengal or the Maulvi of Faizabad or Maulvi Karamat Ali of Jaunpur, all in the first half of the nineteenth century, were influenced by the *Wahabi* movement and concentrated their attention on 'un-Islamic' practices prevalent among Muslims such as: the folk practices of joining each other's festivals, modes of saluta-tions and greetings, common customs and etiquettes influenced by the surrounding Hindu ethos, and, above all, worship of saints as *Shirk* (associating other powers with Allah) and so on. They wanted to wean away the Muslims, especially the new converts, from residual Hindu practices and replace these with a purified form of Islam unadulterated by 'foreign influences'.[9]

Another form of intervention, which comes later in the second half of the nineteenth century, is best represented by Sir Saiyid Ahmad Khan. Instead of a retreat into the past and interpretations oriented to the times of Prophet Muhammad and his close associates, Sir Saiyid's vision was one of a Muslim community, staying away from the emerging struggle against the British, achieving rapid modernization with a conception of Islam in consonance with reason, science and technology, and the demands of the modern era. This trend had many regional echoes but was especially pronounced in Bengal and was personified by Sir Abdul Latif.[10]

Whatever differences which can be discerned with respect to historical time, internal thrust, and intentions or motivations, there are certain common features and consequences of these interventions from above. The more salient features that can be discerned are, firstly, a thought-out and planned move towards addressing the people directly instead of relying on or looking to the court or the aristocracy to defend Islam, as, for example, the orthodox did in the conflict between Aurangzeb and Dara Shikouh. Now, some set out to build bridges between the Muslim gentry and the lower ranks of Muslims to provide enduring channels of communication within the community. Secondly, these interventions sought to bring a shift from the terrain or site of theological arguments addressed to the learned to political appeals to and some form of mobilization of the people on broad themes. Thirdly, there was a consistent effort to reconstruct a 'healthier' version of Islam as the ground on which the newly sought identity of Muslims could stand. It may perhaps be correct to see that these two trends within the interventions taking place then crystallized in the shape of the Deoband School ('Traditionalist') and the Aligarh Movement ('Modernist') which took diametrically opposite stands towards the nationalist movement even while looking at Muslims as a distinct cultural community.

The contradictory consequence involved in all this are worth noting. While these developments were slowly drawing the Muslim community away from the rest of the society, they were also slowly bringing them as a people into the public arena as active participants, insistent on being heard. The people were becoming, in an active sense, the subjects of the history. This was a development, democratic in essence, of far reaching consequences. When seen in conjunction with developments in the rest of Indian society, especially the Hindus, we can more clearly see the manner in which political contentions were taking shape in the society. What is important to apprehend is the nature of Hindu response to the conditions imposed by colonialism.

One feature that stands out about the Hindu response is its greater variety and range and a much higher degree of polemical exchanges. Each position was critically scrutinized and all philosophical trends were closely contested. What is also crucial was the greater emancipator thrust if we look at it in totality; this has been so from Raja Ram Mohan Roy, to the contemporary period. But at a certain point, around the 1880s, there were also highly restrictive and, potentially, divisive moves within this totality. In a broad sense even these restrictive moves can be seen also as part of the 'cultural counter-offensive' to overcome the sense of 'subordination and humiliation' as a result of colonial domination.[11] It is, I believe, not enough simply to recognize this if we have to understand how the Muslim communal response got patterned. Within the wide range of response amongst the Hindus, there were tendencies, muted in some and pronounced in others, which extended the feelings of subordination far back into history before the beginning of the colonial rule; the temporal frame extended backward to include the period of Muslim rule in India as well. The 'foreigners' were now not only the British but all those non-Hindus who had become as much Indians as any others. Now the British and Muslims were almost on par, with Muslims more and more displacing the British as foreigners as the 'cultural offensive' took a clearer shape.

The subordination was seen not simply as a result of colonial rule but also something quite intrinsic in having been ruled by the 'Muslims'. I do not want to pursue this point any further for its implications, including for nationalism, but would like to point out that it gave rise to the creation of the 'other' in Indian society. Engagement with this 'other' became, unfortunately, something necessary for one's own self-awareness. The *other* as a presence in Indian society was also viewed as something bestial and malignant. To elaborate this I will take only two very powerful voices whose ideas had a wide ranging and deep refraction in the society—Vivekananda, one of the more radical of the Hindu social reformers, and Dayanand Saraswati the more sectarian and conservative in terms of influence on society. Much more than novelists and other intellectuals, they had a more direct influence in structuring popular sentiments and responses.

But before we do this it will be useful to ask a further question: what made these interventions possible and effective in the first place? Elites, in whatever period of history, are not omnipotent in society. They cannot, when they feel like it, sponsor a complete change in the way people relate to one another. People are not mere objects to be acted upon as and when it pleases the powerful sections of society. Under the worst of situations, they retain a certain capacity to reach their own judgments and understandings.

The one factor that made these interventions possible as well as effective was the politicization of life in society. Expanding on this we can say, that the strength of the composite culture was its being limited to spheres of life not involving questions of power. Once power became, with the colonial impact going deep down, the central concern of different groups, it became imperative for those in a position of vantage to rally the people behind them. Thus came the phase of political mobilization in Indian society and those who were in the race acquired a new salience. It is this situation which allowed for the effectiveness of elite interventions in Indian society.

Let us now go back to the Hindu response, and how within a wide horizon of debates and contentions, restrictiveness also became one of its features, especially when viewed in relation to the Muslims. First, there was the perspective of the sober, if more radical of the reformer-thinkers. To Vivekananda, Muslim rule had been a foreign presence in India. This is how he pictures it:

> ... The final victory of royal power was echoed on the soil of India in the name of *foreign monarchs* professing an entirely different religion from the faith of the land.[12]

In contrast to Muslim rule his assessment of British rule is revealing:

> Of course, we had to stop advancing during the Mohammedan *tyranny*, for then it was not a question of progress but of life and death. *Now that the pressure has gone*, we must move forward.[13]

Compared to the Muslim 'foreign' rule, the British rule is obviously relatively benign. Not only this, the Muslims because of their religion are an intolerable presence in India. Consider how Vivekananda defines 'Muhammad' and Islam:

> Now the Mohammedans are the crudest in this respect, and the most sectarian. Their watchword is: 'There is one God, and Muhammad is his prophet.' Everything beyond that is not only bad, but must be destroyed forthwith: at a moment's notice, every man or woman who does not believe in that must be killed; everything that does not belong to this worship must be immediately broken; every book that teaches anything else must be burnt. From the Pacific to the Atlantic for five hundred years blood ran all over the world. That is Mohammadanism.[14]

This presence becomes especially malignant because Hinduism is so tender and fraternal in contrast.

You know that Hindu religion never persecutes. It is a land where all sects
may live in peace and amity. The Mohammedans brought murder and
slaughter in their train, but until their arrival peace prevailed.[15]

While the Muslims are bestial, they do not have to fear the Hindus; for
the Hindus can provide the kind of shade under which all can flourish.
This theme of tolerance within the interpretative reworking of Hindu
tradition has, since then, became the basis of filling up the 'other' with
negative features. Dayanand does not look at Muslims and their religion
very differently, only his language is much worse. See, for instance:

> ...They have to their charge the greatest sin of killing innocent people. The
> non-acceptance of Moslem's religion they call heresy and they hold slaughter
> superior to heresy; that is, they say that they will put to death those persons
> who do not accept Islam. This they have been all along doing.[16]

Or

> Now see. This is also a lesson of betrayal of confidence that God is teaching
> to the Moslems. Whether a man be a neighbour or a servant, they should
> fight him or betray him whenever there be a chance. Such things have often
> been done by Moslems.[17]

Having said all this, Dayanand goes on to refer to the prophet of Islam,
'Bravo. Muhammad Sahib, Bravo.'

This two-sided process of interventions from above within the
religious communities in India has been an ongoing process with many
and varied ramifications. It has not come to an end. The controversy
meticulously built over Ram Janmabhoomi-Babri Masjid is the latest
instance of it. The Hindu communalists have found in this a very potent
symbol—the most popular Hindu folk god Ram is given a concrete
manifestation in the shape of bricks and temple—to rally the Hindus.
The Muslim communalists, whatever their other concerns revert more
to the defence of their own history and the notion of the community as
one with that history.

The intervention from above is invariably, unless as a part of the
revolutionary struggles of the people, a ruling class-élite manoeuvre.
It leads to bifurcation of common concerns and interests. It not only
destroys the common heritage, from history in general and of the history
of anti-colonial struggle, but gives rise to two further consequences.

First, it destroys tradition as a resource with people to renew themselves or to bring people together. Tradition in such a situation becomes
more and more a weapon with the dominant to exercise power; and
people become more and more a means for such power to be attained.
Tradition becomes a restrictive imposition, an authoritarian device even

when not felt by the people in this way. Now I do not want to suggest here that all the syncretic traditions at the local levels, which have been so very well researched,[18] have disappeared or been appropriated; far from it. The thrust of my argument is that the militant and politicized forms of the re-worked tradition have completely filled up the public sphere, and the mass mobilization now in the name of tradition, unlike those of Gandhi, are all around these. It has pushed the lived experiences of the people into the corners of their private lives; in other words, these have been domesticated.

And, even within this domain, the re-worked Hindu militancy has created confusion and uncertainty among the people. An indication of this uncertainty is the bias of those poor Hindus, let us say returning from Ajmer Sharif, who have not the slightest hesitation in saying that Muslims are 'dirty' or 'bad' and so forth. Confusion is easy to create because a good bit of the syncretic tradition was also founded on the superstition of the poor and illiterate. Ask those returning and often you hear from them that they had gone to pray for a son or a cure for illness or some other boon. It is not that people have ceased to think in opposition to the monopolistic definitions of tradition being imposed on the society. But within the terrain of their habitual cultural day-to-day life, they do not find avenues to contest or contradict these monopolistic definitions. A disjuncture exists such that on one side there is a feeble presence, a presence which has no larger social canvas on which the political contestations and struggles take place.[19]

Secondly, emancipatory concerns in the domains of economic and social relations, gender questions, cultural enrichment of life, and so on recede more and more into the background. Instead, a communal narcissistic self-contemplation gains in prominence. In other words, a second disjunction emerges between the socio-cultural life of the people which is subjectively getting divided and the socio-economic processes which produce on the objective plane unified structures for existence and struggle. People tend to occupy the same space more and more without becoming part of the same historical order of time.

Endnotes

1. The first major work on this problem was written, to the best of my knowledge, by Tara Chand in 1920 but was published in 1963 after the debate on this problem was revived in the 1960s. See his *Influence of Islam on Indian Culture* (Allahabad, 1963); and also Humayun Kabir, *The Indian Heritage* (Bombay, 1946); and Jawaharlal Nehru, *The Discovery of India* (Calcutta, 1946). It is interesting to note that in the cases of Humayun Kabir

and Nehru, the stringency of the demand for Pakistan provides the immediate background.

The debate was revived in the early 1960s, as noted above, as a part
of the struggle against the communal uses of history from both the Hindu
and Muslim viewpoints. Between 1957 and 1961, The Pakistan Historical
Society published a four volume edition entitled, *A History of the Freedom
Movement (Being the Story of Muslim Struggle for Freedom of Hind-
Pakistan, 1707–1947)*. I.H. Qureshi in his 'Introduction' (vol. 1, pp. 1–57)
tried to show the distinct and parallel paths of developments among the
two communities; he debunked the efforts made by certain kings, especially Akbar, as detrimental to Muslims; and castigated the Mughal kings
before Aurangzeb for the crime of lulling the Muslim community. Around
the same time the Bharatiya Vidya Bhavan, under the editorship of K.M.
Munshi, published the *History and Culture of Indian People* (1960) from
a distinctly Hindu point of view. R.C. Majumdar explicitly argued that
Hindus and Muslims can never come together, that there was 'no-sign that
the twain shall ever meet'; see (vol. IV, no.17, p. 636) of the above cited
work. In C.H. Philips (ed.), *Historians of India, Pakistan and Ceylon*
(London, 1961) Majumdar wrote that 'the newly acquired ideal of a
'secular state' is opposed to all known facts of Indian history' (p. 426).
Peter Hardy in Theodore de Bray (ed.), *Sources of Indian Tradition*,
endorses the position of Qureshi and Majumdar.

The renewed interest in finding the common grounds and synthesizing
processes in history was both a result of and an effort to combat this kind
of communal and pre-judged use of history. Interestingly in both periods—
the 1940s and 1960s—when writings on this theme multiplied, the shadow
of Pakistan looms in the background.

2. Chand, *Influence of Islam*.
3. Kabir, *The Indian Heritage*.
4. Nurul Hasan, 'Presidential Address, Medieval Period', *Proceedings of the
Indian History Congress* (Calcutta, 1963).
5. See for instance symposium: 'The Contribution of Indian Historians to the
Process of National Integration', in *Proceedings of the Indian History
Congress*.
6. For a detailed discussion of the specific features see Rasheeduddin Khan
(ed.), *Composite Culture of India and National Integration* (Simla, 1988).
7. For an analysis of the Bauls see Hugh B. Urban, 'The Politics of Madness:
The Construction and Manipulation of the 'Baul' Image in Modern
Bengal', *South Asia*, vol. XXII, no. 1 (1999), pp. 13–46.
8. Refer to notes 1 and 5 above.
9. Among many others see for instance, Shah Waliullah and his Times. For
a specific region where syncretic traditions were particularly strong, see
Rafiuddin Ahmed, *The Bengal Muslims 1871–1906. A Quest for Identity*
(New Delhi, 1981). But to get a rounded view of the problem it is important
to read the above cited work together with A. Roy, *Islamic Syncretic
Tradition in Bengal* (Princeton, 1983).

10. For details see M.M. Ali (ed.), *Autobiography and Other Writings of Nawab Abdul Latif* (Chittagong, 1968) and K.K. Aziz (ed.), *Amir Ali, His Life and Work* (Lahore, 1968). To understand the differences in the character and outlook of these organizations see Salahuddin Ahmad, 'Muslim Thought and Leadership in Bengal in the Nineteenth Century', in Barun De (ed.), *Essays in Honour of Prof. S.C. Sarkar* (Delhi, 1971).

11. See among others Gyan Pandey, *The Construction of Communalism in Colonial North India* (New Delhi, 1991).

12. All citations are from the *Complete Works of Vivekananda* [hereafter *CWV*], 8 vols (Calcutta, 1962), vol. 4, p. 448.

13. Ibid., p. 373.

14. Ibid., p. 126.

15. Ibid., p. 190.

16. Swami Dayanand, *The Light of Truth*, trans. by Ganga Prasad Upadhaya, (Allahabad, 1981), p. 667.

17. Ibid., p. 707.

18. I have already referred to A. Roy's work on Bengal which is a comprehensive account of one province in India. J.J. Roy Burman, 'Hindu-Muslim Syncretism in India', *Economic and Political Weekly*, 18 May 1996, has given a brief but quite exhaustive survey of these local syntheses from across the country. There is a considerable body of literature for different regions of India and the various syncretic traditions within these. All of these still remain strong.

19. I have tried to handle some of these questions in my 'Tradition in India Under Interpretative Stress: Interrogating its claims', in *Thesis Eleven*, no. 39 (1994).

3

Impact of Islamic Revival and Reform in Colonial Bengal and Bengal Muslim Identity

A Revisit

ASIM ROY

I

PROBLEMATIC HISTORIOGRAPHY

One cannot but begin this discussion with the most obvious question—
why revisit Islamic reform and revival movements in Bengal under the
British—an area that is likely to give an impression of being already
overdone in terms of academic curiosity? Should this be the general
impression, a close scrutiny would not bear it out. Islamic revival and
reform, generally speaking, is undeniably a well-trodden academic, as
well as a popularly attractive site, especially since the Arab petro-
power induced the Western politicians and media to rediscover an
ominous linkage of power and faith in Islam. This trend has seen a
dramatic and tragic escalation because of the spate of violent extremism of political Islam in recent times. The archives of Islamic studies
would indeed have a great deal more material to offer on revivalism
than on many other facets of Islamic development. Islamic revival in
India is certainly no exception. The eighteenth century has, in fact,
earned—very largely on this ground—the distinction of being considered at a serious academic level as Islam's 'Indian century'.[1] And yet,
it may come as a surprise to many students of Islamic revival in South
Asia that the Bengal field has not been as rich, in terms of the range,
depth, and substance of its historiography, as one may be given to
expect, and as some other parts of the subcontinent, especially northern

India. One may be quick to recount a number of major and minor studies on the subject in the region of Bengal, and it would be entirely proper to do so. It is my firmly held view, however, that Islamic revival in Bengal has not yet found its 'great narrative', unlike in northern India.[2]

The Bengal revival has been covered both in English and Bengali languages. Aside from a very limited number of Bengali works,[3] most serious studies are in English, though not all of these are wholly focused on this problem or exclusively confined to Bengal.[4] Despite at least some of these studies being based on a hard core of basic research, a discerning critique of this literature encounters very serious problems with its clarity and consistency, in so far as it relates, in particular, to one of the main academic concerns of these writers—namely, the short- and long-term impact of the reform and revival movements in Bengal, in special reference to their bearing on the development of Muslim cultural and political identity in the region.

It appears that there are two major areas in which the prevailing scholarship remains rather deficient and unsatisfactory for discerning students. The first and the most critical area of persisting opaqueness, obscurity, and confusion in both the serious academic and popular literature on this subject relate to the issue of a clear determination of the role, place, and salience of religious and spiritual concerns underlying the movements of reform and revival in colonial Muslim Bengal, which have been presented more from a secular than a religious perspective. The historiography in this area reveals an utter confusion and even insouciance in seeking a clear determination of, rather than making an uncritical assumption about, the salience of Islam in these reform and revival movements. This literature shuns a detailed and sustained examination and analysis of the actual religious underpinning of the reform and revival movements, taken together with their multi-dimensional impact on Muslim Bengal. Even the religious reference in them is very often thoughtlessly reduced to, and entwined with conveniently categorized and compartmentalized non-religious domains—social, economic, and political.

The second area of problematic scholarship, closely interrelated with the first one mentioned above, concerns the more basic issues of the prevalent academic perception and analytical notion of Islamization held out by every writer on the subject as constituting the essence and the fundamental basis of the impact of reform and revival, with special reference to the murky issue of the nature of the reformed Muslim identity. Both these broad areas of inadequate scholarship have indeed vital bearings on the twin issues of Islamization and Muslim identity in Bengal.

II

ISLAMIC SALIENCE OF THE REFORM AND REVIVAL MOVEMENTS IN BENGAL

The Issues

Most studies in the area care to mention, in some form or another, the significance of reform and revival in religious terms, although there is very little that one could find and call an adequate 'explanation' or 'analysis' of this religious process, as noted above. The observations are usually, and frustratingly enough, quite brief and highly generalized. Besides, individual movements are often reduced, as also noted above, to an aggregate of variegated elements, such as religious-spiritual, social, economic, and political, not essentially seeking to explore the integrative role and place of Islam. Such an approach clearly disregards and distorts, in the process, the holistic picture of this significant Islamic development and hence the totality and integrity of the whole. A brief examination of some writings of this genre is likely to elucidate this matter.

On the impact of the Tariqah-i Muhammadiyah movement, Jagadish Narayan Sarkar notes: 'as a religious force it stirred the entire Indian Muslim society to its foundations.' On that of the Faraizis he maintains:

> By his life-long mission Shariat Allah revived Islam in Bengal from its stupor.... the Haji found Islam in a dying state for lack of water of faith... but he revitalized the tree of faith... Herein lay his contribution... after effecting some permanent changes in the religious life in Bengal for nearly half a century, gradually began to decline in importance.[5]

Under the heading 'Significance of the Movements', he concludes:

> ... it must be admitted that the Islamic religious revivalist and reformation movements of the first half of the 19th century... introduced a new life among the Muslims in Bengal. In many cases it was a protest against the British administration and economic exploitation of the masses of the Muslims. Thus religious reform became a many-sided affair—social, economic, political and communal.[6]

Azizur Rahman Mallick, who differentiates the 'political aim', as well as the 'religious' and 'spiritual', finds 'most of the followers [of the revivalist leaders] drawn from the lower orders of society', who 'dissatisfied with the existing orders of society and finding no way out of their miseries, naturally, became easy converts to the social and political doctrines preached in the name of religion.[7]

Two major writers on the subject differ fundamentally in their perceptions of the religious significance of the revival movements.
Muinuddin Ahmad Khan, unquestionably the first major researcher in
the area of Islamic revivalism in Bengal, does attach religious significance to these movements, but only in broad general terms, and also
presents the success of the rival movements in non-defined and de-
aggregated 'spiritual' and 'political' spheres. To quote him:

> ...the Islamic revivalism in the nineteenth century represented a supreme
> attempt on the part of the Muslim society to rehabilitate its lost glory, and
> this was sought through remodelling the Muslim ways and thoughts in
> accordance with the original teachings of Islam. In this endeavour...the
> reformed schools succeeded considerably in awakening the political as well
> as spiritual consciousness of the masses...the reformists were able to rouse
> great enthusiasm among the masses, who pinned their hope for the recovery
> of their past glory on the success of revivalism.[8]

The position of Rafiuddin Ahmed, the other major scholar in the field,
is an intriguing one in that he seems to have shifted his ground quite
significantly between his earlier and later writings. Ahmed seems, in
his earlier studies, clearly inclined to canvas a position that underrates
the religious significance of the movements, claiming that the attainment of their broad religious objective of 'Islamization' has been
minimal or a failure.[9] His subsequent writings present a *volte face* in that
he emerges there as a strong proponent of the view of an unprecedented
form of 'Islamization' in South Asia since the nineteenth century—an
Islamization process which emanated from the reform and revival
movements of the time, and proved highly consequential in the social,
cultural, and political fields. To quote Ahmed:

> ...it may even be said that the Islamisation of the average Indian Muslim
> only *began* [emphasis in the original] in the nineteenth century with the rise
> of the revivalist movements. Bengali Islam stands as a case pre-eminent.[10]

We intend to follow up later in a separate section this highly complex
and shadowy question of the Islamization process in Bengal. We need
for now to return to Ahmed's dichotomization between the religious-
spiritual and social or political in Islamic reform and revival in colonial
Bengal. In his curious words;

> Whether they [the revivalists] succeeded in their principal task, that is
> Islamisation of the soul, is doubtful, but they did transform his social world.[11]

It raises the immediate question of whether a historian is either equipped
or even expected to delve into the quality of the 'soul'—such meta-
physical issues are clearly unhistorical, and hence irrelevant. Even

leaving aside the issue of historicity of the question, one wonders whether it was possible for the Bengal Muslim's 'social world' to have been transformed without causing some changes in his religious and spiritual consciousness. The elevation of the 'social' at the expense of the 'religious', and the clear underrating of the 'religious' by Ahmed is even more forcefully brought out in the following comment:

> The social basis of the reformist effort partly explains the failure to 'Islamize' fully the Muslim masses of Bengal. To the landless cultivator or the depressed weaver, the theological controversies were often of little significance even when they joined these movements from a combination of religious and economic motives. The reformist platform initially offered them a rallying point from where to express their grievances against the social and economic injustices they had suffered long; the possibility of a heavenly abode after death was perhaps an additional bonus.[12]

In pursuance of the same objective of separating the socio-economic activity of the revivalists from their religious reform program, Ahmed elsewhere maintains that 'the socio-economic programmes of the movements had priority over much of their religious work during the early phase', and that 'their religious programmes suffered a major set-back as a result of this shift in emphasis.'[13] An assertion of this nature does typify the serious limitations of this fragmented perception of the nature and impact of revivalism.

The Alternative Methodology

Most of our writers above clearly entertain a disjunctive view of what is an essential unity underlying the multi-faceted phenomenon of Islamic revivalism. They arrive at their fragmented position by ignoring a fundamental truth in Islam of the close, and even inseparable nexus between the temporal and the spiritual. Ahmed himself raises above the issue of 'social and economic injustices',[14] which is so integral to Islam.[15] If the 'reformist preachers could easily exploit the poverty of the Muslim peasantry', as noted by Ahmed,[16] or 'the denunciation of the exactions proved to be strong incentives and powerful appeals to the simple and oppressed peasantry', as Sarkar observes,[17] the revivalists and reformers needed only to invoke, in self-justification, the Quranic provisions against 'endemic injustice' in society. Given the nature of the historiography of Islamic revival in Bengal based on the pervasive assumption of a cleavage between 'religious' and 'social' concerns of the revivalist programs, it is rather important to reinterpret this development and explore the essential integrity and linkage between the social-political and religious life of the Bengali Muslims as expressed in their response to the messages of reform and revival. There is the further issue of the writers of Ahmed's ilk taking an unduly restrictive view of Islamization in the sense and form of conformity to an ideal notion of Islam, and showing eagerness to pronounce the failure of the revivalists in terms of this unrealistic and unattainable religious goal. Ahmed and others observe that the 'heretical' practices and beliefs continued to have a powerful hold on the Muslim masses and that idolatry remained persistent. This is then their yardstick for measuring Islamization that 'the vast majority remained steadfastly opposed to any new dogma and faithful to the traditional system.'[18]

The actual religious impact of the revivalists is clearly underrated in this approach. There are more than one way of looking into the truth of this statement. To begin with, it is highly imperceptive to ascribe a narrow definition such as that proffered by the above writers to the complex and protean process of Islamization, as we shall explore it below in greater depth. It suffices for our purpose here to point out at the very outset that the process of Islamization unleashed by the revivalists came to acquire an almost subjective meaning open to various interpretations, having some understanding and validity in the minds of individual Bengal Muslims, though not complying with the definition and expectation of the revivalists. The individual could well have come to believe and feel that his life had become more Islamized because his understanding of being a Muslim had taken on a new meaning. The continued adherence to traditional custom-oriented life remained external to and in harmony with this new commitment.[19]

Moreover, the revivalist movements must not be viewed purely as agencies of puritanical religious reform, as they gave the poorer Muslims a new awareness, a corporate voice, transformed the people into a community, and paved the way for later political changes, as most writings on the subject do underline. What is critically important here and not to be overlooked is that all these changes, regardless of whether they involved a new spiritual awakening or a desire for greater material rewards, all occurred under the umbrella of Islamic revivalism. Hence it is not possible to separate this new worldview from religious changes and the new understanding of Islam. By looking carefully at the different changes caused by the early revivalists, it is possible to show that change in one sector of life did influence changes at other levels. What is ultimately important is that the Muslim society was at least responding to the revivalists' message.

The issue of socio-economic justice as a core element of Islamic ideology has been already raised above. Haji Shariat Allah, Dudu Miyan, and Titu Mir all became involved in the socio-economic battles

of the Bengali Muslims by protecting their religious rights. The two
strands of Muslim life must have become more meaningfully inter-
twined through the relationship with the revivalists. The right to demand
equality and justice is a fundamental aspect of Islamic ideology, which
easily became translated into the demand for economic justice and
greater equality. These new aims, when combined with the concept of
Islamic brotherhood, gave the movements potential for becoming revolutionary organizations. Also associated with the development of this
economic and religious awareness was the growing idea that the Bengal
Muslims were a deprived group in the society. The psychological
impact of this would be to add resentment and frustration to their
demands for justice. Thus revivalism awakened negative feelings in the
ordinary Muslim which could be used, positively reinforcing his growing economic and social expectations. Alternatively, these negative
qualities could undermine his self-confidence and make him more
reliant on the revivalists. Thus the possibility for alternative perceptions
clearly exists, and again one must be careful of drawing a general
interpretation of the impact of the revivalists on Bengali Muslim lives.

It is indeed commonplace among all writers to see the revivalists
acting as a catalyst for later Muslim activity which helped to bring the
masses in line with *ashraf* (the highborn) aspirations and pave the way
for the politicization of the Bengal Muslim community. For Rafiuddin
Ahmed the real process for Islamization began in the post-Mutiny
period at the close of the Wahibi trials and with the denunciation of the
holy war or the smaller and external *jihad-i asghar* by Keramat Ali, in
1871.[20] In reference to the two separate movements in the late nineteenth
century—a push for the achievement of political goals and another for
the realization of the earlier revivalist goals—Ahmed shows how these
two strands became linked together with the 'traditional' religious
leaders, the *mullahs* and preachers, acting as mediators between the
urban elite and the rural Muslim masses of Bengal.[21] He does not seem
to adequately recognize that this link between the rural Muslims and the
urban elite was only possible because the earlier revivalists had already
significantly contributed to the process of Islamization. This is also to
deny the fact that the political elite also had religious goals, to ignore
the very real link between religion and politics in Islam, and hence in
revivalism, and finally to diminish the pervasive impact of Islamic
ideology on Bengali Muslim society. Regardless of the stated aims of
the revivalists, they were genuinely concerned with rectifying the balance between the temporal and spiritual, the civic and corporate aspects
of the community. There is clear evidence that the urban elite Muslims
were also concerned with achieving political goals in a 'correct' Islamic

manner.[22] There was, however a great deal of confusion and conflict over what was actually the 'correct Islamic manner', but the spirit of Islam had been awakened and was stirring Muslim minds throughout Bengal at least to think again about their religion and how they should live as Muslims. Since the early revivalists in the nineteenth century took the initiative for reviving Islam, they must also be given responsibility for determining the shape of future change in Bengal and hence for the Islamization process which followed.

One only has to look at the activity, ideology, and attitudes of these early revivalists to see how important their role was in getting the whole Islamization process on the road. Although their roles were stated as primarily religious they used this word in a total and more comprehensive Islamic sense, as stated above. Hence politics remained an intrinsic and inescapable part of revivalism. Also the very nature of the revivalists' activity made it impossible for them not to become more fully involved with the lives of ordinary people. Haji Shariat Allah had 'aimed at reforming the old socio-religious order by purging it of un-Islamic elements', and emphasized 'the necessity of observing *Faraid* or the obligatory duties prescribed by Islam.'[23] Although he intended the Faraizi movement not to become political, it was impossible in the particular socio-economic and political circumstances to prevent this from happening. His followers 'naturally looked upon him for the redress of their grievance', and he was ineluctably drawn into political action by his own religious conviction to defend the rights of the Muslim community, as he 'directed his disciples to withhold the payment of idolatrous cesses and encouraged them to slaughter crows'.[24] Drawing the line between defending the religious rights of the Muslims and becoming involved in their socio-economic battles was indeed neither easy nor meaningful for these popular Muslim icons either on ideological or practical grounds.[25]

The Bengal Muslim masses were clearly in need of protection because the government had created a situation, which gave the *zamindar*s excessive powers, which they abused for their own ends. Shariat Allah, Dudu Miyan, and Titu Mir all became involved in the Muslim battles with the Hindu zamindars, if not the European planters as well. The Hindu zamindars were frightened by the growing unity amongst Muslims as they attempted to resist the increasingly unjust oppression. Rafiuddin Ahmed writes: 'the *zamindars* awakened in the oppressed peasantry a consciousness of social injustice and economic oppression and thus threatened the status quo in the rural society.'[26] M.A. Khan says that Dudu Miyan and Titu Mir met in about 1830–1, and thus the Tariqah-i Muhammadiyah movement came to influence the later style and method of the Faraizis under Dudu Miyan. Dudu Miyan is said to have perfected the method which Titu Mir used and 'struck awe and terror in the minds of his enemies and brought relief to his friends and followers.'[27] Although there are doctrinal differences between the different revivalist movements there exists a shared sense of the same religion and ultimately the same social goals. Thus the conflicts took on two distinct characters. The underlying socio-economic problems and the local demand for justice was first permeated and sublimated by its linkage with the issue of religious justice, thus leading to a second aspect of the conflict—its ethnic or communal aspect. As the nineteenth century progressed, the conflicts were steadily brought, like the general process of Islamization and politicization of the Muslim community, under a common Islamic umbrella reinforcing and deepening the distinction between the Hindu and Muslim communities.

The outcome of Dudu Miyan's battles with the Hindu zamindar family of Ghosh proved to be a remarkable victory for the Faraizis, in contrast with Titu Mir's relative lack of success. Madan Ghosh, the Hindu zamindar, was supposed to have been killed and buried at the bottom of a river, and the Faraizi sources say: 'Henceforth, the Hindus were terror stricken, ... dared not resist the march of Islamisation which then proceeded without hindrance'.[28] Even allowing for some exaggeration in this statement, it is obvious that the threat from the Faraizi revivalists was not simply social, economic or even physical, but was also regarded by the Hindus as a threat to their religious beliefs. Even under Haji Shariat Allah the Faraizi threat to Hinduism was felt, and it was believed that if he was allowed to continue 'the Hindu religion will soon be destroyed which will bring also the world destruction.'[29] Thus the religious impact on Bengali society was being felt even before Haji Shariat Allah died in 1842, and contradicts Ahmed's argument that the revivalists had little direct religious impact on Bengali society. As a consequence of Dudu Miyan's bold actions against the Ghoshes, he rose 'high in the esteem of the down trodden peasantry, who hailed him as their saviour, and as the champion of their cause.'[30]

These revivalist leaders shared similar features to modern day fundamentalist leaders seen in Western countries. First they were aware of the impact, which they needed to make on the masses to achieve certain religious and possible political goals. Secondly, they chose to appeal through their charismatic personality; and finally, to present themselves in a saviour-like role. In view of the conditions, which prevailed in the nineteenth century and the failure of traditional ashraf leaders, the Muslims felt the dire need of an alternative leadership and hence became susceptible to the charismatic appeal and approach of the revivalists.[31] Islam thus became invigorated and renewed because of its association with visions of heroic action, because of leaders like Saiyid Ahmad Shahid at the Frontier and Titu Mir and Dudu Miyan at the mass level in Bengal. R. Ahmed reminds us that Bengal's link with the jihad was very real, and points to the 'great popularity of the Frontier movements, specially in the districts of middle, south and east Bengal.'[32]

Saiyid Ahmad Shahid's defeat at the Frontier by the Sikhs signified not only that the Sikhs were a superior fighting force, but also the naivety of the early revivalists who expected too much too soon of their revivalist programs. Shahid, like Titu Mir, Shariat Allah, and Dudu Miyan, lacked the breadth of vision of men like Shah Wali Allah and did not understand that revivalism and jihad were futile responses in the struggle against the new order. In the late nineteenth century, the more educated and pragmatic Muslims would show that revivalism would need to develop political as well as religious goals if it was to effectively remedy the Muslim condition. However the revivalists in the early nineteenth century gave Islam a new virility because of the intensity of their activities, their persistence, and their attitude of self-confidence, together with the notion of jihad. After Saiyid Ahmad Shahid's death the Ali Brothers—Maulana Wilayat and Maulana Enayat—continued the Tariqah movement. Because of their organizational skills, and their dedication to the doctrinal principles and to the example set by Saiyid Ahmad Shahid, they were able to stir up the Bengali Muslims. Jadunath Sarkar opines:

'Once stirred, their intellectual superiority prevailed and the movement became to a great extent a Bengali Muhammadan revival' and that between 1830 and 1870 they succeeded in rousing a strong religio-political consciousness amongst the Bengali Muslims and encouraging the growth of a civic and corporate spirit, a policy of civil disobedience to government and boycott of government organs, especially the courts. The village mosque under its Imam became the centre of this corporate spirit.[33]

As the mosque took on a more meaningful role in the lives of ordinary Muslims they tended to see themselves more and more as a distinct community from the Bengali Hindus.

While the more colourful leaders such as Dudu Miyan, Titu Mir, and Saiyid Ahmad Shahid appealed to the masses, and the Patna school maintained this heroic tradition, Maulana Keramat Ali began to offer an alternative form of revivalism. He tried to steer a middle course and displayed a more moderate and tolerant revivalist spirit.[34] In this way revivalism was gaining new strings to its bow, and able to appeal to Muslims at different levels. The tendency to moderation reflects, first, a more pragmatic tendency creeping in; secondly, a realization that the

British were indeed in India to stay; thirdly, the possibility that the revivalists may have to collaborate with them; fourthly, that current revivalist methods may not be enough on their own for either the religious aims to be achieved or for the Muslim community to become unified; and finally, the value of revivalist ideology as an instrument of Muslim mobilization was perhaps beginning to penetrate into the wider Muslim community. But beneath this increased moderation and perhaps a more unified revivalist aim, the tension between idealism and pragmatism was nevertheless still unreconciled, as it has remained to this day, reflecting a basic lack of consensus at the theological level of Islam. Although this tension inhibits Islam from easily achieving harmony, it keeps the ideology in full view and provides Islam with the necessary dynamism to sustain it.[35] Although the conflict led to splits it also created a more vigorous atmosphere of competition, and the revivalist groups, despite their differences, gained 'the motive for what was in fact their common work of revitalization and re-definition.'[36]

Inasmuch as the socio-economic battles involved the revivalists and peasants in conflicts with zamindars and European planters and consequently with the law, the condition of the peasantry became a focus for concern. In this way the revivalists emphasized the plight of the peasantry, and the British were finally forced to look at the causes of the insurrectionary behaviour.[37] The Indigo Commission in 1860 should be seen as an outcome of the revivalists' role in bringing the situation to the attention of the authorities. Thus revivalism was having a positive social impact on Bengal Muslim lives. The sequence of developments followed a pattern which is typical in class-based conflicts where self-consciousness, a sense of deprivation, and finally, militant activity act as a natural prelude to final engagement and resolution. The religious ideology and programs of the revivalists were central to the new awareness and the growing sense of community amongst Muslims, rather than separate to it, as we have sought to establish above. Bengal Muslims might not have been drawn towards Islamization out of a greater sense of commitment, but the internal and external conflicts facing them made it necessary for them to identify with the movements for protection. This process of identification involved also the question of loyalty and hence a greater commitment to the movements. Thus it was the negative elements of fear and conflict which were critical to the process of Islamization. This negative psychological impact of revivalism was reinforced by the revivalists' emphasis on exclusiveness or sectarian activity. This would also aggravate the developing communal conflict at the local level. The revivalist programs of Haji Shariat Allah and Titu Mir and later, Dudu Miyan and the organizational activities of the Patna school all emphasized the need for Muslims to distinguish themselves as followers of Islam, and from non-Muslims and non-believers. The early revivalists were motivated by the nativistic aspect of revivalism, the desire to purify Islam and rid it of alien cultural elements. At this stage their goal was to strengthen Islam by emphasizing Islamic principles, whereas later the same process would be used to shape the Muslim community into a distinct political group. This sense of exclusiveness not only aggravated communal conflict but possibly also reinforced the deprivation and injustice felt by the Bengali Muslims. Muslim exclusiveness must have had a very significant impact on the Bengali Muslim's self awareness, as they came to see themselves as rather special in the eyes of the Islamic community while held in contempt by non-Muslim zamindars and planters. At this stage all the forces at work seemed to be consolidating the Muslim's lack of self-worth on the outside, while, as Metcalf says, they gained a sense of worth and community within the revivalist community.[38]

The revivalists played an important part in counteracting the individual's sense of political, social, and cultural alienation caused by the impact of the new rulers. However this positive affect is offset by the defensive action of the revivalists and the tendency to alienate themselves as a community from the rest of society. In Bengal, because of the roughly equal number of Muslims and Hindus, this religious or ethnic division would have a marked social impact on society. Islamization therefore seems to be occurring at great cost to the psychological well-being of the total Bengali community. In a similar way present-day fundamentalist groups in the West provide greater cohension in the community of believers (or likely believers). The sense of power gained by the group comes from a sense of belonging and being a part of the group and the holders of a special ideology with its God-given promises of salvation. In this way the group fulfils an important role in times of crisis. Although the potential for these groups to exploit their religious appeal and the fundamental promises for economic gain is strong, the Bengal revivalists remained quite puritanical in their approach. They attacked the existing corruption of the traditional religious leaders. Hence they were challenging not only the economic corruption of the zamindars and planters but also the religiously corrupt *pirs* and mullahs, who used to make money from administering un-Islamic practices.[39]

It is not surprising that the revivalists' attack on these practices was not as welcome as their attack against the zamindars for exploiting the peasantry, and was as unwelcome as their attack on the Bengali Muslims' own practices and customs. Ahmed believes Bengali Muslims rejected the revivalists because of such puritanical attacks on existing corruption.[40] While his observation here is correct, he is only presenting one side of the picture. He does not consider that their resentment may have been offset by either the gratitude felt towards the revivalists for intervening in their economic battles, or by the heroic vision created through the notion of jihad and the Frontier activities from Saiyid Ahmad Shahid right through into the last quarter of the nineteenth century.

The general atmosphere of growing unrest, tension, and conflict in Bengal was not only external, but was also within the hearts of the Bengali Muslims. On the one hand, the Bengali Muslim was being offered leadership and protection and gaining a sense of certainty and self-worth through his involvement with these movements. He was, on the other hand, having the core of his value system, and the very layout of his mental map, his view of the world, or *weltangshuung*, brutally [sic] attacked and disturbingly challenged. In Erikson's well-known psychosocial analytical model, when an individual feels uncomfortable about any part of his psychosocial identity resulting in inner conflict or self-hatred, he attempts to minimize the conflict by projecting this onto the external world.[41] When the revivalists attacked the Bengali Muslims' un-Islamic practices, which were regarded as borrowing or innovations from the Hindu culture, they were filled with a mixed feeling of unease, shame, and guilt, causing inner conflict. But by directing it against the Hindus and blaming them for their plight, Bengal Muslims sought to ease this inner conflict. Bengali Muslims' dual identity, which had all this time been integrated into their worldview, now possibly rested uneasily.

The exclusiveness, the communal conflict, anxiety, and threat to their traditional and harmonious identity, all created tension and contradiction within the Bengali Muslim society. Although Ahmed believes the Bengali Muslims rejected the revivalists as a consequence of these attacks, it seems more likely that they were in no position to reject any assistance that was offered. What was probably more likely was that they felt an ambivalence towards the revivalists and torn between a sense of obedience and duty to these religious reformers and a sense of resentment and confusion. From Ratnalekha Ray's work it is very obvious that we must be careful about generalizing. She shows that not all Muslims were suffering from oppression and worsening conditions and some were clearly able to use the Faraizi organization to secure economic benefits, so 'the sectarian organization of the Faraizi moment fulfilled a genuine local need',[42] for the Muslim peasants engaged in a struggle for power with the zamindars in the altered socio-economic conditions. For both the prospering and suffering peasantry, revivalism offered a positive message of hope, and the assurance that the solution lay in their own hands; if they followed the word of God they would be assured of rewards, if not in this world, at least in the next. Was this powerful and simple message able to counter the comparatively austere nature of Islam for the ordinary Muslims? The fundamentalist movements everywhere today do offer the same message of hope and empowerment to essentially powerless people ground down with a sense of worthlessness and subjection.[43]

Revivalism must therefore be seen as an attempt to preserve the traditional cultural values of the Muslim community. Events in the second half of the nineteenth century show that the other areas of Muslim lives, the economic, social, and political changes underwent Islamization before the culture itself changed. If we view this sequence of change as Talcott Parsons does, as the normal way in which change occurs, then the events in the late nineteenth century take on quite a different meaning; allowing also for a different interpretation of these events to that made by Ahmed that religious-cultural components of the revivalist program were aborted, while social, economic, and political changes successfully resulted. Had the revivalists not intervened, the Bengali Muslims, might have adapted, like the Hindus, more easily to the British. Regardless of what might have ensued, the rate of cultural change would still have been gradual in comparison with the economic, political, and social changes, which occurred. The backwardly directed cultural changes towards the pristine purity of Islam were still likely to be slow and uneven. It is important to consider the reluctance of peasant societies to respond to cultural change. They were, as an inward looking, conservative, and largely leaderless and powerless community, particularly attached to their cultural traditions and to their traditional world view. In Bengali Muslim society, the Islam, which the revivalists were offering, was rather different to their traditional syncretistic tradition, and hence their reluctance to accept it would have been substantial. This does not mean that they were deaf to the message of the Prophet which being revived, or unmoved by the religious enthusiasm of the revivalists. All it means is that they were reluctant to give up the culture which was familiar and meaningful to them. Hence the rate of cultural change was likely to be slow rather than non-existent. The Bengali Muslims were not simply pawns in the political games of the Muslim elite and the elite in turn was not simply manipulating religious ideology for their own ends. The increasing complexity of the situation, the diversity of Muslim society provoked complex reactions, which defy simplistic interpretation. What we do see happening was that the Muslim society in Bengal was becoming Islamized in a new and non-traditional sense through a sense of shared religious ideology and an increasingly similar Islamic outlook. The aspirations of the *atraf* (the commoners) were moving in line with those of the ashraf. This does not mean however that the great class difference between ashraf and atraf had disappeared or that their social, economic, and political needs were now identical, or even that the overall cultures of the two communities resembled one another. By the third decade of the twentieth century, however, the two classes had come to share a closer sense of Islamic identity.

It is important, therefore, to recognize that the religious activities of the revivalists in the early nineteenth century were as important as their socio-economic and political activities in changing the outlook of Bengali Muslims and paving the way for these later changes. The revivalists involved the Bengali Muslim peasants in a variety of activities aimed at reforming their practices, their material well-being and especially at re-invigorating the Muslim community. Behind all this, the question of restoring Muslims to power remained an ultimate but unrealistic goal. Judging by the progress of the revivalist movements and the response of the Muslims, the early revivalist had used the classical Islamic model to achieve a great deal. They had informed the Bengali Muslims of the right way to live. They had aroused in them a more self-conscious awareness and understanding of themselves and their lowly condition, and of their relation to the wider world and especially to the world of Islam. They had also aroused in them a desire for equality and justice and the demand to have their needs met, and along with this the Bengali Muslims' expectations of a better life were heightened.

The revivalists therefore influenced the thinking, the attitude, and the opinion of the peasants. But this gaining of a new awareness of life was also accompanied with internal and external conflict. The revivalists caused Bengali Muslims to feel a sense of guilt and shame because of their attachment to a syncretistic culture. This internal conflict was likely to have caused the Bengali Muslims to suffer long-term psychological discomfit, ambivalence, and uncertainty about their true identity and make them more, rather than less vulnerable to Islamization. External conflict on the other hand, caused them to become further alienated from non-Muslims, and the social roots of the partition of Bengal were being laid. Later the British could use these 'natural' divisions as part of their divide and rule policy. But the conflicts were not only between Muslims and the zamindars and Europeans, and between Muslims and Hindus, but also between the revivalists themselves, and finally between the revivalists and the authorities.

On the positive side, the revivalists provided the much-needed leadership and gave Bengali Muslims an Islamic assurance and a sense of communal identity. The intense emphasis on Islam, the Islamic world, and an Islamic pattern of living all forced the Bengali Muslims, whether they liked it or not, to be exposed to the persistent, and therefore pervasive and finally even persuasive ideology, and in this way a process of Islamization was initiated in the early nineteenth century.

In general then we see the revivalists involving Muslims in their reform programs, preaching to them, building mosques for them, publishing religious literature and persuasive propaganda, and becoming involved in their socio-economic activities. At this stage we see something like a spontaneous publicity campaign to promote Islam. In the late nineteenth century, this campaign became better organized and coordinated, and consequently more effective. One might have expected the growing conflict and tension to have inhibited this first flurry of fundamentalist revivalism, and hence explain why Islamization was minimal or non-existent at this stage as Ahmed suggests. However, it seems to have had the opposite effect. Conflicts between the various parties grew and tension mounted, but rather than undermine the religious impact of the revivalists it seems to have reinforced their revivalist ideas, and invigorated Islam. Metcalf says of the conflict between revivalist movements in north India, 'Conflict was, in fact, positive; it was satisfying to those involved... sectarian affiliation provided a sense of unquestioned value.'[44] Ahmed expresses a similar view, though one cannot miss the recurrent point that he persists in differentiating between the social from the religious impact of revivalism:

> Conflict and tension, paradoxically, acted as a catalyst in social integration, creating in the individual an awareness that they were integral parts of a social group much wider than their immediate circle.[45]

By the mid-nineteenth century, the reformist goals were being extended to cover all aspects of Muslim life. Revivalism began to take on new meanings and new goals, and its functional value began to outstrip its spiritual significance. In other words, it was becoming more pragmatic and less idealistic. In the process a tendency towards moderation, greater adaptability, and hence greater effectiveness was also seen in Maulana Keramat Ali, who broke away from the jihad campaign. In the same way as Keramat Ali adapted his actions to his doctrines and the changing circumstances, revivalism itself gradually adapted to the changing conditions. Out of the conflict emerged fundamentally important Islamic ideas, which transcended in importance the doctrinal differences and the individual aims of the various movements. Ahmed concedes:

> Despite the persistence of unorhodox beliefs and practices, co-operation between the diverse social elements became possible on the basis of this ideology and the newfound consciousness of solidarity.[46]

But the fact, which Ahmed seems to ignore is that this ideology gave the necessary unity to revivalism and to the community which would ensure greater Islamization in the late nineteenth century. Islamic revivalism in the period prior to 1871 has been shown to be largely a spontaneous movement from below, reflecting the shared attempt by both revivalists and the Bengali Muslim masses to adapt to changed circumstances. This common goal of adaptation overcame the revivalists' initial and excessive emphasis on religion and culture, allowing them to accommodate to the socio-economic needs of the ordinary man. Thus it was through the course of everyday human interaction that revivalism adapted and moderated, allowing the Bengali Muslims to benefit socially and economically.

Despite the conflicts and tensions involved in their experience with the revivalist movements, their worldview and understanding of Islam changed. Rather than arguing that Islamization was incomplete, or failed to meet the ideal standards of revivalism, it has been shown here that Islamization was a religious and cultural change which followed naturally from the economic, social, and psychological changes, and the beginning of a political consciousness. Although the fundamentalist challenge did not succeed in eradicating the mullah's hold on Bengal Muslims, the revivalists re-invigorated Islam and gave it new meaning for the ordinary man. They firmly laid down an Islamic pattern for future change and in this way they initiated a revival of Islam in Bengal. However, the Mutiny signalled a turning point in Muslim, and therefore revivalist history. Muslims would continue to follow an Islamic path, but the new political goals of the Muslim elite were to become linked with religious revivalism, causing Muslims to move towards a political community rather than recreating the idealized Islamic community of classical Islam.

III

REVIVALISM AND MOBILIZATION OF THE BENGAL MUSLIM POLITICAL COMMUNITY

A second wave of Islamization occurred in the post-Mutiny period between 1871 and 1906, for which the impetus came from the elite Muslims rather than representing a spontaneous force from below as in the previous phase of Islamization. The nature of revivalism and its outcome for the Bengali Muslim masses in this phase proved, therefore, significantly different. The egalitarian concepts of Islam played an important part in influencing people to hear the early revivalists' message. Once the elites gained a greater control of the Islamization process, the emphasis was placed on the more conservative aspects of Islam, the outward display of 'correct' Islamic behaviour. As revivalism changed course, the aims of the original revivalists and their followers were lost in the broader elite controlled movement. By identifying with elite interests in the new phase of Islamization, the Bengali Muslims followed once again the older pattern of emulating the elite aims and aspirations. They lost the independence and potential for challenging the elite control and for gaining real socio-economic advantages which they had just begun to experience as a consequence of the radical program of the early Islamic revivalists.

There are several factors which explain why revivalism changed course in the late nineteenth century. First, the political circumstances of India had begun to change from the 1860s. The traumatic impact of the Mutiny on India, the government, and Muslims in particular, caused the British to re-assess their position and policy towards Muslims. The government sought to make itself aware of the entire Muslim situation, and distinguish between loyal and subversive Muslims, and treat each accordingly. Thus the government implemented a twin policy of reform and repression. This was also part of a larger plan to subdue the Indian population by a policy of divide and rule.

Secondly, with the replacement of the East India Company's government, after the Mutiny, by the direct rule of India under the British Crown, the British could no longer be regarded as temporary rulers, and the Muslims were compelled to adapt to the changed circumstances. Corresponding with this turn of events revivalism itself had also changed and prepared the way for further changes. After the death of Dudu Miyan in 1862, his sons showed a much greater willingness to collaborate with the British. The more extreme and doctrinaire members of the Patna school broke away in 1864 and became known as the Ahl-i Hadith. This final split in the Tariqah-i Muhammadiyah movement was important because it removed this more radical and anti-British element from the mainstream of Islamic revivalism. The Ahl-i Hadith on their own also served another important purpose. By keeping the spirit of uncompromising revivalism alive in theory, it provided a model of militant revivalism, and Saiyid Ahmad Shahid's vision of a religious leadership that would carve out, militarily if need be, a new and autonomous society, as an alternative to modernization and colloboration.[47]

Another factor that called for a change in revivalism was the reaction from both the Muslim modernizers and the 'traditionalists' to Islamic revivalism. The Muslim modernizers did not aim at Islamization but favoured a reconciliation between Islam and the West. They wanted 'to usher the well-born Muslim into the modern age weaning him from the faded dreams of Mughal glory.'[48] Nevertheless, their emphasis on Islam helped to focus attention on the concept of Islamization and on the idea of giving Muslims special privileges. The modernizers wanted to compete, not just with Hindus, but with the West itself and wanted to adapt to modernity. Their outlook was quite distinct from the retrogressive view of revivalism and they represented another enlightened form of revivalism, since both aimed at a cultural awakening. The response of the 'traditionalists' to revivalism was much more pedestrian. They resented the attack on their cultural practices, and the traditional reformers objected bitterly to having both the source of their income and their status challenged. They responded by mounting their own campaign for reform in opposition to the either revivalists. The 'traditionalists', like the British, were happy to support an alternative and less threatening form of revivalism. The Muslim elite also saw in revivalism a means of getting the support of the masses for their own social, economic, and eventually political goals, by using the revived ideology as the common ground to unite all Muslims. Religious reform would ensure greater unity to the Muslim community and a basis for later political solidarity. This link meant that Islamization took on new goals and hence new meanings. As the diverse aims and aspirations of the Muslim community all became linked to the concept of Islamization, the process became complicated, contrived, and manipulated. Islamization became an instrument of upward mobility and domination and lost its potential to benefit the masses, along with its original purity and former freedom to adapt.

In general then, the second stage of Islamization meant that revivalism changed from being a spontaneous mass movement to becoming an elite controlled movement. It became pragmatic rather than idealistic, emphasizing overtly political than religious goals. Since these goals represented those of the elite, they were conservative as opposed to the more radical demands of the masses, especially under Dudu Miyan and the Tariqah order. As elite Muslims moved from a position of aloofness towards a more collaborationist position with the British, circumstances and the nature of revivalism also changed dramatically. Although clear differences were observable, the essential continuity of revivalism was still present there. Elements of intolerance and uncompromising attitudes still persisted in the outlook of some of the traditional religious reformers, and what Ahmed interprets as greater Islamization could well be seen as a more heightened sense of Muslim exclusiveness and greater intolerance towards Hindus. The revivalists' unrealistic aim of

returning to the golden age of Islam was no longer stressed nor were
the revolutionary aims of jihad and the overthrow of British rule. The
emphasis was on re-invigorating Islam and purging everything that was
local. The changes that occurred during the first stage of revivalism
contributed largely to the process of Islamization. As the Muslim
community developed a much greater consensus about Islamization in
the second stage, the transition from religious to political goals became
easier. The revivalist ideology and organizational infrastructure for
mobilizing the masses were already in place for the elite to manipulate.
But more importantly, the Bengali Muslims were psychologically prepared to respond to this second wave of revivalism and to the elite
because of the work done by the earlier revivalism. Events in the second
stage of Islamization must be seen as dependent upon, and a continuation of the earlier revivalism. At that stage Muslims were offered a
more exciting and more rewarding concept of Islam, with its heroic
vision, promise of equality, Muslim brotherhood, and justice. A new
invigorated spirit had been injected into Islam, and without this, the
second stage of Islamization could not have occurred.

Among some of the most important factors responsible for increasing the Bengali Muslim's understanding of the correct practice of Islam,
were the religious debates, or *bahas* that began in the 1860s. The
debates symbolized the more pragmatic factual approach rather than the
idealistic and spiritual tone of the earlier revivalism. They were not
concerned with struggling against the injustices suffered by Muslims,
the issues were less emotional and aimed at getting Muslims to conform
to the correct standard of Islamic behaviour rather than rouse them to
wage jihad. Although some debates ended in brawls or turned into
fiascos, the social value of the debates was important. It provided
Bengali Muslims with Islamic occasions on which to meet with other
Muslims beyond their own villages and became better informed about
their religion and develop greater social skills.

Another way of raising the religious awareness of the masses was
through the proliferation of cheap religious books called *nasihat namahs*
(manuals of religious instruction). Besides aiming to distinguish Muslims from Hindus, they sought to enhance their identity with the Muslim
world and they contributed to the communal conflict because of their
openly anti-Hindu tone. The early revivalists had aimed at purification
of Islam rather than communal hatred. Conflict between Hindus and
Muslims had been a corollary of their cultural, social, and economic
consequences rather than being deliberately encouraged. This outcome
in the late nineteenth century, must be seen as one of the 'unintended'
consequences of the early revivalists' activities. The rigid Islamization

of the second period was symbolized by these orthodox, didactic writings. Later this propaganda literature would be used as part of the elites' attempt to get the support of the masses. But the renewed campaign of Islamization was not restricted to the masses. The upper class Muslims also wished to see their religion reformed, and religious literature written in modern Bengali prose also proliferated for educated Muslims and higher ulama in this period.

Another important type of organized religious activity seen in the late nineteenth century and designed to strengthen Muslim communal solidarity and self-confidence, and contribute to the Islamization of Muslims was the *wai'z mahfil*. These called upon Muslims to revive the true spirit of Islamization, change their lifestyle, and work ardently for the welfare of the community. The wai'z mahfils, often directed against the threat of the Christian missionary activities, were ironically modelled on the Christian missionary organizational structure. Thus revivalism can be seen to be adapting, even in these small ways, to Western influence, although its purpose was to defend itself against the West.

The cumulative effect of all this was the manifestation of a more rigid Islamic outlook, a more exclusive Islamic identity, and greater uniformity and conformity, which also tended to polarize Muslims from their Hindu brothers in Bengal. This contributed to the growing Hindu–Muslim communal conflict, sharpened the dual Muslim Bengali identity, and further undermined the traditional syncretistic culture.[49] The increasing tendency of Muslims to identify with the Muslim world and to become more exclusive,[50] was also seen at the local level, as Bengali Muslims sought to imitate the Arabic culture or, the next best thing, to emulate the Muslim elite in their dress, their names, their language, and literature.[51] Thus Islamization seemed to be taking on a more superficial appearance, but if we look a little deeper what we see is the continuing Muslim insecurity: the upper class Muslims had lost their former political power, been conquered by the British, and now were being left behind by the Hindus. The attitude of paranoia and inferiority showed itself in their struggle for position and power, especially in the late nineteenth century right through to Independence. Now these attitudes were seen to be spreading to the masses, and the impact of increased Muslim exclusiveness and paranoia would further alienate Muslims from Hindus. Only by recognizing that the psychological problems of the early nineteenth century continued to linger on, can we properly understand the impact of revivalism at this later stage.

By the end of the nineteenth century, the consequences of revivalism for the oridinary Muslims were becoming tragic. The early revivalists like Haji Shariat Allah, Saiyid Ahmad Shahid, Titu Mir, Dudu Miyan,

Maulana Enayet, Maulana Wiliyat Ali, and Maulana Keramat Ali perhaps had been motivated by a genuine concern for the welfare of the
masses which became incorporated into their reform programs, as
shown above. They had been prepared to enter into the socio-economic
battles between the Muslims and the zamindar and thus help the peasant
Muslims. By the late nineteenth century, the needs of the masses had
been submerged by the concerns of the elites. The 'traditional' reformers were conservative and prepared to conform to the aims and aspirations of the ashraf rather than involve themselves in more radical
behaviour. This led also the masses to accept the new conservative
revivalism, and regard themselves as part of the exclusive community,
identify with the Muslim world and the Arabic culture, and also with
the social expectations of the elite. They no longer had their own leaders
or a separate peasant-based movement and had to accept the goals of
the elite. In a subtle yet complex way, the process of Islamization
became contrived and manipulated by elite Muslims so that the Bengali
Muslim masses lost the position of strength which they had formerly
enjoyed for a brief period under the early revivalist leaders like Dudu
Miyan and his sophisticated organization of Bengali peasant society.
Instead of becoming mentally and socially more aware of themselves
in a positive and affirmative way, the negative elements of earlier
revivalism were exacerbated, and the masses experienced a new form
of psychological oppression under the Muslim elite. To understand this
tragic and unintended consequence of revivalism, it is necessary to look
at the new political goals and developments by the end of the nineteenth
century and into the early decades of the twentieth century.

The Muslim community in general had become more interested in
religion and reform by the late nineteenth century. The actual understanding of the masses of their world had been enriched because of their
social, economic, psychological, and political experiences with the
early religious movements. As a consequence, the meaning of religion
changed, providing Bengali Muslims with a different understanding of
life. Their religion now demanded a more intense and active commitment from the individual, both socially and spiritually. Hence Islamization meant that the masses were offered an alternative to the traditional
syncretistic culture, and a call to rise from the case and comfort of the
time-honoured tradition. But they became more firmly tied to a different
and demanding ideology, which prevented them from adapting comfort-
ably to the new age.

A natural concomitant of the changing Muslim society and Muslim
solidarity based on this ideology was a push by the Muslim elite to
regain their lost power. By the late nineteenth century, Muslims had

gained enough confidence through revivalism to try and recover something of their former glory. Education, employment, and Muslim solidarity had been the first steps. The next step was to politically mobilize the Muslim community. The ideology and the organizational infrastructure created by early revivalism provided the means by which this political goal could be achieved. But to make the Muslim political goals a reality something more than this was also needed. To begin with, they needed extra help—special circumstances to be created by the British to overcome the advantage of the Hindu community, and the authorities were eager to assist by treating all Muslims in India as a special category.[52] Secondly, they would have to become more in tune with the need and goals of the masses to know exactly which symbols of their culture to manipulate to advantage.[53] Islamization in the second stage had moved the aims and aspiration of these two classes closer and all that was needed was for the elite to reinforce the existing social and psychological consequences of revivalism namely, to emphasize identification with the Muslm world, urge Muslims to emulate upper class Muslims, and reject alien non-Muslim cultural ideas. This gave them a sense of superiority as Muslims, but created communal hatred, a sense of Muslim deprivation and inferiority in the eyes of non-Muslims. Next they had to confirm the opinion that the problems of the masses stemmed from exploitation by the Hindu community. By arousing these fears and their loyalty to the Muslim world, the Muslim elite attempted to mobilize the Muslim community. The ground work for political mobilization had been carefully prepared by the revivalist, although without realizing how fertile the soil would prove to be, or indeed what would actually grow.

Having seen the course which elite Muslims were taking by the early decades of the twentieth century, we need to look at the course on which Bengali Muslims were set because of the impact of Islamic revivalism between 1871 and 1906. Despite the impression of the enhanced political and cultural unity resulting from the heightened sense of sharing in an Islamic identity, Bengali Muslim society was still deeply divided. The essential class differences between Muslim masses and the elites made a mockery of the concept of a unified Islamic community. Because the illusion of Muslim unity underlay the political unity, attempts to form shared political goals revealed the idealistic nature of Islamic revivalism, and the fragility of shared religious ideology as a cohesive factor. As Bengali Muslims moved towards modernity and away from the traditional social structure with a sharpened religious ideology they would have to compete more, rather than less, with the conflicting social and economic needs of the different classes of Muslims.

Further, Islamic ideology as the basis of political unity has not solved the problems of Muslim identity, which faced Muslims in East Pakistan and Bangladesh. The Bengali revivalists could not have foreseen these unintended consequences of reviving Islam and initiating the process of Islamization. Looking forward from the position of the early nineteenth century, they could only judge change with regard to the past and especially the classical ideals. Modernity and the accelerated pace of change would have been inconceivable to the revivalists. The revivalists clearly did not understand, let alone value the history of the Bengali Muslims. These historical roots have remained 'a cultural core that persists through time',[54] thus preventing Islamization from becoming a complete process in the Bengali setting.

In summary, the events in the late nineteenth century show certain obvious changes occurring in the pattern of Muslim society in Bengal. Since the post-Mutiny days we see something of a Thermidorian reaction against the purist challenge of Muslim society. This reaction meant that the religious goals of the early revivalists changed to benefit Muslim society as a whole, especially the elites. The different threads of revivalism became woven together, resolving much of the conflicts within the Muslim community but increasing the overall conflict in Bengal because of its anti-Hindu tone. Secondly, the Muslim community was politicized by using the revivalist ideology, but the way in which this finally happened must be seen as one of the unintended consequences of revivalism. For the ordinary Bengali Muslim masses, the later stages of revivalism resulted not in the resolution of the sharpened Bengal Muslim dual identity, but in an additional form of psychological oppression. By being manipulated into seeking elite and therefore unrealistic goals they conformed to the demands of the conservative revivalists. And in this way they ignored the fundamental class differences. Consequently, the wrongs of the Muslim community were not rectified by revivalism and the Islamic promises of equality and Muslim brotherhood remained an illusion. For long after the revivalist period—right up to the present—'endemic injustice' remained a feature of ordinary Bengali Muslims' lives.[55]

IV

ISLAMIZATION AND BENGAL MUSLIM IDENTITY— A REVISIONIST PERSPECTIVE

While the foregoing analyses underscore the critical importance and interconnection of the triple issues of revivalism, Islamization, and identity, the issue of Islamization most clearly emerges as the crux, with its direct and close bearing on the construction of Bengal Muslim identity. And here again, the discussion above clearly underlines a need for re-examination and re-definition of what is so widely, divergently, and uncritically presented in these historical writings as 'Islamization'. We have adduced considerable evidence to reveal boundless confusions among writers on the subject of 'Islamization', either making an uncritical assumption about a radical religious transformation of Bengali Muslims to approximate to the normative and pristine ideal of revivalist Islam, or taking an equally uncritical amorphous view of 'Islamization' as a mixed baggage that holds heterogenous material ranging from models of religious authenticity to social, economic, and political benefits from which Muslim people and groups could pick and choose. Proceeding from the perspective of a dichotomized view of Islamization, on one hand, in the sense and form of conformity to an ideal notion of Islam, scholars like Rafiuddin Ahmed moved on to proclaim the failure of the 'religious' program of the revivalists, while attributing success to their 'social' and 'political' objectives on the other. This is not only being unable to explore the essential unity of Islam (*tauhid*) between religious and non-religious; the approach is no less flawed for underrating the role and salience of Islam. We have taken pains above to situate Islam in Muslim revivalist developments in colonial Bengal. We have sought to establish that individual Muslims, regardless of, and even despite non-conformity with the revivalist-prescribed normative Islamic life and practices, could well have become 'Islamized' because of the impact of Islamic ideology and that this understanding of being a Muslim had taken on a new meaning. Their continued adherence to traditional custom-oriented life, which is strongly evidenced in the historical literature,[56] remained external to and in harmony with this new commitment. We have, in this way, been able to return Islam, where it belongs in a critical and thorough study of revivalism in Bengal.

The restoration of the linkage between spiritual and temporal in Islam, as we have sought to achieve in our approach to the problem, does not, however, put an end to all questions. One of the remaining questions relates to the tendency towards overreaching the boundaries of religion and 'Islamization' in Bengal Muslim developments. Most studies in the growth of Muslim separatism in South Asia, especially Bengal, focus on the religious-cultural process of 'Islamization' leading to the separatist political development. The subsequent participation of Bengal Muslims in the growth and development of the separatist Muslim politics, culminating in the partition as its logical outcome is a common refrain and grand *finale* to this story. The story in its outline is not untrue. Serious problems do, however, surface when the light of historical research is turned on any flat and linear presentation of a rather complex history. The narrative of a steady onward and victorious march of 'Islamization', starting from the vantage point of a 'revitalized' land in the nineteenth century, and ending up with the seizure of the coveted crown of the truncated 'Muslim homeland' is a highly romanticized, monolothic, and linear presentation of a rather complex, uneven, and conflicting history. There are many serious problems of omission and commission in this prevailing and dominant version of Bengal Muslim history. We have, at the beginning of this essay, mentioned Rafiuddin Ahmed's dramatically reversed position on the religious impact of revivalism and his new-found championship of the 'beginning' of Islamization of Bengalis following in the wake of the revivalist movements in the nineteenth century.[57] A bald, uncritical, and unhistorical observation of this nature raises a whole range of questions. It raises questions about the state of pre-revivalist Islam in Bengal, as well as the very basic concomitant question about the meaning of 'Islamization', not merely from the point of view of an academic, but more importantly, from that of the people whose faith is in question. Given the unquestionable fact of Muslims living in Bengal for many centuries before the nineteenth, one is obliged to ask: who were those people before the nineteenth century, if not Muslims? In reference to the syncretistic beliefs of Muslims in pre-revivalist Bengal, Rafiuddin Ahmed clearly expressed *his* view: 'Surely, this was not quite Islamic.'[58] A judgmental historical position of this kind calls into serious question the academic freedom and purpose of studying and questioning the piety of people who know and call themselves believers.

The nineteenth-century-centred version of the history of Bengal's Islamization is also flawed to the extent that it fails to recognize the strength and resilience of the syncretistic religious-cultural forces among Bengali Muslims even in the post-nineteenth-century developments in Muslim Bengal. It does not provide adequate room to consider and evaluate the role, in the nineteenth and the twentieth centuries, of a considerable section of the educated middle class Bengali Muslim intelligentsia, who unequivocally canvassed an alternative model of an inclusive 'Bengali' identity.[59] Failure to take cognizance of such critical expressions of dissimilar thoughts and ideologies can only weaken the explanations for many divergent and conflicting trends and developments in Muslim politics successively in Bengal, East Pakistan, and Bangladesh. A close investigation of the Muslim Bengali literature in the late nineteenth and early twentieth centuries reveals indeed a profound tension, vacillation, and even clear opposition and conflict in Bengal Muslim's self-perceptions and self-statements—uncertainties that are clearly reflected in the contemporary and subsequent politics. It cannot be overemphasized that if the partition of Bengal (1947) is seen as the vindication of the Bengal Muslim's 'Islamic' identity, the rise of Bangladesh (1971) on the ashes of the 'Islamic brotherhood' of Pakistan does fly directly in the face of many of those 'Islamic' assumptions. The developments in Bangladesh since its inception seem to reinforce the persistent image of a people still groping for a commonly acceptable identity. The story is indeed a continuing one—one of an epic proportion, and at times rather turbulent and tragic—of the Muslim's search, in history, for being a Muslim and making a home in Bengal as well.[60]

The most serious problem with the current perception of Islamization relates to the treatment that many scholars and lay observers share in common of the phenomenon of 'popular', or 'folk', or local custom-centred Islam. The continuance and persistence of custom-driven religious practices alongside what must be seen as a significant change in the Muslim's civic and corporate worldview in the post-revivalist period demands convincing explanations. Scholars like Muinuddin Khan would bypass the question on the presumption of an 'Islamic revolution' of a religious as well as non-religious nature. Scholars of Rafiuddin Ahmed's mould, on the other hand, would invest an essentially secular meaning to the Islamic revolution, with an implicit hope in a gradual transformation of the religious life in tune with the demands of High Islam, or the Islamic great tradition.

There are some basic reasons, however, to account for the remarkable strength, resilience, and continuity of the custom-oriented tradition in Muslim Bengal. A probe into this question must necessarily raise other relevant issues of the nature of the interrelationship between such popular local practices and High Islam, as well as the most significant question about the nature and meaning of Islamization. Given the confusion and inadequacy in the current historiography in this area, a probe into these areas calls for a revisionist perspective.

V

FUNCTIONAL UNITY UNDERLYING THE DICHOTOMIZED ISLAM IN BENGAL—A REVISIONIST PERSPECTIVE

The conventional understanding of the process of Islamization has been a simple, uniform, unilinear, and unidirectional movement, transforming the 'popular/folk' or 'heterodox' tradition to the 'high' or 'orthodox' one. On the basis of my own studies, as well as a host of other historical and empirical investigations into this field in the context of both South and Southeast Asia, I began to be increasingly sceptical about the universal validity of this position, and inclined to canvas a revisionist perspective on this issue. The revisionist position rejects a necessarily conflicting position between the two in favour of a non-dichotomous and complementary relationship, and also argues for a complex—rather than a flat and uniform pattern of interrelationship between the twin complex of the so-called high and popular Islam in Bengal.[61]

In a contribution on South Asian Islam, Ali Asani differentiates between two distinct Muslim traditions in this region: one is a 'rustic', or 'folk, low or little tradition', with its 'appeal and popularity among the rural, illiterate masses', and the other is the 'more sophisticated, intellectual facet of Islamic civilization that developed in urban areas under the cultural influence of the immigrant Muslim elite of Persian or Central Asian origin.'[62] The inner divergences in Indian Islam are of course evident from sundry historical sources from the medieval times, especially through the occasional outbursts of 'purist' sentiments and reactions of both the religious and non-religious elites.[63] As for Bengal, there has been a virtual unanimity among observers that the dominant version of the religion, as practised by the overwhelming majority of its votaries in traditional or pre-modern Bengal was rather 'lax' and 'spurious'.[64]

The common perception of the dichotomous nature of Indian Islam is obvious, but the current nature of our understanding and explanation of the divergence is dubious and deficient. The predominant attitude is to discard everything that fails to measure up to the norms and prescriptions of 'scriptural' Islam, into the shadowy and bottomless pit of 'folk' or 'popular' Islam, which again is, in its turn, traced to the most specious logic of 'incomplete conversion'. At the popular level, according to Aziz Ahmad, 'Indian Islam represents a mosaic of demotic, superstitious and syncretistic beliefs...'[65] Further, 'Animism in Islam, as in other religions throughout the world is to some extent rooted in popular beliefs,' while in India 'it may have been influenced to some uncertain extent by Hinduism.'[66] In Muhammad Mujeeb's perception they were only 'partly converted.'[67] Francis Robinson refers to them as 'half-Islamized peoples.'[68] Peter Hardy dubs them 'census Muslims' and adds:

> ...the real challenge to purity of belief and practice in Islam in medieval India was to be found...in the convert's countryside—in the ignorance of new Muslims of the requirements of Islam and in the insidious infiltrations of 'creeping Hinduism' into the daily life of the convert.[69]

A similar perception is shared by other Bengali Muslim historians as well. Momtazur Rahman Tarafdar observes:

> Islam, in its simple and austere aspect, does not appear to have characterized the life of the people [of Bengal]...a careful study of the literature of the time shows that there prevailed a sort of folk Islam having hardly any connection with the dogmas of religion.[70]

Rafiuddin Ahmed likewise takes the conventional position of differentiating between an 'Islamic orthodoxy' and 'folk beliefs and practices,' and writes: 'The adherence to folk beliefs and practices, however, should not be interpreted to mean that the orthodox traditions had no place in Bengali Islam.'[71] Azizur Rahman Mallick's is perhaps the strongest and the most rigid restatement of the orthodox position. He mentions Islam in Bengal 'where corrupt and irreligious practices gained considerable ground.' He speaks of the 'ignorance' of the 'half converted Muslims' and identifies 'incomplete conversion' as 'a channel through which un-Islamic practices passed' into Islam. 'Incomplete conversion in the rural districts of Bengal', Mallick writes, 'left these people only nominal followers of the Faith...' He raises the issue of the Mughal decline and the 'loss of political power' which, in his opinion, 'undoubtedly contributed to the degeneration of Islam...'[72] Mallick, in an intriguing statement, betrays his inclination not even to count 'the half-converts from Hinduism' among 'Muslims':

> Thus long years of association with non-Muslims who far outnumbered them, cut off from the original home of Islam, and living with half-converts from Hinduism, the Muslims had greatly deviated from the original faith and had become 'Indianised'.[73]

There seem to be two broad lines of reasoning in all this for the Islamic divergences. The theory of 'incomplete conversion' or 'semi-conversion' is rather similar in nature to that of 'folk Islam', both pointing at the level and the limit of the cultural attainments of the masses of indigenous converts. The theory of 'degeneration', on the other hand, offers a much different kind of reasoning.

None of these explanations could, however, be sustained either by logic or history. The argument of incomplete conversion and degeneration contradict each other. Degeneration could not have logically followed from a situation which was already regarded as inadequate and 'incomplete'. Besides, the descriptive labels such as 'half-converts,' 'census Muslims,' or 'nominal Muslims' raise serious questions about the place for value judgments in academic pursuits. To call a Muslim something less than a Muslim is a value judgment and not a description or analysis of the meaning of being a Muslim from the point of view of one who calls himself a Muslim and claims the religion as his own. Such presumptuous views on the nature and profundity of piety of individual believers seem more akin to a religious posture than academic objectivity. Finally, the most serious objection to the theory of Islam's degeneration in Bengal is that is it patently unhistorical. There is no historical evidence to suggest that Islam as practised by the masses of its votaries in Bengal, in the declining years of the Mughals, was anything different from what it had been there in the past or that the so-called 'corrupt', 'degenerate', and 'Hinduized' Islam, confronted by the Islamic revivalists and reformists since the nineteenth century, was a sharp deviation from a golden or classical age of Islam in Bengal lying in the past. On the contrary, the earliest extant Muslim Bengali literary sources, dating largely from the sixteenth century, provide the clearest possible evidence of the early existence in Bengal of masses of believers who, having been linguistically cut off from the Arabic and Persian sources of Islamic tradition, and denied of such tradition in their vernacular Bengali, continued to remain steeped in the locally popular non-Muslim tradition readily available in the vernacular Bengali. The authors of this early Muslim Bengali literature were themselves instrumental in recasting Islamic tradition in syncretistic moulds.

It is possible to detect several strands in the formulations of the orthodox position, academic or otherwise. One of them is to treat religious heterogeneities in a Muslim society as 'aberrations,' 'anomalies,' and 'accretions' to be overlooked and ignored, being of little importance and consequence; or as 'festers' that ought and can be 'cured.' Aziz Ahmad's prescription for a 'proper perspective' in which the 'folk-beliefs should be viewed' is that these 'should not be over-emphasized or over-rated.' He sounds a note of assurance:

> They are specific to microscopic Muslim communities and are generally the exception rather than the rule. They were challenged by the fundamentalist, orthodox and modernist movements alike in the nineteenth and twentieth centuries. They have completely ceased to exist in the Westernized upper class and nearly so in the orthodox lower middle classes. In the predominantly Muslim regions which now constitute West Pakistan their hold was not very strong even in the lower classes, and fundamentalism is now rooting them out.[74]

Another distinctive, and academically popular, effort in bringing together the two large religious complexes of Islam is within the broad conceptual frame of 'great' and little traditions,' conflated with the corresponding concepts of 'orthodoxy' and 'heterodoxy.' In the words of Imtiaz Ahmed:

The process of Islamization understood as an increasing tendency amongst Muslims towards new identity formation based on an increase in conformity to orthodox Islamic principles in social and cultural life and a conscious rejection of syncretic elements that previously persisted as remnants of their pre-conversion orientations and beliefs, was said to link the orthodox and heterodox religious complexes, resulting in a gradual shrinkage of the sphere of the heterodox complex of the little tradition.[75]

Ziaul Hasan Faruqi is another to adopt the great-little-tradition model.[76] In regard, however, to the vital question of the interrelationship between the great and little traditions, and the corresponding one between orthodoxy and heterodoxy, both Faruqi and Imtiaz Ahmed's position diverges very little from the lines of the orthodox scholarship. Faruqi maintains that 'Muslim communities belonging to the Little tradition, with all their distinct cultural traits, have always aspired to relate their social and cultural values to those of the Islamic Great Tradition...'[77]

It is my contention that Islam in Bengal has not been a 'primary' but a 'secondary' culture, that is, exogenous and not indigenous to the region. Also, here in this region, Islam has not been a 'single' or the only 'great tradition' since it entered a land which was not culturally virgin, and confronted the long-established indigenous great tradition. Islamic conversion forced a break in the pre-conversion cultural continuity between the great and little tradition of the would-be converts. To remedy the situation, the Bengal Muslim literati constructed a rather rich alternative model of great tradition for the Bengal Muslim masses in the Bengali language and on a syncretistic model, and restored thereby the broken continuity between the great and little traditions of the converts. The obvious implication of this finding has been to reveal the inadequacies of a simple and uniform model of great and little tradition relationship.

The revisionist viewpoint—seeking a complementary rather than a conflicting interrelationship between the great and little traditions as well as between the so-called orthodoxy and heterodoxy in Islam—is being steadily reinforced by many empirical investigations into the South Asian situation. Their findings are full of implications for a fuller appreciation of the process of Islamization in the South Asian setting. The weight of the evidence, first of all, is clearly against 'the conceptualization of religious beliefs, values and practices in terms of a dichotomy of orthodoxy and heterodoxy altogether...'[78] The boundary of 'orthodoxy', howsoever well defined in Islamic scriptural works or by the religious professionals, does not appear often to coincide with the one that is locally determined. Quite often, elements of the little tradition, 'rather than being rejected or eliminated', are actually accepted through Islamization, either in their original or somewhat modified form, and 'incorporated into the corpus of the orthodox religious complex.' Imtiaz Ahmad finds that 'beliefs and values...not derived from the Islamic literature' and not necessarily 'always [in] accord...with orthodox Islam,' are 'regarded by Muslims who hold them as truly Islamic.' He concludes:

> Popular Islam in South Asia is not merely the heterodox side of the Great Tradition of Islam. Looked at from the viewpoint of those who subscribe to its corpus of beliefs and values, it is as much orthodox as the Islamic beliefs derived from the religious texts.[79]

In her illuminating studies on the Tamil-speaking south Indian Muslims called Labbais, Susan Bayly raises some seminal issues concerning the 'actual meaning' of the terms 'purist' and 'syncretic' as well as their 'usefulness' as analytical 'categories.' She also queries 'the relationship between 'purist' and 'syncretic' religious behaviour within individual Muslim communities,' in particular reference to 'the idea of a confrontation between distinct sets of 'purist' maritime Muslims and 'syncretic' peasant or rural Muslims—the sort of people who are so often dismissed as 'half-Islamized' or even degenerate, 'backsliding' or simply 'bad Muslims'.[80] Her findings and observations are emphatic endorsements of the revisionist critique. She totally rejects the 'notion of distinct and opposing realms of Muslim worship, of 'high' and 'low' or 'scriptural' and 'non-standard' Islam...[81] Closely paralleling Ricklefs' attempt to set Javanese Islam in the wider contexts of the indigenous social and religious systems, Bayly sought 'to trace some of the ways in which the Islam practised by Tamil Muslims was shaped and moulded by an equally complex local religious system.'[82] On the basis of her findings, she warns us:

> ...it is no longer satisfactory to conceive of the Tamil country—and indeed many other parts of south and southeast Asia—in terms of separate and distinct religious cultures confronting one another across rigid communal boundaries. Surely the traditions and practices enacted at these Labbai centres indicate that there has long been a close and subtle relationship between religious traditions which are often thought of as distinct and mutually exclusive. Certainly the population of this region cannot be divided into the old bald categories of purist/maritime traders ('santri') and 'syncretic' hinterland peasants ('abangan').[83]

She writes further:

> ...it must not be thought that this Tamil Muslim trading elite had evolved by the eighteenth century into a population of 'Islamized' Muslims who had divorced themselves from the values, culture and religious motifs of the

wider society.... It is clear that the maraikayyar [maraikkayar/the Tamil maritime traders] retained very complex links to a world of elite and exclusive Muslim piety, but they also pursued much wider ranging religious connections.[84]

Islamization, contrary to earlier assumptions, is no longer considered unilinear, unidirectional, or even continuous. It has not always advanced 'orthodox Islamic beliefs and practices at the cost of little traditional ones.'[85] Aziz Ahmad, whom we quoted earlier as speaking so vehemently about the eradication of 'folk beliefs,' concedes that 'movements of mass reform...have tried to erase' those 'demotic, superstitious and syncretic beliefs,' but not with complete success.'[86] 'In the lower classes of East Pakistan [now Bangladesh],' he writes, 'some folk-beliefs still persist despite the fundamentalist Fara'idi movement's success in the nineteenth century, and the Jama'at-i Islami's growing influence on religious life today.'[87] Ismail Lambat's investigations into the conditions of the Sunni Surati Vohras (Bohras) reveal an intensification, in recent years, of a 'struggle between custom and religion,' but 'the customary rites and ceremonies,' he adds, 'continue to hold a very strong hold on the group and have not been replaced by alternate [sic] religious practices.'[88] Partap Aggarwal's findings on the Meos of Rajasthan and Haryana, reveal that they continued to oppose, in the face of sustained pressures of Islamization on the community, preferential cousin marriage, as prescribed in the *sharia*.[89] Likewise, Muslims of Tamilnadu, as observed by Susan Bayly, were inclined to the Tamil system of patrilocal *murai* marriage or preferred marriage to father's sister's daughter. Not permitted under 'orthodox' Muslim law, murari marriages are 'common among Muslims in inland Tamilnadu.' In the trading ports, which harboured Islamic 'orthodoxy,' 'marriage is based on a distinctive matrilocal system which is unknown elsewhere in the region.'[90] Mattison Mines, in his studies on Tamil Muslims, notes that they 'marry among themselves and only rarely marry Muslims from other groups.' According to Mines, this is 'largely a result of Tamilians' marriage preference for kinsmen...,'[91] and thus, 'what is considered orthodox by Pallavaram's Muslims is influenced by local beliefs.'[92]

Lina Fruzzetti and Jean Ellickson's studies relative to the Bengali-speaking Muslims likewise, clearly reveals the co-existence and inter-penetration of the twin religious complexes of orthodoxy and heterodoxy. Fruzzetti's perceptive study of the *rites de passage* and rituals among Muslims of Bishnupur in West Bengal leads her to the conclusion:

Bengali Muslims adhere simultaneously to the fundamental orthodox principles of Islam and to a Bengali culture. They state that one can be a 'Muslim' and a 'Bengali' without creating any contradiction or conflict between the two spheres, though both the boundaries are sharply defined by their ideology and practice...the universalistic aspect of Islam is not the only concern of the Muslims; in everyday practical life, the Muslims share in a 'Bengali culture', which is common to both Hindus and Muslims Bengalis.[93]

Besides 'the prescribed Islamic rules' concerning lifecycle rites, Fruzzetti notes that 'a number of local rules, loosely defined as *desher adat* (customs of the land) accompany the rituals.' Both the Islamic and local culture are 'maintained and followed by the Muslims...'[94] They seemed to have 'forged a unique culture' based on a combination of 'Islamic precepts' with 'the experience of everyday life...and the elements that come from a non-Islamic culture.' They see 'no contradiction between strictly Islamic and non-Islamic practices,' and

> ...whatever does not fit into the one fits into the other. Whatever is not in the Koran is *niom* [*niyam*] (Bengali), complementing though never contradicting, the spirit of Muslim *dharam* [religion].[95]

While Fruzzetti's evidence came from the Hindu-majority area of West Bengal, Ellickson's field study embraced the Muslim-majority area of Bangladesh, and the findings of both reinforced each other. Ellickson reports a substantive conflict between Islamic personal laws and the customary practices of rural Muslims, who perceived no serious violation of Islamic injunctions in their customary acceptance of inheritance by a grandson. The same perception is corroborated by their customary attitudes to divorce. Here again, Ellickson reports no perceived sense of conflict between the family laws of the sharia and the dominant social values obtained locally, disfavouring divorce by the wife. In the words of the locals: 'According to our *religion*, 'a woman cannot divorce her husband'.'[96] The underlying rationale, which Ellickson offers for this position, is a clear vindication of the revisionist model of a shifting boundary between orthodoxy and heterodoxy. In her highly perceptive observation: 'The argument was couched in terms of what a good Muslim should do...and all that is required is general local consensus as to what 'good Muslims' do.'[97]

The revisionist perception does indeed uncover the variety, subtlety, complexity, and dynamism of the highly protean process of Islamization in South Asia. This it does, as shown above, primarily by pulling down the time-honoured notional barricade between the so-called 'orthodox' and 'heterodox' Islam, raised and sustained uncritically by the academic orthodoxy on South Asian Islam. In its existential, historical, and living ramifications, the regional Islam commanded a great deal more elasticity, plurality, tolerance, and accommodation than fathomed by its orthodox observers.

Such views are, however, not exclusive to the world of South Asian Islam. Clifford Geertz's conventional and dominant notion of a dichotomy between a 'high,' 'orthodox,' and 'purist' *santri* Islam and its 'low,' heterodox,' and 'syncretic' *abangan* version,[98] as well as a logical extension of this notion that 'the typical mode of Islamization' involves a 'linear' and 'unidirectional' progression of the transformative effects of the Islamizing process, have been countered in some recent studies.[99] A more subtle process of interplay and interpenetration between Islam and *adat*, in the context of Indonesia, have been offered by others like Ricklefs, Christine Dobbin, and Peter Carey.[100]

The linkages between the two broad strands of Islam have indeed been there if one is looking for them and caring to read serious meanings into them. As amply evident from our discussions above, many writers—consciously or unconsciously—attest, either historically or empirically, to the presence of such contacts, but scarcely stop to probe deeply the nature of their interrelationship and their meanings. We examined above the variety of orthodox academic positions in this matter, the central assumptions underlying them being a common acceptance of their dichotomous relationship—a dichotomy that, in their perceptions, should either be ignored as inconsequential, or must be remedied by means of 'purging,' 'transforming,' and 'purifying' the folkish 'aberrations,' 'anomalies,' 'accretions', or 'degenerations'. There is undeniably a normative, monolithic, and macro-perception of Islam that informs the rationale of such orthodox positions. The inadequacy, rigidity, and even hollowness of this as an analytical model have been clearly exposed in many recent studies, as analysed above. The issue is clear: it is patently a simplistic and flawed academic exercise to resort to the convenience of denying everything in the Islamic developments that one is unable to accommodate easily within the framework of an 'ideal monolithic orthodoxy,' defined essentially in Sunni scriptural terms. The Islam as practised by teeming millions of believers in South Asia, clearly emerges in our study with much greater elasticity, flexibility, tolerance, accommodative spirit, richness, and diversity than what is encapsulated in this rather limited and doctrinaire view of Islamic orthodoxy. One cannot help feeling that this narrow and idealistic perception of Islamization seeks, ironically, to save Islam from what they regard as its weaknesses by turning away from where the real strengths of Islam lay—its dynamism and creativity at the operative level on the world stage. Imtiaz Ahmad expresses similar sentiments when he says:

...while Muslim fundamentalist may assert and maintain that there is one, and only one, version of what is orthodox from the Islamic point of view and whatever does not conform to it is to be dismissed as heterodox, the people's own beliefs and behaviour admit of much greater variety in what they regard as truly 'Islamic'. Clearly it seems to me that the Islamicists' vision has tended to obscure the inherent and underlying pluralism within Indian Islam as a practised religion.[101]

In the light of the mounting evidence to the contrary, the hoary notion of a quintessential polarity between the religious complexes of the so-called orthodoxy and heterodoxy or that of the elite and the folk does appear increasingly indefensible. It is difficult to see that the 'purist' champions in South Asian Islam would be able to hold their ground much longer and continue to deny the rightful place of the regional and syncretistic developments as 'a part and parcel of an integrated and unified religious system... in Indian Islam'.[102] In its empirical develop-ment, no system of ideology, beliefs, and practices could be divorced from its spatial-social context. The social and cultural mores of the believer invest particular meanings and symbolism into those beliefs and practices as far as possible as a means of accommodating them to his worldview, and leave the rest of his previous cultural baggage to co-exist, generally harmoniously, with his new acquisitions. A student of this phenomenon is more meaningfully challenged to unravel this complex interface between the old inheritance and the new acquisition. In his critically important study in the popular 'sufi poetry' in the Sindhi language, Ali Asani emphasizes the 'seminal role' of the so-called 'folk, low or little tradition,' in 'propagating Islamic ideas within this population.' He writes:

> Most studies of Indian Islam, while focussing on the elitist facet, have treated the folk tradition marginally—a treatment that is rather surprising considering the traditions' impact on a substantial proportion of the Muslim population, not to mention... its seminal role in propagating Islamic ideas within this population.[103]

Islam's encounter with Bengal, in the same manner, has its own specific social and cultural contexts which proved determining in re-casting Islam into its distinctive regional mould. The Islamic revivalists and other observers encountered a situation in Bengal that resulted, not from a later debasement of Islam, but from the original conditions of culture-contact in the region. Nurtured and nourished by a rich combi-nation of social, cultural, and political circumstances in the history of medieval Bengal, the dominant form of Bengal's Islamic response blossomed, over a long period of time, into a rich syncretistic and acculturated tradition. The so-called degenerate and devitalized Islam in later Bengal was nothing but an embodiment of an earlier perception and formulation by Bengal Muslims of their religion in a syncretistic frame of reference—a perception that confronted its first major challenge in the wake of the revivalist movements.

Given the complexities and malleability of the concept of Islamization in the context of South Asia in general, and Bengal in particular, as well as its critical bearing on the changing meanings and forms of being and becoming Muslim in Bengal, as clearly evidenced in the foregoing discussion, a discerning student of Islamic revival, Islamization and Muslim identity in Bengal is urged to bring caution, care, and critical sensitivity to bear on one's approach. The nineteenth-century revival and its unquestionable impact on 'Islamization' of colonial and postcolonial Bengal urgently demands an analytical tool to pull down the contrived barrier between the so-called 'religious' and 'secular' domains of Muslim life and find religion its proper place in the totality of Muslim life. One is urged no less caution, care, and balance not to fall an easy prey to the emotive temptation of searching history in the footsteps of a steady, inexorable, lineal, and triumphal march of post-revivalist Islam in Bengal.

Endnotes

1. Albert Hourani, cited in Barbara D. Metcalf, *Islamic Revival in British India, Deoband 1860–1900* (Princeton, N.J., 1982), p. 9.
2. See Metcalf, *Islamic Revival*; Saiyid Athar Abbas Rizvi, *Shah 'Abd al-'Aziz, Puritanism, Sectarian Polemics and Jihad* (Canberra, 1982); Qeyamuddin Ahmad, *The Wahabi Movement in India* (Calcutta, 1966).
3. Biharilal Sarkar, *Titumir ba Narkelbediyar Ladai/Titumir* or *The struggle of Narkelbediya*, Swapan Basu (ed.), 3rd edn (Calcutta, 1997, originally published in 1897); Abdul Gaphur Siddiki, *Shahid Titu Mir* (Dhaka, 1971).
4. Anon. (identified as O'Kinealy), 'The Wahhabis in India, Nos 1–2', *Calcutta Review*, vol. 51, no. 101 (1870); W.W. Hunter, *The Indian Muhammadans* (London, 1871; Calcutta, 4th edn. 1945); M.A. Bari, *A Comparative Study of the Early Wahhabi Doctrines and Contemporary Reform Movements in Indian Islam* (Unpublished D. Phil thesis, Oxford University, 1953); and 'The Reform Movement in Bengal', in Mahmud Husain *et al.* (eds), *A History of the Freedom Movement*, vol. 1 (Karachi, 1957); Muinuddin Ahmad Khan (ed.), *Selection from Bengal Government Records on Wahhabi Trials, 1863–70* (Dhaka, 1961); *History of the Faraidi Movement in Bengal, 1818–1906* (Karachi, 1965); and 'Research in Islamic Revivalism of the Nineteenth Century and Its Effect on the Muslim Community of Bengal', in P. Bessaignet (ed.), *Social Research in East Pakistan* (Dhaka, 2nd rev. edn, 1974); Shamsun Nahar, 'The agrarian uprising of Titu Mir, 1831', *Journal of the Institute of Bangladesh Studies*, vol. 1, no. 1 (1976); Azizur Rahman Mallick, *British Policy and the Muslims in Bengal 1757–1856* (Dhaka,

1977); Rafiuddin Ahmed, *The Bengal Muslims, 1871–1906. A Quest for Identity* (New Delhi, 1981); 'Islamization in Nineteenth Century Bengal', in Gopal Krishna (ed.), *Contribution to South Asian Studies*, 1 (New Delhi, 1979), pp. 88–120; and 'Conflict and Contradictions in Bengali Islam, Problems of Change and Adjustment', in Katherine P. Ewing (ed.), *Shari'at and Ambiguity in South Asian Islam* (Berkeley, 1988); Abhijit Dutta, *Muslim Society in Transition, Titu Meer's Revolt, 1831* (Calcutta, 1987); Narahari Kaviraj, *Wahabi and Farazi Rebels of Bengal* (New Delhi, 1982).

5. J.N. Sarkar, *Islam in Bengal (Thirteenth to Nineteenth Century)* (Calcutta, 1972), p. 48.
6. Ibid., pp. 55–6, 73.
7. Mallick, *British Policy and the Muslims in Bengal*, pp. 157–8, 162.
8. Khan, 'Research in Islamic Revivalism', p. 64.
9. Ahmed, *Bengal Muslims*; and Metcalf, 'Islamic Revival'.
10. Ahmed, 'Conflict and Contradictions in Bengali Islam', p. 115.
11. Ahmed, *Bengal Muslims*, p. 115.
12. Ahmed, *Bengal Muslims*, p. 70.
13. Ibid., p. 44.
14. Ibid., p. 70.
15. Metcalf, *Islamic Revival*.
16. Ahmed, *Bengal Muslims*, p. 47.
17. Sarkar, *Islam in Bengal*, p. 59.
18. Ahmed, *Bengal Muslims*, p. 70.
19. I take the opportunity of acknowledging here with great pleasure many hours of intellectual engagement with my postgraduate students, especially Jill White, and their individual and collective contribution to a critique of Islamic revivalism in colonial Bengal.
20. Ahmed, *Bengal Muslims*, p. 71.
21. Ibid., p. 162, Ahmed distinguishes between the traditional preachers in Bengal and the fundamentalist revivalists.
22. Mustafa Nurul Islam, *Bengali Muslim Public Opinion as Reflected in the Bengali Press 1901–1930* (Dhaka, 1973), p. 79.
23. Khan, *Faraidi Movement*, pp. lxxxix, 11.
24. Ibid., p. 17.
25. Khan is eager to point out that Shariat Allah was put under police custody only because of 'his opposition to the oppressive and illegal taxes levied by the *zamindars* on the helpless peasantry,' ibid., p. 21.
26. Ahmed, *Bengal Muslims*, p. 50.
27. Khan, *Faraidi Movement*, p. 23.
28. Ibid.
29. Ibid., p. 19.
30. Ibid., p. 29.
31. G. Marsden, *Fundamentalism and American Culture, The Shaping of Twentieth Century Evangelism, 1870–1925* (Oxford, 1980). This idea of leadership is a common theme of Marsden's work on American fundamentalist movements.

32. Ahmed, *Bengal Muslims*, p. 42.
33. Sarkar, *Islam in Bengal*, pp. 65–6.
34. Khan, *Faraidi Movement*, p. lxiii.
35. Metcalf, *Islamic Revivalism*, p. 314.
36. Ibid.
37. Kaviraj, *Wahabi and Farazi Rebels*, p. 98.
38. Metcalf, *Islamic Revivalism*, p. 12.
39. Ahmed, *Bengal Muslims*, p. 65.
40. Ahmed, *Bengal Muslims*, ibid.
41. E. Erikson, 'Identity—Psychosocial', *International Encyclopaedia of Social Science* (New York, 1968), vol. 7, p. 62.
42. Ratnalekha Ray, *Change in Bengal Agrarian Society, 1760–1850* (New Delhi, 1979), p. 244.
43. Marsden, *Fundamentalism*, p. 50.
44. Metcalf, *Islamic Revivalism*, p. 357.
45. Ahmed, *Bengal Muslims*, p. 105.
46. Ibid., p. 72.
47. Metcalf, *Islamic Revivalism*, p. 293.
48. Ahmed, *Bengal Muslims*, p. 95.
49. Ahmed, *Bengal Muslims*, pp. 75, 101ff.
50. Islam, *Bengali Muslim Public Opinion*, p. 218.
51. Ahmed, *Bengal Muslims*, p. 169.
52. Paul R. Brass, 'Elite Groups, Symbol Manipulation and Ethnic Identity among the Muslims of South Asia', in David Taylor and Malcolm Yapp (eds), *Political identity in South Asia* (London, 1979), p. 54.
53. Ibid., p. 43.
54. Ibid., p. 68.
55. Metcalf, *Islamic Revivalism*, p. 5.
56. Asim Roy, 'Islam in the Environment of Medieval Bengal' (Ph.D. thesis, Canberra, Australian National University, 1970); 'Social Factors in the Making of Bengali Islam', *South Asia*, no. 3 (August 1973); *The Islamic Syncretistic Tradition in Bengal* (Princeton, N.J., 1983); 'The Bengal Muslim 'Cultural Mediators' and the Bengal Muslim Cultural Identity in the Nineteenth and Early Twentieth Centuries', *South Asia*, vol. 10, no. 1 (1987), pp. 11–34; also *Islam in South Asia. A Regional Perspective* (New Delhi, 1996), ch. 5, pp. 123–46; Ahmed, *Bengal Muslims, passim*; Sarkar, *Islam in Bengal*, p. 75; also Mallick, *British Policy and Muslims in Bengal*, p. 163.
57. See '...it may even be said that the Islamization of the average Indian Muslim only *began* (emphasis in the original) in the nineteenth century with the rise of the revivalist movements. Bengali Islam stands as a case pre-eminent.' Ahmed, 'Conflict and Contradictions in Bengali Islam', p. 115. See also Asim Roy, 'Being and Becoming a Muslim, A Historiographical Perspective on the Search for Muslim Identity in Bengal', in Sekhar Bandyopadhyay (ed), *Bengal Historiography, A Revisit* (New Delhi, 1999).

58. Ahmed, ibid., p. 126; also Roy, ibid.
59. See Roy, 'Bengal Muslim Cultural Mediators'.
60. Roy, 'Being and Becoming a Muslim'.
61. For this part of the analysis I have drawn on my earlier contributions. See Asim Roy, 'Islamization in South Asia with Special Reference to the Bengali-speaking Region, A Conceptual and Historical Revaluation', *Indo-British Review*, vol. XIX, no. 1 (1993), pp. 21–41. (A special issue on the theme of 'Religious Traditions in South Asia, Interaction and Change', G.A. Oddie (ed.) also in Roy, *Islam in South Asia*, pp. 45–73.
62. Ali S. Asani, 'Sufi poetry in the folk tradition of Indo-Pakistan,' *Religion and Literature*, vol. XX, no. 1 (Spring, 1988), p. 81.
63. See Roy, *Islam in South Asia*, p. 52.
64. Ibid.
65. Aziz Ahmad, *An Intellectual History of Islam in India* (Edinburgh, 1969), pp. 44, 46.
66. Aziz Ahmad, *Studies in Islamic Culture in the Indian Environment* (London, 1964), pp. 163–4.
67. Muhammad Mujeeb, *The Indian Muslims* (London, 1967), p. 22.
68. Francis Robinson (ed.), *Atlas of the Islamic World Since 1500* (Oxford, 1982), p. 119.
69. Peter Hardy, *Muslims in British Indian* (Cambridge, 1972), p. 27.
70. Momtazur Rahman Tarafdar, *Husain Shahi Bengal, 1494–1538* (Dhaka, 1965), pp. 163–4.
71. Ahmed, *Bengal Muslims*, pp. 54–5.
72. Mallick, *British Policy and Bengal Muslims*, pp. 3, 7–8, 9.
73. Ibid., p. 29.
74. Ahmad, *Intellectual History of Islam*, p. 51.
75. Imitaz Ahmad, 'Unity and Variety in South Asian Islam. A Summary', in Dietmar Rothermund (ed.), *Islam in Southern Asia*, pp. 6–8.
76. Ziaul Hasan Faruqi, 'Orthodoxy and heterodoxy in India Islam', *Islam and the Modern Age*, vol. 32 (1979), p. 34.
77. Ibid.
78. Imtiaz Ahmad (ed.), *Ritual and Religion among Muslims in India* (New Delhi, 1981), p. 12.
79. Ahmad, 'Unity and Variety', pp. 6–7.
80. Susan Bayly, 'Islam in Southern India, 'purist' or 'syncretic'?, in Chris A. Bayly and D.H.A. Kolff (eds), *Two Colonial Empires* (Dordrecht, 1986), pp. 36–7.
81. Susan Bayly, 'The Limits of Islamic Expansion in South India' (Paper presented at a Conference on 'Regional Varieties of Islam in Pre-Modern India', held in Heidelberg in July 1989), p. 6.
82. Bayly, 'Islam in Southern Asia', pp. 36–7.
83. Ibid., p. 57.
84. Bayly, 'Limits of Islamic Expansion in South India', p. 3.
85. Ahmad, 'Unity and Variety', p. 6.
86. Ahmad, *Intellectual History of Islam*, p. 44.

87. Ibid., p. 51.
88. Islmail A. Lambat, 'Marriage Among the Sunni Surati Vohras of South Gujarat', in Imtiaz Ahmad (ed.), *Family, Kinship and Marriage among Muslims in India* (Delhi, 1976), p. 80.
89. Partap C. Aggarwal, 'Changing religious practices, their relationship to secular power in a Rajasthan village', *Economic and Political Weekly*, vol. IV, no. 12 (1969), pp. 547–51.
90. Bayly, 'Islam in Southern Asia', p. 40.
91. Mattison Mines, 'Islamization and Muslim Ethnicity in South India', in Rothermund (ed.), *Islam in Southern Asia*, p. 72.
92. Ibid., p. 69.
93. Lina M. Fruzzetti, 'Muslim Rituals, the Household Rites vs. the Public Festivals in Rural India', in I. Ahmad (ed.), *Rituals and Religion*, pp. 91–3.
94. Ibid., p. 91.
95. Fruzzetti, 'Muslim Rituals', p. 111.
96. Jean Ellickson, 'Islamic institutions, perception and practice in a village in Bangladesh', *Contributions to Indian Sociology*, vol. VI (New Series, 1972), p. 62.
97. Ibid., p. 58.
98. Clifford Geerts, *The Religion of Java* (Glencoe, Illinois, 1960).
99. John D. Legge, *Indonesia* (Sydney, 2nd edn, 1977), pp. 59–61.
100. M.C. Ricklefs, *Jogjakarta Under Sultan Mankubumi 1749–1792. A History of the Division of Java* (London, 1974); also 'Islamization in Java', in Levtzion (ed.), *Conversion in Islam*, pp. 100–28; Christine Dobbin, *Islamic Revivalism in a Changing Peasant Economy. Central Sumatra, 1784–1847* (London, 1983); Peter Carey, *Babad Dipanagara. An Account of the Outbreak of the Java War, 1825–30* (Kuala Lumpur, 1981).
101. Ahmad (ed.), *Rituals and Religion*, p. 18.
102. Ibid., p. 14
103. Asani, 'Sufi poetry in the folk tradition', p. 81.

4

Islamic Responses to the Fall of Srirangapattana and the Death of Tipu Sultan (1799)

KATE BRITTLEBANK

It is almost two hundred years since Tipu Sultan Fath Ali Khan, ruler of the powerful south Indian kingdom of Mysore, died defending his capital against the forces of General Harris. Over these years, Richard Wellesley's *bete noire* has become a mythological figure of extraordinary proportions. To the victors, the British, who had a need to justify their actions, Tipu was a tyrant and a usurper, an Islamic bigot who had received his just desserts; more recently this image has re-emerged, in the rhetoric of those Indians who hold anti-Muslim sentiments today.[1] So tenacious is this negative representation that even now it continues to be cited by some scholars.[2]

In a more positive vein, for the Muslims of the subcontinent, too, Tipu's role in their myth-making has been enduring. In the south, as a 'universal figure of power', he features in Tamil texts and oral traditions relating to sufi saints, with the Muslim holy men described as 'shahid-companions' of the late ruler,[3] and an early Muslim modernist, 'Abdur Rahim Dahri (1785–1850), saw Tipu as a heroic example to follow, glorifying his deeds in a Persian *mathnawi* entitled *Saulat-i Zaigham* (*The Ferocity*—or *Onslaught*—*of the Lion*).[4] Later, during the rebellion of 1857, Tipu's courage is said to have inspired Ahmadullah Shah Madrasi (1789–1858), who played a prominent role in the uprising in Awadh,[5] and Muhammad Iqbal (1877–1938), who has been described as 'the spiritual father of Pakistan', portrayed him as the 'martyr sultan' in his poem, *Jawidnama*.[6] In present-day Pakistan, he continues to be revered.[7]

In the main, though, these are later representations, their roots lying in the nineteenth and twentieth centuries, as Indian Muslims struggled with the loss of hegemony and the impact of colonization.[8] At the time of Tipu's death, the re-exploration of values identified by Barbara Metcalf, which occurred over the following one hundred and fifty years or so, was still in its infancy.[9] The fall of Srirangapattana and the subjugation of Mysore was, nonetheless, a crucial event in the rise of British paramountcy, and it follows then that it was a time of crisis in Indian history, particularly in the south. This essay will present therefore a preliminary analysis of how Muslims at the time, both locally and further afield, appear to have reacted to the event.[10]

The final defeat of Mysore and the death of its ruler was the result in part of a subsidiary alliance formed in late 1798 between the British and Nizam Ali Khan of Hyderabad, which led to the involvement of Hyderabad troops in the subsequent aggression against Tipu. The governor-general, Richard Wellesley justified his invasion on the flimsy ground that Tipu had been plotting against the British with the French. There was also the self-righteous argument, put forward after the fall, that the defeat of Tipu enabled the restoration to the throne of the rightful ruler of the kingdom, a child member of the Hindu Wodeyar dynasty. The attack on Mysore was surprisingly effective. Ordered to march on the kingdom in early February 1799, General Harris stood victorious in Tipu's palace three months later, leaving many Indians, particularly Muslims, to grapple with the implications of what had occurred.

Tipu Sultan was, of course, a Muslim, although his kingdom was predominantly Hindu; the Nizam of Hyderabad, who had always had very strained relations with Tipu, whom he regarded both as an upstart and a threat to his own power in the region, was a Muslim.[11] In the same area, the rulers of the Carnatic were Muslims, while the Marathas, a significant political force, were Hindu. What this essay will ask is how did religious affinity affect the Muslims' response to Tipu's death? Does it have any significance? The British, naturally, were non-believers and yet the Nizam had allied with them against Tipu. The Marathas on the other hand, although Wellesley had attempted to recruit them to his cause, did not become involved in the hostilities.

C.A. Bayly has argued that prior to the mid-nineteenth century there was perhaps no 'identifiable "Muslim", "Sikh" or "Hindu" identity which", as he puts it, "could be abstracted from the particular circumstances of individual events or specific societies'". Bayly prefers the *Annales* term '*mentalite*' which implies, he writes, 'a more variable, ambiguous or fragmented form of consciousness and one that is partly

contingent on social and economic circumstances rather than constructive of them.'[12] And the alliance of the Nizam with the British against
Tipu would seem to support this view. The Hyderabad ruler's self-
interest apparently overrode any loyalty he may have felt to his Mysore
counterpart and fellow Muslim, in the latter's struggle against the
infidel. In this he was not unusual. From pre-Mughal times to the
eighteenth-century incursions of Nadir Shah and Ahmad Shah Durrani,
the history of the Indian subcontinent is littered with incidents of inter-
Muslim conflict.

The complexity of the issue is underlined by early findings. Two
themes have emerged from the material examined so far: that of betrayal and that of destiny. It is generally accepted that Tipu was betrayed
to the British by some of his officers, particularly his Diwan, Mir Sadiq,
who was actually killed by enraged Mysore troops during the siege.
What is most interesting, though, is that even writers of the opposing
camp, associated with Hyderabad, condemn those who betrayed Tipu
as false and worthless creatures. Ghulam Muhammad, one of the
Nizam's men, in a long letter written shortly after Tipu's death to Nawab
Alif Khan of Kurnool, an ally of Hyderabad, talks of 'the seditious
people', like Mir Sadiq and others, 'who were on the lookout for their
opportunities', and condemns also 'the low-born commandant, Mir
Nadim', 'that offspring of a whore'.[13] Purnaiya, Tipu's leading Hindu
officer, who as Diwan under the new regime virtually became regent,
is described as a 'faithless infidel.' The terminology in the letter is
essentially that of jihad, with two loyal Mysore officers attaining
martyrdom and Tipu wielding his 'blood-sucking sword'.[14]

Mir Hussein Ali Khan Kirmani, who wrote a chronicle of the reigns
of Haidar 'Ali and Tipu, completed in 1802, and who had been employed
by them for a short time in the early 1780s, also raises the issue of
betrayal. Kirmani is not usually regarded as particularly pro-Tipu, being
a pensioner of the British when he wrote his work. He does not accord
Tipu the epithet *shahid* or martyr, unlike the chroniclers of the Nawabs
of the Carnatic, for example, who do refer to him thus.[15] Nor does he
describe him as Padshah, which is how Tipu styled himself, but reverts
to the titles bestowed on him by the Mughal emperor, which Tipu did
not acknowledge or use. But Kirmani, too, refers to the falseness of
some of the Mysore officers and concludes his account of the siege by
describing the interment of Tipu's body in his father's tomb, where, he
says, it 'rested from the treachery and malice of faithless servants and
cruel enemies.'[16]

Kirmani also regarded Tipu's defeat as being his destiny, against
which he could do nothing. Of an early engagement of the siege, in

which the Mysoreans came off worst, he concludes, 'This undoubtedly was all predestined and under the power and control of no one.'[17] Further, he states, the Mysore ruler's difficulties were compounded by his lack of judgment and failure to listen to the advice of his loyal officers. While Kirmani does not explicitly link this to his destiny, a north Indian writer, Abu Taleb, does. Abu Taleb made his comments in an account of his travels in Europe during the years 1799 to 1803. In a wider assessment of British victories in India, he writes that Tipu was 'led on by his evil destiny' to inappropriate actions and poor judgment. Critical of Tipu's tactics, he refers to the Mysore ruler's pride and his resolve to die in defence of his honour. He then cites a verse:

> When Fortune turns away her face from a man,
> he does precisely that which he ought not to do.[18]

Similarly, Kirmani concludes, 'In short the agents of fate and destiny did what they willed, or what was in their power.'[19]

There is a sense in these writings of the inevitability of the death of Tipu at the hands of the British but one also has the feeling that the authors recognize the tragedy of that death. There is perhaps discomfort with the knowledge that a Muslim had been defeated by unbelievers and all that it implied, and also perhaps a dawning realization of the significance of the ever-growing influence of the British on the subcontinent, the dangers of which both Haidar and Tipu had well understood and constantly fought against. It must be remembered that to Muslims the world is divided into *dar ul-islam*, the house or abode of Islam, and *dar ul-harb*, the house or abode of war. The house of Islam is territory governed by Muslims and subject to Islamic law; the house of war is the rest of the world. As Bernard Lewis notes, 'The unsubjugated unbeliever is by definition an enemy.'[20] Under the Mughal empire, Indian Muslims would have had no doubt that they lived within the house of Islam. By the end of the eighteenth century, with the Mughal emperor reduced to a shadow of his former self, beholden to others for the maintenance of his position, the Nizam, a client of the British, and the last independent Islamic ruler of any potency, now dead, it must have seemed increasingly that the subcontinent was becoming dar ul-harb or the house of war. That this was in fact the case is demonstrated by the requests for rulings submitted during the early years of the nineteenth century to Shah Abdul Aziz (1746–1824)—who had inherited the mantle of his father, the great north Indian sufi and scholar, Shah Wali Allah—on this very subject.[21]

At home in Britain, there was intense interest in the so-called 'great victory of Seringapatam', and Abu Taleb recounted his experience of visiting a theatre in Ireland. 'In my account of Dublin,' he writes, 'I mentioned having seen the principal events of *The Capture of Seringapatam* exhibited on the stage, by which I was much affected.'[22] He does not elaborate but it takes little imagination to realize that he found the images disturbing.

This problem of how to respond to Tipu's death is very clearly articulated in a letter from a certain Muhammad Mustafa Khan to Mir Alam, one of the Nizam's most senior officials and the man who had commanded the Hyderabad troops during the invasion. According to Ghulam Muhammad, the author of the letter to the Nawab of Kurnool, Mir 'Alam had been highly pleased with the outcome of events and had stated that 'through the grace of God a great victory was achieved and through the good fortune of His Excellency [presumably the Nizam] a great disturbing aggrandisement was removed.'[23] Muhammad Mustafa, however, did not see things in quite so simplistic terms. He talks of Tipu's pride in his pomp and power, arms and wealth, and writes that he was a unique personality in India, resembling Nadir of Persia and second only to Tamuchin of China—that is Chinggis Khan. While admitting that Tipu disgusted believers and non-believers alike by his violent temper, he argues that 'he was so firmly resolved on bringing glory to Islam and carrying out the divine behests that he established his claim by his valour, intrepidity and martyrdom.'[24] Probably suspecting that Mir Alam would not agree with him, Muhammad Mustafa acknowledges it is not clear whether the former regarded Tipu as a martyr or as 'one neither of faith nor of the world'. His view, though, is that 'the mother earth will not be able to produce such a Rustam-like hero for a period of 130 years. If the Muslims simultaneously smile and weep like a candle-stick', he concludes, 'and rejoice and mourn at the same time like a rose it will not be improper.'[25]

As Muhammad Mustafa points out, one thing that could never be said of Tipu was that he lacked courage and he proved this to the end, dying a hero's death rather than capitulate to the British, as so many of his contemporaries had done. Also, over the years he had portrayed himself in his letters to other Muslims as a defender of the faith, appealing to the bonds of Islam when attempting to form alliances against the infidels, be they Marathas or Europeans—although one should not read too much into this, since he also, like the Nizam, entered into alliances with non-believers if it suited him, such as the French, and he courted the Marathas on more than one occasion. But he clearly saw his struggle against the British in terms of jihad, or what is known in the West as holy war, and this would have been well-known by Islamic observers, as is demonstrated by Muhammad Mustafa's letter. He had, then, all the attributes of the archetypal Muslim warrior, who achieves martyr-dom in defence of Islam, a figure highly revered in the Muslim world. It is quite probable that the anguish demonstrated by some of the writers is a direct response to this, irrespective of whether they were friend or foe.

As noted earlier, this essay is merely a preliminary analysis and it may become clearer through further research why, for example, in the responses there is such an emphasis on betrayal. This is something that has fed into the later mythology. The traitor Mir Sadiq is frequently mentioned along with Mir Ja'far, whose treachery was believed to have led to Clive's victory at Plassey. The two feature side by side in Iqbal's *Jawidnama* and are cited together by Mujeeb in his book *The Indian Muslims* as 'symptoms of a fatally common disease' in the eighteenth century.[26] Even today, Muslim historians regard Tipu's betrayal as an issue; both Mohibbul Hasan and Sheikh Abdur Rashid emphasize Mir Sadiq's role in his downfall.[27] While the focus on betrayal by the later writers is perhaps understandable, that it should also have been a preoccupation of contemporary writers is less so. Kingship in India was generally regarded as open-ended in nature, with rulers constantly facing challenges to their authority if they were perceived in any way to be weak by tributaries and subordinates. So acts of betrayal would hardly have been unusual. Yet the betrayal of Tipu is clearly regarded as problematic, perhaps underlining again the difficulty encountered by Muslims in responding to his death.

For the writers to see the hand of destiny in Tipu's demise is, however, to be expected, being entirely consistent with Islamic thought. In Muslim chronicles, events are frequently explained as being the will of God. Further work is needed, though, to establish whether Islamic observers saw Tipu's death as a manifestation of God's displeasure, another frequent theme in chronicles. It is clearly evident, nonetheless, that not all Muslims responded negatively to Tipu's death. We have already seen that Mir 'Alam was delighted with the turn of events, and this no doubt reflects the 'ambiguous or fragmented' consciousness identified by Bayly in his article. As Bayly emphasizes, it is futile to attempt an analysis of consciousness without regard to context,[28] and it certainly seems that those who benefited from their association with the British were not troubled by the circumstances of Tipu's demise. As founder of the Fort William College in 1800, Richard Wellesley was eulogized by the Islamic writers who found employment there. Within only a few years of the fall of Srirangapattana, as Rizvi notes with some astonishment, they dedicated their books to him in the sort of language previously reserved for Mughal emperors.[29]

But for some Muslims, particularly those who were closely associated with the events themselves or witnessed depictions of the events, how to respond to the death was far less straightforward. Both Paul Brass and Francis Robinson, in discussing Muslim identity on the Indian subcontinent, have accepted the view that members of communities have attachments to 'primordial' symbols and meanings that stay with them throughout life, and which can play some kind of role in the definition of national or ethnic identity.[30] It would not be difficult to argue that the figure of the shahid or martyr is a strong primordial symbol for Muslims everywhere and that the emotional reactions referred to above are direct responses to that attachment.[31] For those writers, on the other hand, whose experience of the fall was less dramatic or more distant, the emotive impact of Tipu's death could well have been diminished.

Returning then to the question of whether religious affinity affected Indian Muslims' responses to the death of Tipu Sultan, we can see that to some extent it did but only within the context of the observer's experience of the event. Certainly at this time, as Bayly suggests, Muslim solidarity or identity were not strong enough to overcome self-interest, or even disinterest; however, it also seems clear that under certain circumstances it would be wrong to discount the significance of religious allegiance altogether.

Endnotes

1. For an expanded discussion of the re-emergence of Tipu as tyrant, see Kate Brittlebank, *Tipu Sultan's Search for Legitimacy: Islam and Kingship in a Hindu Domain* (Delhi, 1997), pp. 1–2.

2. See, for example, Peter van der Veer, *Religious Nationalism: Hindus and Muslims in India* (Berkeley, 1994), p. 32. Although van der Veer recognizes that this image is part of Hindu nationalist rhetoric, he appears to believe its origins lie in fact, rather than in the constructions of British colonialism.

3. Susan Bayly, *Saints, Goddesses and Kings: Muslims and Christians in South Indian society 1700–1900* (Cambridge, 1989), pp. 187–8, 190–1.

4. Mujeeb Ashraf, *Muslim Attitudes Towards British Rule and Western Culture in India* (Delhi, 1982), p. 217.

5. Ibid., pp. 169–70.

6. Annemarie Schimmel, *Islam in the Indian Subcontinent* (Leiden-Koln, 1980), pp. 164, 168–9.

7. See Brittlebank, *Tipu Sultan's Search for Legitimacy*, pp. 2, 4, for further discussion of Tipu's image in Pakistan today.

8. Summaries of Islamic responses to the rise of British power in the late eighteenth and early nineteenth centuries, particularly in north India, can

be found in P. Hardy, *The Muslims of British India* (Cambridge, 1972), pp. 31–60; Barbara D. Metcalf, *Islamic Revival in British India: Deoband, 1860–1900* (Princeton, 1982), pp. 16–86; Schimmel, *Islam in the Indian Subcontinent*, pp. 177–84. More detailed analysis is contained in Saiyid Athar Abbas Rizvi, *Shah 'Abd al-'Aziz: Puritanism, Sectarian Polemics and Jihad* (Canberra, 1982).

9. Barbara D. Metcalf, *Moral Conduct and Authority: The Place of Adab in South Asian Islam* (Berkeley, 1984), pp. 17–18.

10. The essay takes it as given that Indian Islam is not homogeneous. However, it also recognizes, as others have, that the idea of community for Muslims generally is a strong one. Francis Robinson, 'Islam and Muslim Separatism', in David Taylor and Malcolm Yapp (eds), *Political Identity in South Asia* (London and Dublin, 1979), p. 83; Gail Minault, *The Khilafat Movement: Religious Symbolism and Political Mobilization in India* (New York, 1982), p. 3.

11. The Nizam referred to Tipu as 'this villain', while to the Mughal emperor, Shah 'Alam, he was '*maqhur*', 'destined to be vanquished'. Intelligence received from Pondicherry, 1 September 1787, Foreign Secretary, Consultations. 10, National Archives of India; Rizvi, *Shah 'Abd al-'Aziz*, p. 43. Tipu, on the other hand, is believed to have referred to the Nizam on at least one occasion as a *kafir*, or unbeliever. Mahmud Husain, tr. *The Dreams of Tipu Sultan*, (Karachi, n.d.), p. 87.

12. C.A. Bayly, 'The Pre-history of "Communalism"? Religious Conflict in India, 1700–1860', *Modern Asian Studies*, 19, 2 (1985), pp. 202–3.

13. Syed Hasan Askari, 'Some Letters of, and Relating to, Tipu Sultan', *Proceedings of the Indian Historical Records Commission*, vol. 32 (1956), pp. 54–5.

14. Ibid., pp. 55–6.

15. Muhammad Karim, *Sawanihat-i-Mumtaz*; See also S. Muhammad Husayn Nainar, *Sources of the History of the Nawwabs of the Carnatic* (Madras, 1939–50), vol. 3, p. 133, ch. 4, p. 132.

16. Meer Hussein Ali Khan Kirmani, *The History of the Reign of Tipu Sultan Being a Continuation of The Neshani Hyduri*, trans. by W. Miles (London, 1844), p. 272. It is interesting to note that earlier in his work Kirmani, too, like Ghulam Muhammad, is critical of Tipu's appointment of 'low-bred, vulgar' men. Ibid., p. 98, 156. Rizvi points out that an increased preoccupation with nobility and low birth (the ashraf/*ajlaf* division of Islam on the subcontinent) seems to have accompanied the declining economic position of Indian Muslims in the eighteenth century. Kirmani's and Ghulam Muhammad's comments may well be a reflection of this trend. Rizvi, *Shah 'Abd al-'Aziz*, p. 177.

17. Kirmani, *History*, pp. 258–9.

18. Charles Stewart (trans.), *Travels of Mirza Abu Taleb Khan in Asia, Africa, and Europe, During the Years 1799, 1800, 1801, 1802, and 1803*, 2nd ed. (London, 1814), pp. 201–5.

19. Kirmani, *History*, p. 273.

20. Bernard Lewis, *The Political Language of Islam* (Chicago, 1988), p. 77.
21. Rizvi, *Shah 'Abd al-'Aziz*, pp. 226–31, 236–7, 577. Discussion of the Shah's *fatawa* on this issue can also be found in Metcalf, *Islamic Revival*, pp. 50–2; M. Mujeeb, *The Indian Muslims* (London, 1967), pp. 390–1. As Metcalf notes, 'Abdul 'Aziz's rulings are ambiguous; nor was there unity amongst Muslims on the topic. See Anwar Moazzam, 'Indian Muslims' Attempts at Self-Definition', C. W. Troll (ed.), *Islam in India: Studies and Commentaries*, (New Delhi, 1985), 2, p. 27. Rizvi notes, though, that by the second half of the nineteenth century Islamic scholars, on the basis of classical authorities, issued fatawa ruling that India under British rule was not dar ul-harb. Rizvi, *Shah 'Abd al-'Aziz*, p. 531.
22. *Travels of Abu Taleb*, p. 205.
23. Askari, 'Some Letters', p. 56.
24. Ibid., p. 57.
25. Ibid.
26. Mujeeb, *Indian Muslims*, p. 502. On Iqbal, see Schimmel, *Islam in the Indian Subcontinent*, p. 164.
27. Mohibbul Hasan, *History of Tipu Sultan*, 2nd ed. (Calcutta, 1971), pp. 313–14, 323–4; Sheikh Abdur Rashid, *History of the Muslims of the Indo-Pakistan Sub-Continent (1707–1806)* (Lahore, 1978), 1, pp. 265, 365.
28. Bayly, 'Pre-history of "Communalism"?', p. 203.
29. Rizvi, *Shah 'Abd al-'Aziz*, p. 63.
30. Paul R. Brass, 'Elite Groups, Symbol Manipulation and Ethnic Identity among the Muslims of South Asia', in Taylor & Yapp, *Political Identity*, pp. 35–77; Robinson, 'Islam and Muslim Separatism', pp. 78–112. Brass and Robinson differ in their interpretations of the role 'primordial attachments' play in the establishment of ethnic or national identity, including the significance of that role.
31. In this regard, see the discussion in Stephen F. Dale, 'The Islamic Frontier in Southwest India: The Shahid as a Cultural Ideal among the Mapillas of Malabar', *Modern Asian Studies*, vol. 11, no. 1 (1977), particularly pp. 46–7 and n. 26; pp. 52–3.

5

South Asian Muslims and the Plague 1896–c.1914

I.J. CATANACH

At one level, the level of administrative measures and indigenous response to those measures, the story of Muslims in the early plague years in British India can be fairly briefly told. Some parts of that story are, indeed, reasonably familiar. While this paper does not entirely neglect *histoire evenementielle*, its concerns are ultimately more those of the historian of *mentalite*. Plague provides us with a most useful mirror of South Asian Islam in the last years of the nineteenth century and the early years of the twentieth century. But, as is usual in the study of history, we cannot avoid beginning with 'events'.

The existence of plague in the city of Bombay, for some time suspected, was confirmed in October 1896; by the end of the year the disease had shown signs of spreading beyond the city. Vigorous 'cleansing' operations were instituted; in the early days of plague, those found in house searches to be suffering from the disease were bundled off to various temporary and permanent buildings described as 'hospitals', and some attempt was made to 'segregate' their families. Death could occur without the vital rites of passage. In Pune, house-to-house searches were conducted by British soldiers; the result was the assassination of the British official in charge, W.C. Rand.

Plague, it was maintained, would soon be 'stamped out'. The fact was, however, that initially the British had little idea of how to tackle the visitation. Beyond the Bombay Presidency other provinces of British India prepared themselves for the worst while earnestly hoping for the best. Officially, plague did not reach the Punjab until October 1897; the Government of Bengal did not admit the existence of plague in Calcutta until April 1898 and the plains of the North-Western Provinces (soon to become the United Provinces) did not begin to experience the disease until the very end of 1899. But meanwhile regulations for the control of plague had often been promulgated, argued about, sometimes sternly resisted, and sometimes amended.[1]

Although the North-Western Provinces 'plague rules' of early 1897 gave officials the right to remove to hospital any who were suffering from the disease, 'home segregation' was, virtually from the start, permitted in the case of people of high status. Nevertheless in March 1897 an angry crowd, mainly Muslims, assembled at the place known as Shah Mina in Lucknow in protest against the plague rules. Shah Mina—named after, and reputedly the burial place of, Lucknow's 'founding saint'—was in itself 'sacred space'.[2] A deputation of *raises*— one was Mehdi Hasan Khan, from the old Avadh royal family—went from the Shah Mina meeting to Sir Antony MacDonnell, the lieutenant-governor of the North-Western Provinces. They told MacDonnell, to quote his words, that they 'considered the plague a far less evil than separation from plague-stricken members of their families; that plague was a God-sent dispensation, against which they were not at all sure it was not impious to contend; and that happen what might, they would never permit the segregation of their women or the administration of European drugs to their families.'[3]

A little later, in May 1897, MacDonnell visited Aligarh. While he was there, the ageing Saiyid Ahmad Khan came to visit him. MacDonnell reported that Saiyid Ahmad was particularly concerned about the possible breaking of purdah. The 'old gentleman... solemnly warned me that the business was creating more ill-will against us than anything he had known since the Mutiny.'[4]

The Punjab promulgated a set of plague regulations at the end of January 1898. They were in some ways harsher than the contemporary North-Western Provinces rules. In mid-February 1898, during Ramadan, there were rumours in Delhi, then administered as part of the Punjab, that plague would close shops at the Id. A season of gifts and rejoicing could be spoilt. It was claimed that a crowded protest meeting of, 'all the noblemen and raises of Delhi'[5] was held. Then, on the morning of 25 February, four handwritten notices appeared, briefly but dramatically, on the Clock Tower opposite the Town Hall. Bombay, it was said, had been 'looted by these people' (that is, the British); 'they have killed God's creatures by... giving out that plague has appeared in other towns.' There was a reference to recent British defeats by those the notice called 'the Frontier Ghazis'. Another notice cried: 'We are quite prepared to sacrifice our lives for our religion and respect.... The notion will cause emotion equal to that of the 1857 Mutiny.'[6]

In the city of Bombay on 9 March 1898 riots—which were seen to have a distinct anti-European tinge to them—broke out. 'Plague huts', as they were called, were set on fire and an attempt was made to raze the J.J. Hospital. The riots began in protest against an attempt by a Parsi medical student, in the employ of the plague authorities, to examine a twelve-year old Muslim girl; of those convicted after the riots 144 were Muslim and only 61 Hindu.[7]

A few weeks later there were plague-related disturbances—the Government of Bengal insisted, perhaps a little disingenuously, that they were not riots—in Calcutta and its surrounds.[8] Some of the worst troubles occurred on the two days following *Bakr Id*; Calcutta's growing migrant Muslim working class, about whom Dipesh Chakrabarty has written much,[9] were particularly involved.

The events in Bombay, especially, were part of the background to the India-wide easing of the plague rules which came in the middle of 1898[10]—although the fact that the easing was not always widely promulgated may have had something to do with the riots in Kanpur in April 1900. There, as people issued forth from the *Idgah* after Bakr Id celebrations, someone raised the cry (false as it happened) that two plague cases had been carried off to hospital. A crowd swept down on the plague hospital; members of the Muslim Butcher community played a leading role, urged on from a distance, it was alleged, by a Muslim member of the Municipal Board.[11] MacDonnell, who had rushed to Kanpur on hearing news of the riot, and who had hitherto remained apparently unflustered, confident, and one could say, liberal-minded in the face of plague, now confessed to the viceroy that he had begun to understand the feelings of British administrators during the Revolt of 1857.[12]

Punjab can be said to have been spared plague-connected violence, for some time, after bloody police firings at the Muslim-dominated town of Garhshankar in April 1898.[13] (There were further plague-related riots in a few places in April and May 1901, and arguably, plague was part of the background to the Canal Colony disturbances of 1907).[14] In Punjab, Muslims were on the whole much slower than other communities to take to the inoculation against plague, with Haffkine's vaccine, that was increasingly offered to them.[15] And in the Punjab, as in much of the rest of northern India, the observance of purdah remained a problem in plague administration. Purdah, both amongst many Muslim groups and some higher Hindu castes, was arguably as much a matter of male status as of anything else. As an Ambala Rajput put it to Malcolm Darling in the late 1920s: 'What would remain of the Rajputs if they gave up purdah?'[16] But just as for some of the British the very existence of purdah provided some sort of justification for supposedly enlightened British rule, so too, there is little doubt that for the 'high-born' Muslim male, and for some others as well, the defence of purdah was inimitably bound up with defence of a whole way of life.

II

At first sight, then, it might seem that South Asian Muslims put up a formidable and united front against British-sponsored plague measures. In their more 'orientalizing' moments many of the British were inclined to see matters this way; rumoured links between, say, Delhi and Bombay Muslims over plague reinforced such notions.[17] In the last years of the nineteenth century, even such a shrewd observer as Harcourt Butler regularly generalized (in letters to his family, anyway) about 'the Mohammedans'.[18]

Yet in practice South Asian Muslims were anything but united in the face of plague. In the city of Bombay many Aga Khani Khojahs and Daudi Bohras collaborated with the British in plague matters. Wealthy Muslims—the *Muslim Herald* called them mere 'flatterers and honour hunters'—accompanied General Gatacre on his rounds when he was in charge of plague control in Bombay in 1897. Much of the Muslim opposition to plague measures in that city came from one community, the Sunni Konkanis. But the Muslims amongst whom, in Bombay, the violent protest of 9 March 1898 began were, in fact, *Julahas*, weavers, originally from the North-Western Provinces. They were a group of people who, admittedly, were looked on with some disdain by many of the 'well-born', but also a group with, as Gyan Pandey has reminded us, a reputation for 'fanaticism'.[19] Actually, the Julahas in Bombay were divided, partly on economic lines (factory workers as against poverty-stricken home workers)[20] and partly on religious lines (one group was described in colonial documents as 'Wahabi' and one was not).[21] What seems to have happened on 9 March 1898 was that a group of 'young men' amongst the Julahas broke from the control of their 'headman'; they were probably somewhat inebriated[22] as a result of their partici-pation in that three-day social *bouleversement* (as Ranajit Guha has described it),[23] the 'Hindu' festival of Holi. So much, one might say, for Julaha 'fanaticism'. One might note, too, that in its way we have here another example, to add to those from Delhi, Calcutta, and Kanpur, of 'plague troubles' emerging out of religious festivals. As Sandria Freitag has observed, riots in South Asia tend to grow out of gatherings for other purposes.[24]

'Muslims' and 'Hindus' were obviously not always leading entirely separate lives in Bombay. In Delhi and Kanpur, too (but not in Calcutta, where it would seem that differences of language and class were, by the late 1890s, beginning to be superimposed on religious differences in a unique way), Muslims and Hindus were reported by nervous British officials to be 'fraternizing' before and during plague troubles. In other words, they were not behaving according to commonly accepted stereotype. In Delhi, on the Id day, 23 February 1898, 'certain influential Hindus' were allowed inside the Idgah while prayers were in progress. On the following day Hindus attended the Muslim festive gathering known as Tar Mela; in a reversion to a practice that had obtained before the communal disturbances of 1886, a leading Hindu, Sri Kishen Das, provided the venue and the necessary sherbet and sweets.[25] In Kanpur there were, it was said, 'unusual' demonstrations of Hindu-Muslim amity before the Bakr Id outbreak of 11 April 1900.[26] And from Rohilkhand, sullen since the 1857 revolt, came reports of Muslims and Hindus failing to follow stereotypical roles in plague matters; there were similar reports from Ajmer in Rajasthan.[27] It is conceivable that the shrillness of protest from Muslims which followed soon after MacDonnell's so-called 'Nagri' resolution of 18 April 1900 owed something to a feeling of 'let-down' after the seeming communal co-operation over plague of only a few weeks before. A Banaras Hindu newspaper insinuated late in May that twenty thousand Muslims assembled at a mosque in the city, ostensibly to offer prayers in connection with the plague, were in fact offering prayers against the use of the Hindi script.[28]

What the British found in almost every part of India—and it was something that they lamented greatly—was an absence of chains of command amongst Muslims. In Bombay, Gatacre tried to get one of two rival *qazi*s to issue definitive orders to 'his Moulvies' (as Gatacre, the military man, put it) among the Konkanis. A little later Gatacre tried to work on the 'leaders of the "Jamats"', and under their orders the headmen of the streets.' But this was largely to no avail: in any case the formal powers of the Bombay qazis had been steadily reduced by the British over the nineteenth century.[29] A somewhat similar problem arose in Bombay with a personage described in a newspaper as the 'High Priest' of the Bohras. A police officer approached him after the riots of March 1898. 'You did not come to me when the Governor received the leaders of the community', he retorted; 'why do you come to me now?'[30]

In the North-Western Provinces the British tried, at the time of plague, their by now well-worn tactic of attempting to control matters through those they regarded as the 'natural leaders of the people' (although MacDonnell, with his Bengal background, somewhat distrusted those he called 'Durbaris').[31] So, Muslim notables such as Ashgar Ali Khan of Bareilly and Mushtaq Husain of Amroha and Moradabad (Viqar-ul-Mulk) flit across the pages of the plague records, but, generally speaking, leave no real mark there. There are many reasons for this—including the post-conquest and post-Mutiny treatment of so many of the old Muslim 'aristocracy'. But it is possible that such notables could not have led north Indian Muslims in plague matters even if they had tried. Certainly their powers over urban artisan groups were, at least by this stage, often not great.[32] And in the final analysis one is left with the impression that Albert Hourani's argument about the medieval Muslim city is of some relevance to the situation of Muslims in late nineteenth-century Indian towns. 'There was', wrote Hourani, 'an individual believer' [perhaps it might have been better to have said 'an individual male family head'] 'and there was the whole community of believers, but in between there was no stable grouping regarded as legitimate and permanent.'[33] The courtyard of the Muslim notable's house, it is worth remembering, turned inwards, away from the street.

The idea of ruling through local notables had some hold in the Punjab, as well as in the North-Western Provinces. The raises, said the *Civil and Military Gazette* of Lahore in 1898, had to help in plague matters in return for the position he had been given: 'no *khidmat*, no *izzat*.'[34] But in the Punjab, somewhat more than in other provinces, an attempt was made to gain support from the 'scholars' of Islam, the ulama. The Raj had in its confident days of conquest and early rule divorced itself virtually entirely from the ulama, but such a situation had not led to a decline in the importance of the ulama in Indian Muslim life. If anything, the reverse had been the case. Now, in the Punjab, the Raj, in the face of plague, scurried to gain the confidence of the ulama.

Early contacts with Punjab ulama appear to have been made by H.J. Maynard (then a junior secretary, with de facto oversight over plague matters, but due to rise to higher things) and a Captain Aubrey O'Brien[35] (a rare type of intermediary, one suspects, in that he was the son of a notable Punjab civilian, a linguist, an authority of the pirs of western Punjab, and for a time a trustee of a Muslim shrine in an Indian state). At first the concessions gained amounted to little more than fatawa which permitted the use of disinfectant. Such fatawa were, however, 'circulated on lithographed broadsheets' at government expense:[36] printing—especially in the form of the Indian-owned and edited newspaper—could hinder the cause of plague control but it could also on occasion assist it.[37] J.G. Silcock, deputy commissioner of Ludhiana, 'reasoned' (as he put it) with the 'leading Maulvis of Ludhiana town', and apparently managed to obtain a fatawa permitting 'evacuation' in certain circumstances.[38] Finally, Mufti Muhammad Abdullah, president of the reformist but somewhat militant Anjuman Himayat-i-Islam in Lahore[39] (an organization with some of the 'hegemonizing' tendencies that have been detected in the Singh Sabhas and the Arya Samaj),[40] was brought to pronounce that 'segregation' was 'a kind of treatment, for to breathe pure air is one of the best and most beneficial things for health.' Furthermore, 'anti-plague inoculation' was said to be 'allowable by' and 'in accordance with' Muslim law. Muhammad Yar, *imam* of the Sunehri mosque, a small but important mosque in Lahore, signified his agreement with this pronouncement. So, too, did a few maulvis from Gujranwala and Amritsar, and even Shah Suleiman, an important *alim* from Phulwari, in far-away Bihar. But most of the other signatories were comparatively minor teachers in various schools in Lahore sponsored by the Anjuman Himayat-i-Islam.[41]

Maynard touched the crux of the matter so far as British relations with the ulama were concerned when he wrote in 1907: 'Mullas in the rural Punjab appear to recognize no spiritual authority whose pronouncements on the sacred law are regarded as generally binding.'[42] That unity, that chain of command after which the British hankered, was simply not in evidence in Indian Islam.

III

The real problem, said Maynard, was 'the teaching of the small local Mullas that it is impious to resist or evade the will of God.'[43] It was, of course, not just rural Punjabi mullahs who held such views. Plague, said some at a meeting of Bombay Muslims (mainly, it would appear, Sunni Konkanis) in December 1896, was a 'warning from Heaven'. If plague led to death, that would be a 'blessing in its way and not a curse.'[44]

Such reports, like the report of the Shah Mina meeting in Lucknow, have the potential to lead us away from the realms of policy construction and riot 'deconstruction'—so often the main concerns of the colonial records—and into the realms of South Asian Muslim theology and medicine, and popular mentality. These realms are all to some extent related: many an alim had some understanding of medicine; many a *hakim* had some understanding of theology,[45] and 'ordinary people', even in villages, were not totally ignorant of either.[46]

Pious and scholarly Hindus struggled (not very successfully) to find plague described in ancient Hindu medical treatises. Pious and scholarly Muslims, on the other hand, soon had no great difficulty in placing plague in historical and intellectual contexts. It was *waba*, an epidemic disease; specifically, it was *ta'un*,[47] as it had been known in the Middle Eastern world in Umayyad times and in the era of the Black Death, and (in India) in the seventeenth century. Indian Muslims in the 1890s could, in the face of plague, invoke certain principles that had been evolved over many centuries. Plague was a mercy sent by God, which, for the faithful, could provide the blessing of martyrdom. Since plague was decreed by God, a Muslim should neither enter nor flee from a land in which plague was present. And, as with other diseases, there was no 'contagion' (*adwa*), no transmission from one person to another.[48]

As we have seen, the raises of Lucknow were well aware of these principles; the Konkanis of Bombay had at least an inkling of them, too. Yet these principles—especially, perhaps, that of no contagion—had been some time in formation, and had never been fully accepted by the learned, let alone by others.[49] Debate on these principles continued in India in 1896 and the following years.

The Bombay Memon Cassim Mitha may have been something of a 'flatterer and honour hunter'. But he showed that he possessed a measure of theology when he argued that no man had a right to throw away his own life.[50] Whether Cassim Mitha fully realized it or not, he was entering into the debate within Islam over 'freewill' and 'predestination'. God was in control of all—but did He, as the Qadariyya asserted, 'delegate' actions to human beings?[51] Some medieval Muslims had asked whether even petitionary prayer at a time of plague was appropriate. Was it efficacious?[52] Early twentieth-century Indian Muslims—amongst them, in a notable fatawa, Maulana Ashraf Ali Thanavi[53]—argued yet again over the meaning of the well-known story of the Caliph Umar, who had summoned his military commander from plague-stricken Syria. Should he, or should he not, have done so?[54]

Above all, it needs to be said that there was a strong body of opinion which believed that medicine had an important role to play in the understanding and treatment of plague. 'Medicine' might or might not include the 'segregation' which the British for a time desired: that was very debatable. But, it was said, the Prophet himself had permitted the use of 'curing drugs'.[55] The activities of all manner of hakims could thus be justified.

The 'medicine' offered by such men as Hakim Abdul Majid Khan of Delhi, and his ultimately more prominent younger brother, Hakim Ajmal Khan, was undoubtedly of a highly sophisticated variety. Ajmal

Khan set out his views on a plague in a treatise, *al-Ta'un*, as early as 1897.[56] It was written in Urdu; Ajmal Khan was seeking the audience offered by the lithographer. Yet in many ways his treatise followed the format of older medical treatises: it began with a long 'history' of the disease (ostensibly in order to console the afflicted),[57] and it offered prescriptions—both for the wealthy and for the less affluent. But Ajmal Khan devoted much space to the physical care of patients; he was for gentle measures, and was 'strongly' opposed to the blood-letting advocated by some other physicians.

As far as definition of plague was concerned there was, said Ajmal Khan, 'hardly any difference' between *yunani tibb* and western allopathy. He was quite definite that plague was 'infectious' and 'contagious'. If plague broke out 'the first thing to do' was to 'leave the place.'

One can see why one of the placards posted on the Delhi Clock Tower in February 1897 accused Ajmal Khan's brother of 'supporting the Government...following the Christians'.[58] And one can see why, in the second decade of this century, the Lucknavi Abdul Halim Sharar could write that Ajmal Khan's system of medicine, 'apart from the method of diagnosis, includes so many European practices that the original science of Muslim medicine, instead of advancing, seems to be headed for disaster'.[59] But Ajmal Khan was no sycophant. In his relations with the British earlier in his career he maintained a dignified, aristocratic aloofness[60]—his family had been hurt as a consequence of 1857[61]—and politically, of course, he was later to be an ardent supporter of the Khilafat movement and, for a time, the Indian National Congress. In later years, especially, he and his students at the Unani Tibbi College in Delhi concerned themselves to quite a considerable extent not only with western medicine but also with Ayurvedic medicine. The reality of his medicine, and of *yunani* in general, was this: it was, and is, as Barbara Metcalf has pointed out, 'inherently plural in its origin and continuing openness.'[62] It needs to be emphasized that, for this reason, a tradition of conservative opposition to yunani (Greek) medicine stretched a long way back in Islamic history.[63]

Yet it was probably not on these grounds that the teaching and activities of Ajmal Khan and his family, at time of plague, met with objections from others in Delhi who took the title of hakim. Another placard posted on the Clock Tower fulminated: 'Oh! the disciples of Hakim Abdul Majid Khan, you have brought disgrace upon your teacher and yourselves by prohibiting the use of *kachalu..*, *laungchire...*, plums etc., which cure diseases of all sorts.... If the use of these articles be prohibited, how will their dealers maintain themselves.' H.S.P. Davies, acting deputy commissioner of Delhi, was perhaps (again in

an 'orientalizing' way) too quick to suspect mercenary motives in the
activities of 'Hakims and Vaids' whom he believed to be behind the
Delhi agitation.[64] 'Hakims and Vaids' were frequently to be accused of
spreading rumours about plague, for their own ends. But, in this case,
there may have been some basis to British suspicions.

There were, in fact, hakims and hakims—just as there were ulama
and ulama. The potions and (sometimes) the astrology and the amulets
of the less learned hakims belonged to quite a considerable extent to the
world of folk medicine, a world in which the *jinn* (spirits) played a large
part.[65] They could also belong to a comparatively new world, opened up
by the coming of printing, that of the 'advertising hakims',[66] who sought
custom through the newspapers and operated mail-order businesses.
The role of hakims and *vaids* in the British-sponsored system of
medicine in India had been steadily reduced as the nineteenth century
wore on.[67] The urgencies of plague eventually brought, in most parts of
India, a greater, if still somewhat reluctant, readiness on the part of the
British to make use of indigenous medicine—for essentially British
purposes. From 1907 hakims could be paid by the Punjab government
for plague services.[68] A somewhat similar process—but in reverse
direction—was at work amongst some of the hakims. They were beginning to make use of allopathic medicine, for their own purposes. They
acted, doubtless, out of a mixture of conviction (let us not forget Barbara
Metcalf on the openness of yunani) and expediency. Fear may even have
entered the equation: the hakims at Garhshankar in the Punjab, where
the police had spilt much blood at the time of plague's first appearance,
were reported within a matter of months to be 'a most intelligent set of
men', who had quickly learnt to dress festering buboes with antiseptic.[69]

IV

Theology and medicine—even if at times they were imperfectly understood—formed, as we have seen, part of the mentality of quite ordinary
Muslims. But there were many other elements besides theology and
medicine in the South Asian Muslim mentality (or, more correctly,
mentalities) at the time of plague.

In the earliest days of plague sheer horror was a very important
factor—horror at the delirium and death which plague produced. 'I think
on the whole the people were so upset that they did not really know what
they were saying', wrote the civil surgeon of Allahabad as he reported
the first outbreak of plague on the north Indian plains—amongst largely
Muslim weavers in the small town of Mau Aima—right at the end of

1899.[70] A deputy commissioner in the Central Provinces had this to say in 1905:

> I do not know if terror alone can kill or induce disease, but there can be little doubt that terror super-added to disease is fatal, and a native removed for segregation is, to all intents and purposes, dead before he passes through his door.[71]

It is, perhaps, the terror caused by plague that partially explains some of the paths taken by the Ahmadiyya sect—although one of the more recent historians[72] of the Ahmadiyya has neglected plague almost completely. Mirza Ghulam Ahmad, the self-proclaimed 'promised Messiah and Mahdi', claimed for a time to have the 'ointment of Jesus' which could cure plague.[73] Plague, he insisted, would not touch his village base of Qadian[74] (by analogy, presumably, with the way in which Mecca and Medina had ostensibly avoided plague). It is perhaps Ghulam Ahmad's contacts with Christian missionaries which provide much of the explanation for the apocalyptic tone of much Ahmadiyya teaching; if Michael Dols is to be believed, the apocalyptic and the messianic were markedly absent from popular Islamic reaction to plague in medieval times.[75] But we must still acknowledge that Ahmadiyya's rise was, at least partially, a response to a feeling that the times were seriously out of joint—and it is difficult to avoid seeing plague as one of the factors responsible for such a feeling.

While scholarly Muslims could fairly soon place plague in their scheme of things, for the 'ordinary' Muslim plague was as new as it was to the average Hindu. It was, as the Hindustani-speaking Muslim migrants in Calcutta put it, the *naya bimari*, the new disease.[76] It needed to be explained—urgently. So the Muslim editor of a Moradabad newspaper claimed in February 1897 that plague was 'really due to the consumption of rotten grain and vegetables'.[77] It was also frequently said to be a punishment for sin (something which, at least according to Michael Dols, medieval Muslims rarely asserted).[78] Plague, wrote one Sayad Ramzan Ali of Rohtak, originated from 'vice'. When widows or unmarried women became pregnant they tried to produce abortions. In certain cases 'a portion of the *lochia* remains in the womb and begins to rot'.[79] That was why, this Muslim added, rather revealingly, Hindus kept their womenfolk away from such people. 'Warnings to mankind', wrote a correspondent of the *Rohilkhand Gazette*, were 'scattered broadcast throughout the Quran', nevertheless Indians had failed to give up 'drinking, adultery, sodomy, perjury, usury, desecration of the places of worship, bribery, irreligion, etc. etc.'[80] So God had sent a greater punishment. Some said that the city of Delhi, particularly, deserved such a visitation.[81]

The gathering of crowds, in the early days of plague, when news of a new case or a death became known, was undoubtedly part of the search for explanation. But there was also, at this stage, a real element of sympathy and a desire to assist—especially, perhaps, amongst women. 'Around the doors of the two houses there was collected a crowd of women about 150 in number', wrote the Allahabad civil surgeon after he had visited the Mau Aima weavers at the end of 1899. 'On enquiry it was found that those people had collected to sympathise with the inmates of one of the houses who had just returned from burying a child who had died that morning.' There was a feeling of 'community', although it was not necessarily a feeling either for Mau Aima as a whole or for all Muslims within it: 'the whole of the villagers or at least that section of it [sic] in the vicinity of the sick houses appear to have been in and out helping to tend the sick and comfort the afflicted.'[82]

Yet by the time the ubiquitous lieutenant-governor, MacDonnell, reached the scene—within a few days—these same weavers had scattered themselves to nearby villages 'inhabited', as MacDonnell put it, 'by their caste-fellows.'[83] (The language perhaps reveals something about MacDonnell's patterns of thought as well as something about 'caste' amongst Muslims.) The weavers of Mau Aima had fled. They had done what many Indians, Muslim and Hindu, had done and were to do in the face of plague. They had done so, perhaps, in the face of the possibility, or the actuality, of the severe British measures—such as the burning of the plague-stricken houses—which soon followed the outbreak in Mau Aima.[84] Above all, though, they had fled because, in the circumstances, that seemed the most obvious thing to do. They had not followed the instructions of the ulama, if indeed they knew of them—or if indeed the weavers came within the purview of such mullahs as there may have been in Mau Aima (which had a population of some 6000). The weavers had simply followed the dictates of fear and common sense. In this respect, and in others, there was often no distinctive Muslim response.[85]

This is not to deny that there are, later on, many examples of weavers —unwilling to abandon the looms which represented their livelihood,[86] but also very mindful of the dictates of their religion—refusing to leave their homes. And there were many others besides weavers, amongst the well-born and the not so well-born, who refused to leave, sometimes with quite tragic consequences. A correspondent of the Lahore *Tribune* in 1907, the year of peak plague toll in the rural Punjab, visited several villages in Gujrat district and claimed—probably with, it must be admitted, a grain or two of hyperbole—that he 'hardly met a Muhammadan who has not lost more than half the number of his family members.'[87]

In many a Punjab village, when plague first struck, the specifically 'religious' reaction of most of the inhabitants was basically similar whatever their formal allegiance. Indeed, it would seem likely that there was an element of 'syncretism'. H.J. Maynard painted a vivid if perhaps slightly facile picture:

> When an outbreak is apprehended there are signs of religious revival. A Granthi is installed under a canopy or in the village rest-house to recite the Scriptures; 'Havan' is freely practised; public prayers are offered in the village mosque…the poor are collected and fed.[88]

It is, of course, possible that Maynard was the victim of what was, arguably, another piece of British 'orientalism'—this one being peculiar to the Punjab and on the face of it somewhat contrary to that other 'orientalist' notion: that the most distinct division in Indian society (certainly Indian urban society) was the division between Hindus and Muslims. The peculiar Punjab generalization was that, in the villages of the province, 'tribe' was more important than 'religion', that (as Denzil Ibbetson put it, famously) 'where the whole tone and feeling of the countryside is Indian, as it is in the Eastern Punjab, the Musalman is simply the Hindu with a difference.'[89] Certainly, we must not push the case for syncretism too far. But the main point to note from Maynard's generalizations is surely that in the village, whatever people's religion, their first reaction to the new disease of plague could hardly be said to have been one of fatalism,[90] or even (to use Dols' term about medieval Muslims) 'reverent resignation'.[91] It was one of action—even, at times, action to the point of riot. But action also included, amongst Muslims, without any hesitation, petitionary prayer. The same was true in the towns and cities. Prayer could be very public: from Pune, with its comparatively small Muslim population, it was reported that Muslim 'boys' were parading the bazars, with green flags, reading verses from the Quran.[92]

Some of the most detailed accounts of villages under siege by plague in its earliest years come from a study by a member of the Indian Medical Service, C.H. James, of the progress of the disease through the districts of Jullundur and Hoshiarpur, in the Punjab, in 1897–8.[93] At this stage, plague was still thought, by the British, to be spread directly from person to person, so we learn much about people's comings and goings and especially about inter-village relationships, by marriage and otherwise. We learn about people's insistence on visiting in order to express condolences and attend funerals.[94] We learn of a group of Muslim eye-doctors—Rawals—setting out to travel to, of all places, Australia.[95] We learn a little about the relationship of the Lalaris—Muslim cloth-dyers—of the town of Banga with one Pir Bakhsh.[96] (How one wishes to know more about this pir, and the role of pirs generally at the time of plague. One suspects that, if only because the onset of plague, and plague's frequent outcome, were so sudden, there was not much of a role for the pirs as 'curers' of that disease.) We learn from James' report that when Mussamat Jiwan, sister-in-law of Karim Bakhsh, became ill with plague her female neighbours came and visited her. They came, it was said, 'to touch the wound with the "hem of their garment" so as to diffuse the pain over several persons.'[97] Here was a custom well understood by Hindus and Sikhs; it depended upon a notion of the transmutability and transmissibility of 'substances'[98] that could hardly be said to be 'Islamic'. And we learn of the activities of the much revered Qazi Abdulla: a cordon was in place around his home village of Purkhowal, but he 'used, with the connivance of the constables, to go to and from the other villages to read prayers, and to see to the bathing of the dead.'[99] Qazi Abdulla seems to epitomize, in fact, one type of South Asian Muslim reaction to plague about which we do not hear a great deal: he quietly got on with what he felt to be his duty as a Muslim. If the rules and regulations of the Raj stood in his way he circumvented them—but, again, he did so quietly.

V

We also catch a glimpse in James' report of the *niaz* (feast) held in the village of Kanum as the hot weather of 1898 approached, to celebrate the fact that the plague was pronounced to be over.[100] Unfortunately it was not over—or certainly not in the province of Punjab, and in much of the rest of India. It returned, year after year. Plague was at its worst, from the point of view of mortality, in the first decade of this century.

Yet this is the time when plague was, for Indians, no longer the great unknown; it had become part of life. It was also the time when the British relaxed their plague rules considerably. If, for example, people did not want to move when plague struck, then (it was often decided) so be it. Plague had, in fact, become part of life for the British, too. 'The recuperative powers of the social organism become operative at once', Karl Helleiner declared of the years immediately after the devastating plague year, 1348, in Europe.[101] A provincial sanitary commissioner in India, writing in 1908, had this to say: 'India is a country that recovers quickly from calamities, and even tragic events are rapidly forgotten and obliterated by fresh troubles and fresh interest.'[102]

'Calamities': one is reminded that the words 'Encounters and Calamities' were used by Gyanendra Pandey in the title of his pathbreaking
study of the qasba of Mubarakpur, in Azamgarh district, in the nineteenth and early twentieth centuries.[103] As it happens, the mortality rate
for plague, over the whole period 1899–1929, was in Mubarakpur the
highest for any town in India.[104] Yet in Pandey's 'indigenous' sources
(for this period, a Muslim weaver's diary) there is apparently not a
single mention of plague[105]—not even in the entries for 1904, a year in
which more than 10 per cent of the town's population died from the
disease.[106] Instead, the concentration in 1904 is upon a communal riot.

It has to be emphasized that the notion of Muslim fatalism in the face
of plague, in British India, largely springs from this period.[107] The wife
of a young Indian Medical Service officer, who travelled with him on
plague work in the years before the First World War, remembered that,
while some followed her husband's pleas for them to leave their houses,
some did not:

> They hesitate to leave their houses lest their possessions are stolen in their
> absence, or they are afraid that inoculation will bring other diseases in its
> train, and to all persuasion and exhortation will only give the same answer,
> 'Plague comes every year. It is the will of Allah.'[108]

'Plague comes every year': this sentence tells us much. And we should
remember that Gramsci found that 'fatalism' amongst Italian peasants
was 'nothing other than the clothing worn by a real and active will in
a weak position.'[109]

Wendy Doniger has insisted that Hindus often behave as if they do
not believe in *karma*.[110] She quotes the conclusions of the anthropologist
Pauline Mahar Kolenda on some village sweepers: they 'sometimes
pontificate that death is the result of God's fate', but 'in almost the same
breath' say that it is the work of a godling, or of a person who has failed
to appease a godling. In particular, 'anxious wives' often rebel against
'inactivity in such important matters of life and death', especially in
relation to their children.[111] One strongly suspects that similar attitudes,
though often dressed in somewhat different language, were and are to
be found among many South Asian Muslims as well. In the final
analysis it is not so much that Hindus and Muslims share a common
'Indic' civilization; it is, rather, that all share a common humanity.

VI

In Richard Loeffler's village in Iran, so acutely portrayed in his book
Islam in Practice: Religious Beliefs in a Persian Village,[112] there are all

sorts. There is the mullah who feels that if a man has become sick it is because he has eaten the wrong food. There is the rigid young teacher who believes that God exacts most of His punishment in this world. There is the Old Hunter, who claims that he knows the jinn well. And there is the peasant father of a cripple who agrees that it was his son's 'destiny' to be a cripple—but still the Lord may wish to heal him, and so He should be implored, by prayer, to do so.

A similar diversity of views is to be found amongst South Asian Muslims, both in the village and the town, at the time of plague. There are Muslims with leadership pretensions—but often these remain merely pretensions. There are differences within South Asian Islam between the well-born and the rest, between the country and the town, and between regions. There are differences, too, between theology and medicine, and within those fields. But almost always the borders between categories are indefinite—fuzzy, in fact—in spite of orientalist stereotyping by the British, and the vertical links within categories are shaky, to say the least. In the face of plague there is sometimes amongst South Asian Muslims—especially after the first shock has been and gone—a certain amount of what appears at first sight to be fatalism. But there is also a more robust and pragmatic, a relatively untheological, 'common sense'. There is a certain amount—but only a certain amount—of religious syncretism. As always in human affairs there is, at this time, a great deal of basically unsurprising ambiguity and inconsistency. Amidst all this, however, there remains, the figure of Qazi Abdulla of Purkhowal, quietly getting on with his duties as plague took its toll roundabout. For this particular observer, anyway, Qazi Abdulla provides what is ultimately the dominant image of South Asian Islam at this time.

Endnotes

1. On the plague epidemics of 1896 and the following years, see I.J. Catanach, 'Plague and the Indian Village', in Peter Robb (ed.), *Rural India: Land, Power and Society under British Rule* (London, 1983 and Delhi, 1992); 'Poona Politicians and the Plague', *South Asia*, N.S., vol. 8, no. 2 (December 1984); 'Plague and the Tensions of Empire' in David Arnold (ed.), *Imperial Medicine and Indigenous Societies* (Manchester, 1988) [hereafter, Catanach, 'Tensions']; '"Who are your Leaders?" Plague, the Raj and the 'Communities' in Bombay, 1896–1901', in Peter Robb (ed.), *Society and Ideology: Essays in South Asian History presented to Professor K.A. Ballhatchet* (Delhi, 1993) [Catanach, 'Bombay']. See, too, David Arnold, *Colonizing the Body: State Medicine and Epidemic Disease in Nineteenth-Century India* (Berkeley, 1993), chs 5 and 6.

2. On 'sacred space' see Anand A. Yang 'Sacred Symbol and Sacred Space in Rural India', *Comparative Studies in Society and History*, vol. 22, no. 4, (October 1980).

3. MacDonnell to Elgin, 21 March 1897; Elgin Papers [EP], F84/70, India Office Library [IOL]. Mehdi Hasan, though a Trustee of the College at Aligarh founded by Saiyid Ahmad Khan, moved towards the Congress in 1901. See his letter in *Pioneer*, 14 April 1901.

4. MacDonnell to Elgin, 9 May 1897; EP, Ibid.

5. *Wakil-i-Hind* (Delhi), 19 February 1898, Selections from the Vernacular Newspapers published in the Punjab [SNP], 1898.

6. H. Davies, Deputy Commissioner, Delhi, to Commissioner, Delhi Division, no. 55 of 5 March 1898: part of Enclosure 83 in Revenue Sanitary Letter from India, 1898, no. 11; India Office Records [IOR].

7. Catanach, 'Bombay', p. 215.

8. See, especially, W. Finucane, Officiating Chief Secretary, Bengal, to J.P. Hewett, Secretary, Home Department, Government of India, Demi-official of 28 May 1898, enclosed Hewett to Sir Philip Hutchins, India Office, no. 182D of 8 June 1898; J & P 1295/1898, L/PJ/6/483, IOR; and C.W. Bolton, Chief Secretary, Bengal, to Hewett, Confidential Demi-official of 18 June 1898; J & P 1422/1898, L/PJ/6/485, IOR.

9. Dipesh Chakrabarty, 'Communal Riots and Labour: Bengal's Jute Mill-hands in the 1890s', *Past and Present*, no. 91 (May 1981); *Rethinking Working-Class History: Bengal 1890–1940* (Princeton, 1989).

10. Catanach, 'Tensions', pp. 156–7.

11. The most revealing files are India Home Public A Progs, June 1900, 291–302, National Archives of India [NAI], and G.A.D. 486C/1900, U.P. State Archives, Lucknow. See also MacDonnell Papers, Manuscripts English History Collection 355, Bodleian Library, Oxford.

12. MacDonnell to Curzon, 24 April 1900; Curzon Papers, Mss. Eur. F111/201 pt i, IOL.

13. On the Garhshankar riot, see J & P 1372/1898, L/PJ/6/484, IOR. It may be significant that *Paisa Akhbar* (Lahore), 5 July 1898, SNP, claimed that people had 'only gathered at a shrine of a fakir', on a Friday, and that they might have gone to pray for the 'extinction' of plague.

14. John Morley, Secretary of State for India, made a very plausible case for plague as an unsettling influence in 1907, although the advice sent to him from India does not easily lead to such a conclusion: Morley Papers, Mss. D573/12, ff.36–58, IOL.

15. E. Wilkinson, *Report on Plague in the Punjab 1901–1902*, Govt. of Punjab, 1903, p. 9; S. Browning Smith, 'Report on Plague Inoculations, Amritsar District 1902–3', *Indian Medical Gazette*, 39, June 1904, p. 213.

16. Malcolm Lyall Darling, *Rusticus Loquitor*, London, 1930, p. 349.

17. Sandhurst, Governor Bombay, to Elgin; EP, Mss. Eur. F84/72, Appx. B, IOL.

18. In his letters to his family, now preserved in the IOL (Mss. Eur. F116/5), he normally wrote 'the Mohns'.

19. Gyanendra Pandey, 'The Bigoted Julaha', *Economic and Political Weekly*, 29 January 1983, pp. PE19–28. For the Bombay riots of 9 March 1898, and the Julaha role in them, see Catanach, 'Bombay', pp. 213–15.

20. Rajnarayan Chandavarkar, 'Workers' Resistance and the Rationalization of Work in Bombay between the Wars', in Douglas Haynes and Gyan Prakash (eds), *Contesting Power: Resistance and Everyday Social Relations in India* (Berkeley, 1991), p. 121.

21. *Report of the Municipal Commissioner on the Plague in Bombay for the year ended 31st May 1899*, p. 113.

22. See Sir James Campbell, Chairman, Bombay Plague Committee, to A. Wingate, Secretary, General Dept. (Plague), Bombay, no.16864 of 18 March 1898; L/PJ/3/959, IOR.

23. Ranajit Guha, *Elementary Aspects of Peasant Insurgency in Colonial India* (Delhi, 1983), p. 34.

24. Sandria B. Freitag, 'Religious Rites and Riots: From Community Identity to Communalism in North India, 1870–1940' (Ph.D. dissertation, University of California, Berkeley, 1980), p. 7.

25. R. Clarke, Commissioner, Delhi Division, to H.J. Maynard, Junior Secretary, Government of Punjab, no. 63 of 7 March 1898; H. Davies, Deputy Commissioner, Delhi, to Commissioner, Delhi Division, no. 55 of 5 March 1898; see note 6 above.

26. See especially *Pioneer* (Lucknow), 19 April 1900; also note11 above.

27. MacDonnell to Elgin, 16 July 1897; J & P 1657/1897, L/PJ/6/454, IOR; and A. Martindale, Resident, Mount Abu, to Private Secretary to Viceroy, Demi-official Confidential of 21 May 1898; India Home Sanitary Plague A Progs, August 1898, 793, KW VI, NAI.

28. *Bharat Jiwan* (Banaras), 4 June 1900, Selections from the Vernacular Newspapers published in the North-Western Provinces and Oudh [SNNWP], 1900.

29. Catanach, 'Bombay', pp. 208–9 and n. 82.

30. Anon., *Friend of India* (Calcutta), 17 March 1898. On the organization of the Bohra community at this time see Satish C. Misra, *Muslim Communities in Gujarat* (Bombay, 1964), especially p. 50.

31. MacDonnell to Elgin, 4 March 1897; EP, Mss. Eur. 84/70, IOL.

32. See Katherine Prior, 'The British Administration of Hinduism in North India 1780–1900' (Ph.D. thesis, University of Cambridge, 1990), especially pp. 132–5, 266.

33. A.H. Hourani, 'Introduction' to Hourani and S.M. Stern (eds), *The Islamic City* (Oxford, 1970), p. 14.

34. *Civil and Military Gazette*, 30 April 1898 (editorial).

35. H.J. Maynard, Deputy Commissioner, Ambala, quoted E. Wilkinson, *Report on Plague in the Punjab, 1901–02*, Government of Punjab, 1904, p. 27; and Maynard, Commissioner, Multan to Secretary, Government, no. 755 of 13 August 1907; Punjab Home (Medical & Sanitary) Progs, November 1907, 23, IOR. Maynard, later Sir John Maynard, was in retirement a prominent Fabian, Labour candidate, and author of studies on the Russian peasantry.

36. Maynard, quoted Wilkinson, *loc. cit.*
37. On printing see Francis Robinson, 'Technology and Religious Change: Islam and the Impact of Print', *Modern Asian Studies*, vol. 27, no. 1, February 1993.
38. Silcock, quoted Wilkinson, *op. cit.*, p. 55.
39. On the Anjuman, see Edward D. Churchill, Jr., 'Muslim Societies of the Punjab, 1860–1890', *Punjab Past and Present*, vol. 8, no. 1, (April 1974); S. Razi Wasti, 'Anjuman Himayat-i-Islam, Lahore—A Brief History', *Journal of the Research Society of Pakistan*, vol. 3, nos 1–2, (1966).
40. See Harjot Singh Oberoi, 'The Worship of Pir Sakhi Savar: Illness, Healing and Popular Culture in the Punjab', *Studies in History*, N.S. vol. 3, no. 1 (January–June 1987), pp. 52–5; Harjot Oberoi, *The Construction of Religious Boundaries: Culture, Identity and Diversity in the Sikh Tradition* (Delhi, 1994). See also Douglas E. Haynes, *Rhetoric and Ritual in Colonial India: The Shaping of a Public Culture in Surat City, 1852–1928* (Berkeley, 1991), especially Conclusion.
41. See Hakim Ghulam Nabi, *Plague Inoculation from the Muhammadan Point of View* (Lahore, 1903); IOL Tracts, vol. 976.
42. Maynard to Government, no. 755 of 13 August 1907; see n. 35 above. Cf. Peter Hardy, 'The Ulama in British India', *Journal of Indian History*, *Golden Jubilee Volume*, 1973.
43. Maynard to Government; see n. 42 and n. 35 above.
44. Catanach, 'Bombay', p. 206.
45. Cf. E.G. Browne, *Arabian Medicine*, Cambridge, 1921, p. 5; Fazlur Rahman, *Health and Medicine in the Islamic Tradition: Change and Identity*, New York, 1989, p. 83. 'Theology' is used here in a broad sense, which includes both *kalam* and *fiqh*.
46. Cf. S.J. Tambiah, in *Buddhism and the Spirit Cults* (Cambridge, 1970), p. 317, on the supposed 'Little Tradition'/'Great Tradition' binary opposition: 'The idea of two levels is an invention of the anthropologist.' (Quoted Oberoi, *The Construction of Religious Boundaries*, p. 140.)
47. Michael W. Dols, 'The Arabic Terminology for Plague', *The Black Death in the Middle East* (Princeton, 1977), Appx. 2; Lawrence I. Conrad, '*Ta'un* and *Waba*...', *Journal of the Economic and Social History of the Orient*, vol. 25, no. 3 (October, 1982).
48. Dols, 'The Arabic Terminology for Plague', p. 109.
49. Lawrence I. Conrad, 'Epidemic disease in formal and popular thought in Early Islamic society', in Terence Ranger and Paul Slack (eds), *Epidemics and Ideas: Essays on the historical perception of pestilence* (Cambridge, 1992), pp. 88–92, 98 and n. 49; also Conrad, 'The Plague in the Early Medieval Near East' (Ph.D. dissertation, Princeton University, 1981), p. 452.
50. Catanach, 'Bombay', p. 207.
51. *Encyclopaedia of Islam* (2nd edn.), 6; see under 'Kadariyya'.
52. Jacqueline Sublet, 'La Peste prise aux rets de la jurisprudence: le traite

d'Ibn Hagar al-Asqalani sur la Peste', *Studia Islamica*, vol. 33 (1971), pp. 147–8.

53. Ashraf Ali Thanavi, *Imdad al Fatawa*, Delhi, 1346/1927, vol. 3, pp. 157–80. The fatawa in this volume date from 1320 *hijri* to 1323. I am indebted to Dr Muhammad Khalid Masud, of the Islamic Research Institute, Islamabad, for a photocopy of the relevant fatawa, and to Dr M.A. Salam for translation.

54. Thanavi, *Imdad al Fatawa*; Nabi, *Plague Inoculation*, pp. 15–16.

55. Ibid., p. 4.

56. Muhammad Ajmal Khan, *al-Ta'un* (Delhi, 1897). I must thank Professor Mushirul Hasan for procuring for me a photocopy of this tract from the Library of Jamia Millia Islamia, New Delhi, and Mr S.A.H. Rizvi, of the Indian Institute of Islamic Studies, New Delhi, for translating it for me.

57. Cf. Lawrence I. Conrad, 'Arabic Plague Chronologies and Treatises: Social and Historical Factors in the Formation of a Literary Genre', *Studia Islamica*, vol. 54 (1981), p. 86.

58. H. Davies to Commissioner, Delhi; see n. 6 above.

59. Abdul Halim Sharar, *Lucknow: The Last Phase of Oriental Culture*, trans. and ed. E.S. Harcourt and Fakhir Hussain (London, 1975), ch. 14. Sharar's work was originally published, in the main, in the second decade of this century. Dr Claudia Liebeskind, of Royal Holloway, University of London, is working on the distinctive Lucknow tradition of *yunani tibb*.

60. C.F. Andrews, 'Hakim Ajmal Khan' (reprinted from *Biographies of Eminent Indians*), in *Eminent Musalmans* [ed. G.A. Natesan], (Delhi reprint, 1981), p. 293.

61. Ibid., p. 289.

62. Barbara D. Metcalf, 'Nationalist Muslims in British India: The Case of Hakim Ajmal Khan', *Modern Asian Studies*, vol. 19, no. 1, February 1985, p. 5.

63. J. Christoff Burgel, 'Secular and Religious Features of Medieval Arabic Medicine', in Charles Leslie (ed.), *Asian Medical Systems: A Comparative Study* (Berkeley, 1976), p. 44. On nineteenth-century Indian Muslim opposition to yunani see M. Zubair Siddiqi, 'The Unani Tibb (Greek Medicine) in India', *Islamic Culture*, 42, 3, July 1968, p. 170. But it needs to be emphasized also that yunani on the whole flourished in British India, at a time when it was in decline in much of the rest of the Muslim world. See Lawrence I. Conrad, 'The Arab-Islamic Medical Tradition' in Lawrence I. Conrad, Michael Neve, Vivian Nutton, Roy Porter, and Andrew Wear, *The Western Medical Tradition*, Cambridge, 1995, p. 138.

64. Clarke to Maynard, 7 March 1897; Davies to Clarke, 5 March 1898; see n. 25 above. Ajmal Khan himself included plums in one of his prescriptions for the plague-ridden.

65. On the belief in jinn see, especially [H.A. Rose], *A Glossary of the Castes of the Punjab and the North-West Frontier Province*, vol. I, Government of Punjab (1970 reprint), p. 561.

66. On the 'advertising Hakims, whose number is daily on the increase', see *Akhbar-i-Am* (Lahore), 28 June 1898, SNP.

67. John C. Hume, Jr., 'Rival Traditions: Western Medicine and *Yunan-i-tibb* in the Punjab, 1849–89', *Bulletin of the History of Medicine*, vol. 51, no. 2, Summer 1977.

68. Punjab Home (Medical & Sanitary) Progs., July 1907, 32 (IOR). See also *Punjab Plague Manual*, Government of Punjab (1911), p. 13.

69. Surgeon-Captain W. Ronaldson Clark, 'Remarks', in C.H. James, *Report on the Outbreak of Plague in the Jullundur & Hoshiarpur Districts of the Punjab, 1897–98*, Government of Punjab (1899), p. 154; National Documentation Centre, Pakistan (microfilm in IOR).

70. B. O'Brien, Civil Surgeon, Allahabad, to Inspector-General of Civil Hospitals, N.W.P., 1 January 1900; Public Health 404B/76, UP State Archives, Lucknow.

71. Report by E.R.K. Blenkinsop, Deputy Commissioner, Jubbulpore, on Plague in the Central Provinces, n.d., India Home Sanitary A Progs, February 1906, 334, IOR.

72. Spencer Lavan, *The Ahmadiyah Movement: A History and Perspective* (Delhi, 1974).

73. Ghulam Ahmad Kadiyani, *A Revealed Cure for the Bubonic Plague* (Lahore, 1898). For a recent, brief appraisal of the Ahmadiyya see Francis Robinson, 'Ahmad and the Ahmadiyya', *History Today*, vol. 40 (June 1990).

74. *Dafi u'l-Bala*, p. 10, quoted in H.D. Griswold, *Mirza Ghulam Ahmad, The Mehdi Messiah of Qadian* (Lodiana [Ludhiana], 1902), p. 19; Mirza Ghulam Ahmad, *Tadhkirah*, ed. and trans. by Muhammad Zafrullah Khan (London, 1976), p. 185.

75. Dols, *Black Death*, pp. 294–5. There is, however, a note of scepticism about some of Dols' assertions on these matters in Robert E. Lerner, 'The Black Death and Western European Eschatological Mentalities', in Daniel Williman (ed.), *The Black Death: The Impact of the Fourteenth-Century Plague* (Binghampton N.Y., 1982), pp. 105–6, n. 44.

76. *Friend of India*, 5 May 1898.

77. *Naiyar-i-Azam* (ed.), Ibn Ali (Moradabad), 26 February 1897, SNNWP.

78. Dols, *Black Death*, p. 296. See also Dols, 'The Comparative Communal Responses to the Black Death in Muslim and Christian Societies', *Viator: Medieval and Renaissance Studies*, vol. 5, 1974.

79. *Akhbar-i-Am* (Lahore), 19 January 1898, SNP.

80. *Rohilkhand Gazette* (Bareilly), 24 April 1900, SNNWP.

81. *Rozana Akhbar* (Delhi), 25 September 1899, SNP.

82. O'Brien to Inspector General Civil Hospitals, 1 January 1900; see n. 70 above.

83. A.P. MacDonnell, Draft Report to Home Dept., Government of India, 6 January 1900; Public Health 404B/76, U.P. State Archives, Lucknow.

84. H.C. Ferard, District Magistrate, Muttra [Mathura] to Secretary Government of UP, no. 3607/XXVII of 18 August 1905; India Home Sanitary Progs, February 1906, 331/2, IOR.

85. H.J. Maynard reported in 1901–2 that the Jat in Ambala District, whether Sikh or Hindu, was quite willing to 'evacuate' once the winter cold was over, 'and his Muhammadan brother of the Sutlej Valley, who has heard for several years past of the experiences of the Hoshiarpur District, was fairly ready to follow his example'. Maynard quoted Wilkinson, *Plague Report 1901–02*, p. 25.

86. Note by Colonel M.D. Moriarty, Inspector-General of Civil Hospitals, Central Provinces, n.d.; India Home Sanitary Progs, February 1906, 334, IOR.

87. Kashi Nath, 'The Plague in Gujrat District', *Tribune*, 5 May 1907.

88. Quoted Wilkinson, *Plague Report 1901–02*, p. 23.

89. Denzil Ibbetson, *Panjab Castes* (Delhi reprint of 1916 edn., 1974), p. 14. See J.R. Drummond, deputy commissioner, Gurdaspur, 21 December 1900: 'The Jat peasant is still a farmer first, a Sikh or Muslim, as the case may be, in the second place only.' Quoted David Gilmartin, *Empire and Islam: Punjab and the Making of Pakistan* (Berkeley, 1988), p. 30.

90. I have dealt with so-called 'fatalism in the plague situation, mainly amongst Hindus, in I.J. Catanach, "Fatalism"? Indian Responses to Plague and other Crises', *Asian Profile*, vol. 12, no. 2 (April 1984) the present paper extends the argument.

91. Dols, *Black Death*, p. 298.

92. *Poona Observer*, 5 April 1897.

93. James, *Jullundur and Hoshiarpur, 1897–98* (see n. 69 above).

94. See also Wilkinson, *Plague Report 1901–02*, p. 5.

95. James, *Jullundur and Hoshiarpur 1897–98*, pp. 1–2. Rawals often seem to have been 'holy men', of a sort, as well as 'eye-doctors'.

96. Ibid., p. 30.

97. Ibid., p. 80.

98. See McKim Marriott, 'Hindu Transactions: Diversity without Dualism' in Bruce Kapferer (ed.), *Transaction and Meaning* (Philadelphia, 1976); also E. Valentine Daniel, *Fluid Signs: Being a Person the Tamil Way* (Berkeley, 1984).

99. James, *Jullundur and Hoshiarpur 1897–98*, p. 85.

100. Ibid., p. 76.

101. Karl F. Helleiner, 'The Population of Europe from the Black Death to the Eve of the Vital Revolution', *Cambridge Economic History of Europe*, vol. 4 (Cambridge, 1967), p. 9.

102. J. Chaytor-White, *Annual Report of the Sanitary Commissioner, United Provinces, 1908*, p. 12.

103. Gyanendra Pandey, 'Encounters and Calamities': The History of a North Indian Qasba in the Nineteenth Century', in *Subaltern Studies III*, in Ranajit Guha (ed.) (Delhi, 1984).

104. *Report of the Haffkine Institute for the years 1932–35* (Government of Bombay, 1936), p. 83.

105. Gyanendra Pandey, personal communication, 24 February 1984. It seems that the weaver's 'diary' was not a diary in the strict sense; some of it was

composed in retrospect, even as late as the 1920s. It may well reflect the preoccupations of the time of its composition. If this is so, the argument in the text, above, may be in need of some modification. However, the same would also be true of Pandey's original argument.

106. UP Govt. Resolution no. 453/XVI–82, Sanitation, of 29 August 1908; UP Sanitation Progs, October 1908, 29, IOR.

107. On Muslim 'apathy' in the Punjab at the time of the 1902–3 outbreak see E. Wilkinson, *Report on Plague and Inoculation in the Punjab, 1902–1903* (Government of Punjab, 1904), p. 2.

108. 'For Lucinda and Susanna, by their Great-Grandmother, Margaret Muirson', [privately printed, 1969]; Muirson Papers, South Asia Archive, Cambridge.

109. Antonio Gramsci, *Selections from the Prison Notebooks* (London, 1971), p. 337, quoted David Arnold, 'Gramsci and Peasant Subalternity in India', *Journal of Peasant Studies*, 11, 4, July 1984, p. 171.

110. Wendy Doniger O'Flaherty, *The Origins of Evil in Hindu Mythology* (Berkeley, 1976), p. 15.

111. Pauline Mahar Kolenda, 'Religious Anxiety and Hindu Fate', *Journal of Asian Studies*, vol. 23 (June 1964), especially pp. 77–8. There is a good deal to be said for Nita Kumar's assertion that, especially amongst artisans, there is a 'common cultural fund' which both Hindus and Muslims draw upon, often without realizing it. (See Nita Kumar, 'Work and Leisure in the Formation of an Identity', in Sandria B. Freitag (ed.), *Culture and Power in Banaras: community, performance, and environment, 1800–1980* (Berkeley, 1989), p. 165.) At the conference at which this paper was read the phrase 'composite culture' gained some currency. We must avoid pushing this notion too far, however.

112. Richard Loeffler, *Islam in Practice: Religious Beliefs in a Persian Village* (Albany N.Y., 1988).

6

Islam and the 'Moral Economy'
The Alwar Revolt of 1932

IAN COPLAND

I

Why do the subaltern classes in the countryside—the peasantry—structurally subservient, instinctively cautious, and conservative—sometimes put aside their 'passivity' and rise up against their landed masters and (more rarely) against the ruling political order?

Down to the 1970s, answers to that question generally emphasized the primacy of economic factors, or, in the case of Marxist writers, the dynamic of the class struggle. According to this view, people were driven to riot and revolt chiefly out of desperation, of which a common cause in pre-modern times was hunger. Thus the economic historian T.S. Ashton's striking description of the English collier riots of the eighteenth century as 'rebellions of the belly'.[1] However, even for many Marxists, there are some problems with this deterministic approach. One is that the potentially most militant section of the subaltern class, namely those at the bottom, are also the least powerful. While such people might be desperate and violent—having, in Franz Fanon's words, 'nothing to lose and everything to gain'[2]—unaided, they are unlikely to pose a threat to the ruling system. Another, signalled early on by Marx himself, is that the dominant subaltern class in the country-side, the peasantry, has generally played a conservative, even counter-revolutionary role. Indeed Marx was unkind enough in 1852 to liken the French peasantry to a sack of potatoes, a snide reference to their approving stance toward the 'Eighteenth Brumaire' *coup d'etat* of Louis Napoleon.[3] Accordingly, much of the Marxist writing about peasant insurgency since the Second World War has focused not on the landowning (or rich) section of the peasantry nor on the poor (tenant farmer) and landless sections, but on the so-called 'middle' peasantry—usually defined as the peasants who worked their lands as family holdings, using their own labour and who operated just above the margins of subsistence. This middle group, it is said, was the only component of the peasantry which possessed sufficient 'internal leverage' to enter into sustained rebellion.[4] Nevertheless, while the 'middle peasant' thesis is useful in clarifying the question of agency, it does not altogether dispose of the objection of 'peasant conservatism'. Why should even a 'middle peasant' wish to heighten the tempo of political activity, when this might draw attention to the inequalities embedded in the rural economic and social structure and thereby endanger his own (comparatively) privileged position?

Well, in theory anyone can be pushed to breaking point if the pressures are strong enough—even people with interests to protect. It is possible that even rich peasants might revolt if the situation demanded it. What sort of 'jolt' could 'get them moving'?[5] One such might be a massive fall in prices for cash crops, such as happened during the world depression of the 1930s. In this respect, rich and middle peasants would be equally threatened. But the latter, occupying a precarious position on the edge of the capitalist system, would be far more vulnerable than the former to the vagaries of the market.[6]

As a global explanation, the 'middle peasant' thesis appears to fit quite well with the South Asian case, particularly for the late colonial period. For one thing, it is not difficult to identify in early twentieth century India, rural groups which fit the middle peasant profile. For another, many of these same communities became politicized in the 1930s during the civil disobedience movement.[7] Historians have been quick to make a connection between this upsurge of militancy and the commercial effects of the world depression which saw food and cash crop prices in India plummet to half their 1929 levels in the space of twenty-four months—the biggest and fastest fall in living memory.[8]

In other contexts, though, the link between economic downturn and peasant protest in South Asia is rather less transparent.[9] Sumit Sarkar, for example, while initially advancing a mainly economistic interpretation of subaltern violence during the *swadeshi* period in Bengal,[10] has recently revised that view, noting that high grain prices during 1906-7 (on the face of it, beneficial to those *raiyat*s producing for the market) did not inhibit agrarian rioting led by rural magnates. Sarkar concludes that popular outbursts cannot 'be explained by immediate economic factors like price fluctuations alone'.[11] Likewise Eric Stokes' later writings on the rural revolts of 1857 exhibited less confidence than his earlier work in the primacy of material factors. Ultimately, he decided, it was impossible to disentangle 'the economic element from its social and political integument'.[12]

It was European historians, though, who first postulated a theory to explain these recurrent disjunctures between economic cause and political effect. Working on English crowd violence in the eighteenth century, E.P. Thompson and George Rude were struck by the way the rioters they studied typically couched their protests as appeals for social justice—more often than not in terms of a return to a normative *status quo ante*. As Thompson wrote in a pathbreaking essay:

> It is of course true that riots were triggered off by soaring prices, by malpractices among dealers, or by hunger. But these grievances operated within a popular consensus as to what were legitimate and what were illegitimate practices in marketing. milling, baking etc. This in turn was grounded upon a consistent traditional view of social norms and obligations, of the proper functioning of [the] several parties within the community....[13]

Thompson and Rude called this consensus the 'moral economy of the poor'. Implicitly, they meant the urban poor. However in 1976 James C. Scott extended the argument to the countryside—specifically rural Burma and Vietnam during the late colonial period. According to Scott, peasants are spurred to revolt not so much by a craving for food as by a yearning for justice; they rise to defend their right to subsistence.[14] This general approach to Asian peasant rebellions has since been followed by a number of Asian scholars, including some working on colonial and postcolonial India.[15]

Scott's application of the moral economy model to Asia provoked extensive criticism. He was accused, perhaps unfairly, of offering an overly romantic notion of peasant society which ignored the strength of its class-divisions;[16] of underestimating the peasant's capacity for 'rational' action in pursuit of profit; and of arbitrarily selecting case studies to suit his hypothesis.[17] Nevertheless, despite Greenough's reservations about Bengal,[18] features of the little traditions Thompson and Scott describe clearly exist, or existed, in the parochial world of the Indian village. They can be seen in the characteristic institutions of village government; in the joint proprietorship common to many villages especially in north India, under which lands were held and managed jointly by dominant caste 'brotherhoods'; most obviously in the *jajmani* system, under which dependents/clients within the village community were rewarded not according to a market-value placed on their labour but by customary rates, the latter paid not in money but in kind through a seasonal, almost ritual, division of the grain-heap at the conclusion of the harvest.[19] Again, the Indian case offers abundant examples of peasant insurgency where protest appears to have been triggered by landlord/patron actions subversive of accepted social and moral norms. For instance Gyanendra Pandey sees the revolt of the Awadh peasantry in 1921, during the non-cooperation movement, as resting essentially on the idea of a 'just, or moral struggle'.[20] Likewise Indian history is replete, no less than that of Europe, with grain-riots, some apparently actuated by the concept of a 'just price'.[21] Yet in some ways the 'moral economists' are not very different to the 'political economists'. Although they differ about the way the economic equation works, they agree on its primacy. Both schools put material factors squarely at the centre of their analysis. This tends to obscure the important fact that Indian villages have always been shaped by a complex web of interrelationships, some of them non-economic.

Caste relationships are a case in point. They are regulated not just by considerations of wealth or by jajmani ties but by notions of status—of relative 'purity' and 'pollution'—which are at heart not economic but ideological. As Elder has shown, the peak of Ahir caste aspirations in north India during the early twentieth century was not material betterment, but the right to wear the sacred thread, marker of the ritually twice-born.[22] So, too, interpersonal relations at the local level in South Asia are strongly affected by the way people behave in the ritual sphere, and by how they configure their religious identity—what is commonly (and perhaps significantly) referred to in the Indian vernacular as their 'community'. Thus, we find that many South Asian peasant rebellions were launched either in defence of threatened religious values, or to punish violations of sacred space, or in anticipation of the imminent establishment of God's kingdom on earth. Again, it has been observed that religious symbolism often invades the discourse of Asian peasant protest (though as Ranajit Guha points out, the same resource could also be employed by elites to 'sacralize' their authority and thereby to reinforce the hierarchical status quo).[23] Generalizing from these and other Indian cases, Partha Chatterjee has argued that religious doctrine provided the peasantry with a 'code of ethics, including political ethics';[24] we may go further and suggest that it sometimes provided the peasantry with the motive, and the means, for rebellion.

II

Consider the case of Islam—arguably the most 'political' of the major South Asian religions. At a theoretical level Islam makes much of the idea of brotherhood; of the communality of believers. Despite sectarian differences, the theory has substance. The institution of the mosque, and

the tradition of congregational prayer on Fridays, celebrates and rein-
forces the Muslim sense of belonging.[25] So does the custom of the *hajj*,
which, for a month each year, fills Mecca with ecstatic pilgrims from
all over the Muslim world. So too does the practice, widespread in South
Asia, of pilgrimage to the shrines of Muslim pirs. Muslims, then, might
be considered a 'natural' or primordial political constituency, and one
that, thanks to the mosque and the Friday sermon, is relatively easily
mobilized for political action.[26] Last but not least, Islam's emphasis on
the equality of believers in the eyes of Allah arguably constitutes a
powerful levelling ideology, its promise of immediate entry to Paradise
to believers martyred in holy war, a powerful incentive to self-sacrificial
acts of violence. Given the above, we would expect to find, in South Asia,
many examples of revolt by Muslim peasants: and so we do. Modern
Indian history is replete with examples of what British officials liked
to call Muslim fanaticism: the Faraizi movement in early nineteenth-
century Bengal, the Pabna disturbances of 1873, the Moplah rebellion
of 1921, the Kashmir revolt of 1931, and the Tebhaga movement of 1946
being only some of the more notable. However, in the real world of South
Asian Islam things are rather more complicated than this simplistic
presentation suggests. Not only are Indian Muslims divided by doctrine
into sects (Sunni, Shi'ia, Ahmadiyya), they are (or at least were, in pre-
modern and colonial times) a very socially diverse group, embracing,
at the margins so to speak, convert-communities scarcely distinguish-
able from the surrounding Hindu population, some of them quite ignorant about matters of Islamic doctrine.[27] If, as Brass conjectures, there
was no single Muslim 'political community' in the subcontinent before
the twentieth century,[28] neither was there a homogeneous Muslim
religious community in anything but the most abstract sense. Does this
invalidate the claim that Islam has been, during the last century, a
powerful motivating force among South Asian peasant communities?

For some scholars, the answer is a decided 'yes'. Writing about the
Pabna League of the 1870s, K.K. Sen Gupta argues that since the
participants were for the most part unschooled Muslim converts, the
movement could not have been religiously inspired: 'such men', he
avers, would 'not consciously rise' against Hindu landlords 'merely
because the latter were Hindus'.[29] This conclusion appears unduly
pessimistic. As Ranajit Guha remarks, 'ignorance of scriptures' need
not be a barrier to religious fervour.[30] Indeed, it may even be a precon-
dition, given that there is little Quranic sanction for acts of mob
violence against unbelievers. Nevertheless, we should be wary of
attributing every Muslim peasant outbreak simply to religious solidarity
and/or the existence of some millenarian vision of an earthly Paradise.

If religion is a factor, then so is livelihood. At one level, rural revolts in South Asia are always about land-control, rent, tax, and debt. Perhaps the real issue is: how do these two ingredients—the material and the ideological—interrelate?

The Meo revolt in Alwar in 1932 provides an ideal context in which to explore this question. On the face of it, the Meo revolt was a classic peasant revolt in the mould of earlier Rajputana outbreaks such as those in the Bijolia *taluqa* of Udaipur between 1905 and 1922.[31] As in the Udaipur case the trigger was an enhanced *darbari* tax-demand which the Meo peasants could not and would not pay. Again, the timing of the outbreak would suggest that the Meos' recalcitrance had something to do with the economic impact of the Depression which, as we have seen, is widely regarded by historians as the key factor in the (contemporaneous) extension of the civil disobedience movement to the countryside in some parts of British India. Significantly, the first academic to comment on the Alwar revolt—no lesser personage than Harold Laski—interpreted it very much in these economistic terms.[32] On the other hand, the Meos were—at least nominally—Muslims, and, as we shall see, religious demands and communal antagonisms played a considerable part in the later stages of the upheaval. Was Islam, too, a significant shaping factor? Or was the 'Muslim' dimension only incidental, a phantom conjured up by the state's Hindu ruling clique?

III

Alwar lies in the eastern flank of the Aravalli Range, about one hundred kilometres south-west of Delhi. Now a district of Rajasthan, Alwar down to 1947 was a separate kingdom ruled by a dynasty of Kachwaha Rajputs. Like the other Indian princely states, it was linked to the British Raj by treaty and dependent on the 'Paramount Power' for its defence and foreign relations. However, save for the (fairly loose) supervision of a resident based at Jaipur, the local government, or *darbar*, had virtually complete discretion as regards internal administration.

In many ways Alwar in the early twentieth century was a typical middle-sized middle-ranking (17-gun) state, one of about a dozen similar Rajput and Jat principalities within the Rajputana Agency. What made it exceptional was its ruler, Maharaja Jey Singh. By 1932 Jey Singh was one of the most senior and experienced of the major Indian princes, having ruled Alwar for forty years. He was also acknowledged as one of the brightest. After an hour of listening to Jey Singh on 'the transmigration of souls', the vicereine, Lady Reading, noted in her diary: 'altogether the most interesting of the Rajahs, [and the pick of them] as to brains'.[33] Blessed with a lively intelligence, swarthy good looks, and a natural eloquence, Jey Singh had established himself by the 1930s as a leading princely politician and even as something of a statesman. He had represented his country at the League of Nations and the 1923 Imperial Conference; he had participated as a member of the princely delegation in the London Round Table Conference of 1930; he was on the Board of Governors of Benaras Hindu University and president of the Sanatan Dharma Sabha. However, these modest achievements in the public arena were overshadowed, at least in the official mind, by the *maharaja*'s unsavoury reputation for eccentricity and sexual depravity. 'Some day', the viceroy Lord Irwin wrote to a friend in 1926, 'I will tell you tales about him... that will make your hair stand on end. I have heard so many that I cannot believe that some are true.'[34] Amongst other things, it was said that Jey Singh had an unnatural aversion to dogs, that he could not abide the touch of leather or of the ungloved hand, that he was a homosexual and a paedophile, that he took pleasure from torturing animals.[35] As the rumours mounted, the maharaja of Alwar's star began to fade; within the Chamber of Princes, which he had dominated with his rhetoric for a decade, he was increasingly ostracized. Nevertheless, one section of society—the more devout section of the Hindu community—remained staunchly supportive. Among the north Indian Hindu religious elite Jey Singh was acclaimed for his orthodoxy, his piety, and his patronage of Hindu charities. Among the unlettered and the superstitious, the maharaja was widely considered an incarnation or manifestation of Rama. Not surprisingly, many Alwar Hindus saw the maharaja as their natural protector and benefactor.

Nor were they disappointed. The laws and policies of Alwar favoured Hindus over members of other communities. Hindi was the sole medium of instruction in state schools and mandatory in the state public service; while 'dress-code' rules forbade the wearing of beards (which were commonplace among Muslim males). As a result, Hindus dominated the upper levels of the bureaucracy, filling, in 1932, 1716 out of a total of 1,875 senior posts.[36] On the other hand, the Alwar authorities discriminated against Muslims in a number of ways. Urdu, the language of the urban Muslims, was available in schools, but only as an optional subject. Yet new rules promulgated in 1925 restricted the opening of private Urdu-medium schools, or *maktab*s. The darbar persistently refused to allow new mosques to be built and on several occasions fined congregations who attempted to refurbish existing ones without permission. Last but not least, there is evidence that 'the [criminal] courts on occasions had covert orders from the darbar to inflict exemplary sentences in cases where prominent Muslims were the accused'.[37]

To be sure, Alwar was not alone among Hindu states in serving the interests of the majority community. The pattern there was fairly standard practice, just as the reverse practice was standard in Muslim states such as Bhopal, Junagadh, and Hyderabad.[38] But Alwar was unusual among Hindu-ruled states in having a significant Muslim minority. In 1931 over 26 per cent of the state's population of 746,000 were Muslims, a higher proportion than in any other Rajputana kingdom except for Jaisalmer.[39] Here pro-Hindu policies were clearly inappropriate.

They were also potentially dangerous. As we noted above, the tag 'Muslim' carries no necessary implication of political solidarity. But Alwar's Muslims were unusually homogeneous. Most of them—117,381 out of 146,460—were Meos, members of a single extended 'caste'. And the Meos were clannish and territorial. As Table 6.1 shows, they were heavily clustered in several *nizamat*s or districts. At the same time, the Meos' settlement patterns transcended Alwar's administrative boundaries, spilling over into neighbouring Bharatpur state and part of Punjab. Throughout this region Meo villages were grouped according to lines of descent into *pal*s, each under the hereditary leadership of an elder known as a *chaudhuri*. According to their own notions, therefore, the Meos of Alwar were not simply subjects of Jey Singh; they were also, and perhaps more fundamentally, citizens of a broader tribal/cultural configuration, the region of Mewat. What is more, the Meos were 'a people of military traditions'.[40] Having for centuries mixed pastoralism with cattle rustling and raids on caravans plying the highways around Delhi,[41] in the late nineteenth century the Meos moved into agriculture and soldiering, signing up in their thousands for service with the Indian Army. Consequently, by the 1930s every Meo village had its handful of battle-hardened veterans. Clearly this was a community to be reckoned with.

TABLE 6.1
Meo Population of Alwar: Selected Nizamats (1931)

District	Meo Population	Total Population	Percentage
Tapukrah	12,411	27,058	45.8
Ramgarh	15,089	33,036	45.7
Alwar	18,937	43,705	43.4
Govindgarh	11,877	28,176	42.2
Kishangarh	7713	31,083	24.8
Khairtal	7713	31,374	22.4
Malakhera	5722	35,017	16.5
Lachmangarh	8140	49,472	16.4
Mandawar	3580	31,079	11.5
Tijara	13,243	39,620	33.4

Source: *Census of India 1931*, vol. XXVII, Provincial Tables I and III.

Nevertheless, for a long time it seemed that the Meos had well and truly put their social banditry days behind them. During the first forty years of Jey Singh's reign, they caused little trouble. They paid their taxes, obeyed the maharaja's *nazims*, and for the most part kept the peace. So why did the honeymoon come to an abrupt end in November 1932?

IV

Rajasthan generally is a dry area; but the eastern plains and foothills, with an average annual rainfall of around 21 inches, are rather better watered than most other parts, and correspondingly more densely settled. In Alwar, the rural population density in 1931 was 238 persons per square mile, compared to a provincial average of 145.[42] What is more it was, by Rajputana standards, a fairly productive region, capable of sustaining the cultivation of wheat and coarse grains and the grazing of cattle, sheep, and goats. Though mainly, at this stage, a subsistence zone, there was limited crop-production for the local market and quite an extensive export-trade in livestock. As in neighbouring Punjab, smallholdings of between five and ten *bigha*s predominated; the basic economic unit was the family farm. However by no means all rural households had proprietory rights; most of the land was held in perpetual leasehold from the state by village 'brotherhoods' of dominant peasants known as *biswardar*s. In large parts of Alwar, particularly in the nizamats of Tapukrah, Ramgarh, Alwar, and Govindgarh, the biswardars were mostly Meos.

Thus, while the Meos may fairly be regarded as 'subalterns', they can hardly be said to have constituted a rural proletariat. As smallholders, most Meo families made a comfortable living from the land; and many in addition were in receipt of military salaries and pensions. For instance when Subedar Chand Khan retired from the army in 1919 he had Rs 9000 saved up, enough to build a *pukka* house and three irrigation wells in his home village of Saharanpuri.[43] Secondly, as the dominant land-controllers, the Meos occupied a position of power in the local community. The other castes in the village, Muslim and Hindu, were all, more or less, their clients. Even *brahmins* served them by keeping their horoscopes. These jajmani relationships were 'enduring and hereditary'.[44] Thirdly, the Meos demanded the social respect due to people of status. Although converts to Islam, the Meos claimed that they were descended from Rajputs and therefore 'twice-born'. Such was their economic clout, that this claim was, for the most part, freely conceded (or at least not openly contested).[45] On the other hand the Meos treated the low Hindu castes, the Chamars and Bhangis, as untouchables. Fourthly, the Meos had something of a culture of self-improvement. In particular, during the 1920s some Meos took advantage of the opening of a 'high school' at Nuh by a paternalistic British district officer, Frank Lugard Brayne, to acquire a rudimentary education.[46] On all these counts (land-ownership, moderate wealth, respectable status within the village community, and aspirations to upward mobility) the Alwar Meos fit neatly into the 'middle peasant' category as defined by Wolf and Alavi.

The first point to note, then, is that the Meos were a community with a position to uphold and defend. The second point to make is that as biswardars—in effect, tenants of the Alwar state—they were victims of a very iniquitous darbari revenue system. The 1901 assessment of Alwar, carried out by an I.C.S. officer on loan from the Punjab, but within parameters established by the darbar, was characterized by him as 'at least fifty per cent higher than I would dare to impose in a British district'.[47] Nevertheless between 1920 and 1924 the rate was revised upward, in the light of post-war price-inflation, by an average of 22.6 per cent. This represented a state share of the crop, after deductions for expenses, of two-thirds.[48] By the 1930s, Meo peasants in the Nuh *tehsil* of Gurgaon district, just across the Alwar border, were paying basic rates of between Rs 1–10–0 and Rs 0–12–0 per standard *bigha*; whereas their kinsmen in Tijara nizamat were paying between Rs 2–6–0 and Rs 0–14–0 per bigha.[49] Needless to say, the latter felt cheated. But that was not all. Unlike in many parts of British India, cultivators in Alwar were subjected to a variety of additional imposts: these included a grazing tax, an octroi, and an export duty (which alone added some 18 per cent to their tax-burden).[50] Moreover, the fiscal regime in Alwar was administered more capriciously and harshly than in the provinces. The record of rights, being kept in Hindi, was unintelligible to the Meos

TABLE 6.2
Revenue Demand in Selected Alwar Tehsils

(Rupees)

Tehsil	Demand under 1901 settlement	Demand under 1921 settlement	Enhancement (per cent)
Kishangarh	240,294	301,612	26
Ramgarh	298,605	361,089	21
Mundawar	189,860	246,355	30
Behror	214,219	263,524	23
Rajgarh	173,264	197,509	14

Source: IOR R/1/1/2614.

and indeed to most village *patwari*s. The subordinate revenue officers
were frequently ignorant and incompetent, and blackmail and petty
corruption flourished. Peasants who defaulted and could or would not
afford the price of a bribe were introduced to an apparatus called a *katta*,
which crushed its victims under heavy wooden beams.[51]

From the moment the new settlement was first introduced in 1921
there was grumbling and protest among the peasantry—even (at
Nimuchana in May 1925) organized resistance.[52] Despite this, the new
jama did not initially represent a crippling burden for the majority of
Alwar's cultivators. With seasons bountiful and agricultural prices
high, there was generally enough surplus to meet the enhanced demand.
However these optimal conditions could not and did not last. From 1928
eastern Rajputana suffered a succession of poor seasons; then, in 1930,
crop prices plummeted. The results were catastrophic. In Kishangarh,
the area irrigated by wells went down by 19 per cent; in Rajgarh, the
area under irrigation shrank by 23 per cent; in Thanaghazi the total area
under cultivation fell by 29 per cent. Arrears on revenue collections
increased from Rs 8800 in fiscal year 1927–8 to Rs 77,894 in fiscal
year 1930–1.[53] Yet the Alwar authorities refused to help. Down to 1932
not a single rupee of revenue was remitted, nor was any money spent
(as in Gurgaon) on famine relief, nor was any interest waived on
government agricultural loans.[54] When the maharaja's nazims went into
the villages in November 1932 to collect arrears due on the summer
rabi crop they found the Meos sullen, hostile, and defiant.

Even so, it took an act of crass stupidity to push the Meos over the
edge. On 14 November a party of darbari revenue officers arrived at
Damokar, in the Kishangarh nizamat. As elsewhere there was a standoff; but on this occasion the officials refused to accept the peasants'
pleas that they had no cash or grain to spare. Accusing them of acting
like criminals (*badmashe*s), the darbar's men seized hold of the villagers they took to be the ringleaders and threw them in the local lockup.
The few who resisted were handcuffed and beaten. However these
strongarm tactics backfired. Within a couple of hours a large and very
angry crowd had assembled outside the lockup. Anticipating an assault,
one of the darbari party fired, injuring three Meos. Enraged by the sight
of blood the crowd surged foward and attacked the officials with fists,
sticks, and knives. Only one man escaped, and by the time he returned
with police reinforcements the Meos had gathered up their scanty
possessions and fled into the hills.

It was a small beginning; but it was enough. The following day the
embryonic insurgency was joined by Meos from Bidarkar in Alwar
nizamat, who were related to the Damokar Meos by marriage and had

a score to settle with the nazim of Tijara who, some weeks earlier, had tortured one of their number almost to death.[55] After that resistance spread rapidly. By mid-December some seventy villages populated by about 80,000 Meos, perhaps a quarter of them armed,[56] were in open rebellion.

Jey Singh responded to the outbreak with a mixture of coercion and conciliation. On 1 December he announced the appointment of a committee of inquiry headed by revenue minister Raja Ghazanfar Ali to look into the peasants' grievances. Meanwhile, troops were dispatched from Kishangarh with instructions to re-establish darbari authority and intimidate the contumacious villagers. But the Meos stood fast. Labelling the inquiry a transparent sham they set up an early warning system consisting of watchmen on the hills equipped with drums, dug fortifications, cut down trees, and rolled boulders across the roads to impede the passage of the darbar's forces, sent their women and children across the border into Gurgaon district and levied money for a war-fund, soliciting contributions from Hindus and Muslims alike. When an advance party of troops and police arrived at Bhagar village on 3 January they were met with a 'fussilade of bullets' and were forced to retire. Shortly afterwards, another Meo band destroyed the octroi post at Mubarakpur, the first of several attacks on government offices. Then, on 7 January 1933, some 6000 Meos led by a retired Indian Army *jemadar* and First World War veteran Bakhtiwar Khan, launched an overnight assault on soldiers guarding the revenue office at Govindgarh, killing and wounding about a dozen and forcing the rest to beat a hasty retreat to the capital.[57]

With the situation in the eastern districts spiralling out of control, a now rather frantic Jey Singh appealed to the government of India through the resident to provide reinforcements. Somewhat reluctantly, and against the advice of the Punjab government, they agreed. On 8 January a battalion of infantry and two squadrons of cavalry, backed up by four armoured cars, arrived in the disaffected areas from Delhi. Gradually, order was restored. But this British military aid carried a price tag. Before dispatching the troops, the imperial authorities required Jey Singh to agree to hand over control of the Meo nizamats for at least the duration of the military operations, and to undertake such measures as they deemed necessary to ensure that the causes of the rebellion were redressed. In mid January they imposed additional terms, including a demand that the maharaja take on a British revenue minister and a British minister of police. Although Jey Singh resisted this intervention as best he could—avoiding interviews, instructing his officers to withhold information, and covertly putting it about that the loaned officers did not enjoy his confidence—by the end of February 1933 the civil administration of Alwar was effectively in the hands of outsiders. And British control was further tightened in May when Jey Singh was sent into permanent exile.[58] One of the first acts of the new regime was to remit a quarter of the government tax demand on the *kharif* harvest; and in 1934 the revenue assessment was permanently reduced in the five nizamats of Alwar, Rajgarh, Kishengarh, Ramgarh, and Mandawar by amounts varying from 20 to 25 per cent.[59]

It is easy to see why many contemporaries (including Harold Laski) came to the conclusion that the 1932 insurgency in Alwar was essentially a peasant movement, grounded in oppression and material deprivation; it bears all the hallmarks of a classic 'middle peasant' revolt.[60] Yet this economistic interpretation is not without its problems. For one thing, the revolt remained confined to the Meo areas. Other groups of cultivators such as the Jats and the Rajputs, although governed broadly by the same system of revenue administration[61] and equally affected by famine and falling prices, did not rise; indeed in some cases they adopted a stance of outright hostility towards the rebellion. For another, the revolt was not supported with the same ferocity in all the five nizamats in which Meos predominated; its epicentre was in Tijara, Ramgarh, and Kishengarh, significantly, perhaps, the Alwar districts closest to Gurgaon and Delhi. Thirdly, there is a problem of synchronicity. If the world depression was indeed the trigger for the revolt, one might have expected it to break out in 1930 or 1931, by which time crop prices had already bottomed, rather than at the end of 1932. Last but not least, the agrarian explanation takes no account of the possible role of ideas, and of ethnicity. We have already alluded to the fact that the Meos were a tightly knit group. Was it important that they were also defined by ties of religion, that they were Muslims and their oppressors, the state and its officials, mainly Hindu?

V

Early in 1933, particularly after the attack on Govindgarh, allegations began to circulate that the Meos were targeting Hindus and Hindu shrines. In its coverage of the Govindgarh episode the *Times of India* wrote: 'During the night the Meos broke Shivaji's idols in temples, tore up and threw down the Book of Ramayan and tied up one mahatma residing there with ropes and hung him to a tree upside down'.[62] Other reports cited attacks on Hindu shopkeepers who had refused to contribute to the Meos' war-coffers, and to the desecration, in late January, of three temples around Firozepur Jirkha and an image lodged in a *chhatri* in Ramgarh.[63] Soon, scores of Hindu refugees were straggling out of the disaffected areas. For the darbar, the signs were damningly clear: the state was facing a 'communal' agitation.[64] How far does this (obviously propagandist) claim fit the known facts?

As far as the Meos are concerned, not very well. Firstly, the Meos' brand of Islam was, and is, a very heterodox one. The Meos celebrate Hindu festivals—Divali, Dasehra, the birthday festival of Krishna. They venerate saints and the tombs of saints.[65] Meo women do not observe purdah. Wives, daughters, and sisters have no legal right of inheritance, as provided for in the sharia. Conversely, the Meos do not permit cousins to marry, though Islam allows it.[66] Of course, as remarked above, syncretism may not necessarily connote lack of religious fervour. However, the Meos' syncretism seems to have been, not just a pale reflection of the 'real thing', but rather a thing in itself—a sturdy and remarkably durable little tradition. Although, from 1927, the Meos were exhorted by the *tabligh* missionary Maulana Ilyas (1886–1944) to abandon their 'un-Islamic' practices, and to become 'proper' Muslims, Ilyas' propaganda appears to have had little impact, at least before 1947.[67] Indeed, as late as the 1980s, Meo informants told Shail Mayaram gently but firmly: 'Meos are not Muslims'.[68] On the face of it, the Meos are unlikely communalists. Secondly, there is no prehistory of overt communal conflict in the rural areas of Alwar. The newspapers, which at that time were almost obsessed with reporting communal riots, carry no such reports about Mewat.[69] On the contrary, anecdotal evidence suggests that the Meos 'had always lived amicably with Hindus'[70]—a finding that also accords with what we have noted above about Meo patronage of Hindu service castes and more generally about the economic inter-dependence of Indian village life. Thirdly, when the British looked into the cases of temple 'desecration' in Ramgarh, they found no signs of 'deep-seated communal tension' in the town, and concluded that the incidents in question had been engineered by a darbari official, Debi Dayal, in order to cast the Meos in a bad light.[71]

Nevertheless, I think the darbar's propaganda machine inadvertently got it partly right. I think the Alwar revolt *was* a communal—Hindu versus Muslim—episode in at least two important respects. Indeed I would go further, and say that the Alwar revolt was a major milestone in the communal history of princely north India.

Although the revolt clearly had its roots in agrarian distress, consequent upon an iniquitous taxation system, as it spread and became more violent, provoking in turn governmental repression and British intervention, other groups, Muslim and Hindu, Alwari and non-Alwari, jumped in to support the rebels and assist the beleaguered darbar respectively. On the Muslim side, the first to do so were the Sheikhs of Alwar City.[72] Unlike the Meos, the Sheikhs did have a communal agenda. Urdu-speaking and mainly middle class, they wanted more access to the public service and an end to discrimination against Muslims in government schools and the judiciary. Moreover, their campaign to pressure the darbar into changing its policies in these matters soured relations between the communities in the capital. In May 1932, during Mohurrum, a *chaddar* (sheet, i.e. offering) procession led by the Anjuman-i-Khadim-ul-Islam clashed with a procession of Hindu Chamars inaugurating a new Saivite temple. At least three people were killed and over forty were injured in the ensuing riot. Although there was no further violence, relations were still strained at the end of the year, a circumstance that may have contributed peripherally to the Meos' defiant mood in November.[73]

Meanwhile, the Alwar cause had begun to attract the support of influential Muslims in British India. In July Maulana Syed Ghulam Bhik Narang, general secretary of the Central Jamiat-i-Tabligh-ul-Islam of Ambala took it up; in August an inflammatory article appeared in the *Inquilab* newspaper of Lahore; in October Sir Muhammad Iqbal, President of the Muslim Conference, sought to involve the viceroy Lord Willingdon; and in December a much-publicized 'all-India Alwar Conference' at Ferozepur Jirkha in Punjab passed resolutions condemning the Alwar government's discriminatory policies. With the darbari crackdown at the end of the year and the shootings at Govindgarh early in January, which, amongst other things, caused about 10,000 Meos and other Alwari Muslims to flee to Gurgaon and Delhi, the provincial Muslim response went up a further notch, and leaders such as Iqbal and Fazli Hussain now openly called on the government of India to intervene. Yet while voicing their concern for the suffering of Meos, the north India Muslims remained more interested in the issue of communal representation. Significantly, in the Muslim Conference petition of October 1932, agrarian grievances feature well down the list. As the Imam of the Delhi Jama Masjid frankly admitted to the Political Department's George Wingate, the militants in Ambala and Delhi wanted to 'exploit' the Meo situation; their idea was to turn Alwar into a 'second Kashmir'.[74] By 1933 the Meos were the unwitting centrepiece in a much larger political game.

As for the other side in this game, the Hindus, they too saw Alwar as an aspect of a wider communal struggle. As already observed, the Rajput–Bania elite in Alwar conceived the state very much as a Hindu artifact—as a creation of, and for, Hindus. Accordingly, they saw the

Muslim campaign for civil and religious rights as a threat both to their patrimony and their livelihood. When the revolt broke out, they rallied around the maharaja with every bit as much spirit as the the Meos had displayed in defying him; spreading stories of Meo violence which helped to put the darbar in a better moral light; holding counter-rallies; stirring up their co-religionists with inflammatory speeches and provocative acts of desecration such as those in Ramgarh attributed to Debi Dayal. However, as with the Muslims, local leaders were soon relegated to a back seat by outsiders, in this case by the stalwarts of the Hindu Mahasabha, Bhai Parmanand and Dr B.S. Moonje. In January, following the Govindgarh episode, Moonje paid a flying visit to Alwar during which he offered Jey Singh advice on countering the Muslim threat and assistance in procuring an aeroplane for aerial reconnaisance. He left somewhat annoyed at his reception.[75] Nevertheless, over the following months the Mahasabha mounted a vigorous campaign in the press and other forums in defence of the maharaja's government. The party accused the Meos of carrying on a reign of terror against the local Hindu community in furtherance of the 'Panislamic designs of the Muslims of India', and called for an impartial enquiry into the violence. It held an Alwar Day, and tried to organize a conference at Rewari to show solidarity with the Darbar. It collected subscriptions, and distributed the money 'amongst the Hindu sufferers of Alwar'.[76] The Mahasabha's efforts may not have helped Jey Singh, but they did help to politicize the Hindus of Alwar, as evidenced by the formation in 1933 of a Hindu Sabha branch in the state.[77]

The appropriation of the Alwar revolt by outside interests and parties did not, in itself, alter the fundamental nature of the struggle. For the Meos, it remained, first and foremost, a struggle for social justice. Nevertheless the involvement of the Anjuman and the Muslim Conference and the Mahasabha inevitably coloured the way it was perceived by the people of north India; slowly but surely, it became transformed in the popular imagination. This is one sense in which the Alwar revolt can be regarded as a communal episode.

The other sense in which we can speak of the Alwar revolt as communal is in terms of its consequences. The revolt and its aftermath—imperial intervention—polarized the two communities within Alwar. Buoyed by their success in bringing about (albeit indirectly) the demise of the hated Jey Singh, the Meos emerged from the experience more confident, more organized, and, to Hindu eyes, more arrogant. After 1933 they became more demanding of government largesse and, at the same time, more resentful of darbari authority—a stance that reached its logical conclusion in 1946 when Meos from Alwar joined with their kinsman in Gurgaon and Bharatpur to press for the creation of an autonomous Meo state, 'Meostan'.[78] Likewise the urban Muslim communities in Alwar—the Sheikhs and the Pathans—grew more intransigent during the 1930s in matters of religious observance, particularly in respect of routes for *tazia* processions during Mohurrum. Conversely, for Alwari Hindus, the revolt inaugurated a traumatic period of adjustment. Under the new British regime established in 1933 many Hindus in the bureaucracy lost their jobs; many others felt angry and humiliated by the treatment meted out to Jey Singh. At a public meeting in Alwar City in April 1933 one speaker declared: 'unless the pro-Muslim policy is given up, every Hindu will lay down his life in the service of his community'. This outburst of patriotism provoked lusty cheers.[79] Initially the main target of the Hindus' anger was the new British regime; but as time went by, dulling the impact of the presence of British officers in the palace, more and more came to see the refractory Meos as the real cause of their misfortunes. Many lusted for revenge. Necessarily stifled during the interregnum, these resentments erupted after the Alwar darbar was finally released from its imperial chains in 1943, generating a flood of local recruits to the chauvinistic Rashtriya Swayamsevak Sangh. In spring 1947 RSS cadres, assisted by elements of the Alwar army, used the pretext of a second Meo revolt to launch a coordinated pogrom against the state's rural Muslims. Thousands were brutally murdered, thousands more forcibly re-converted, in the worst episode of Partition violence outside the Punjab.[80]

VI

Since E.P Thompson wrote his pathbreaking essay on the English working class in 1971, the idea that pre-modern subaltern societies were regulated by consensual norms of fair dealing—what Thompson called the moral economy—has gained widespread scholarly acceptance, more recently providing the theoretical underpinning for several important studies of peasant rebellion in colonial Asia. Indeed the moral economy notion seems tailor-made for the parochial, inward-looking world of the Asian village, where so much of life and livelihood was regulated by customary shares in the harvest and by ties of interdependence between landholding patrons and labouring or artisanal clients. It is but a short step (and on the face of it a logical one) to see peasant revolts in Asia as primarily restorative movements designed to defend, repair, or resurrect moral economy values threatened by political and economic change, which is in essence what James C. Scott argued in *The Moral Economy of the Peasant*.

But Scott's picture of the Asian village in that book is a somewhat one-dimensional one. It revolves essentially around the issue of live-lihood. 'The purpose of the argument that follows', he writes, 'is to place the subsistence ethic at the center of the analysis of peasant politics'.[81] Accordingly, Scott's case studies are about peasants strug-gling to maintain or restore their rights to subsistence, rights which have become redundant and anachronistic as a result of the encroachments of commercialization and state power. Now, I have no quarrel with the premise that calculations about subsistence, about survival, are central determinants of Asian peasant behaviour (just as they lie, I suppose, at the heart of all human action). However as Scott himself concedes, the peasant's mental world does not begin and end with concerns about his stomach. The study of the moral economy might start with economics, but sooner or later it must embrace the domains of culture and religion—a point Scott himself freely acknowledges.[82] Interest-ingly, a recent exploration of collective violence in South Asia by Stanley Tambiah concludes with the proposition that 'the true "moral economy" of countries such as India' is composed of 'pluralism and multiculturalism'[83]—ideologies of ethnic-religious tolerance.

In this essay I have also tried, in a small way, to unravel the complex interplay of economic and cultural or religious elements in the life of the Asian peasant, focusing, as Scott does, on a major post-Depression rural insurgency: the 1932 Meo rebellion in Alwar. On the face of it, the Meo revolt was a classic 'middle peasant' outbreak triggered by adverse economic conditions; trapped between rising taxes and falling returns, the Meos rose to restore the moral economy that had prevailed in the good years of the early twentieth century, before the Alwar durbar broke its side of the bargain by raising taxes to exhorbitant levels. Nevertheless I don't believe that the revolt can be understood just as an agrarian movement. Whilst the Meos' motivation may have been largely economic, the form that the revolt took and the responses that it evoked from other parties (both within the state and across north India) were indelibly affected by the Meos' communal solidarity and by their status (however nominal in practice) as Muslims. Notwith-standing that the Meos had previously lived, locally, in relative harmony with their Hindu neighbours, the movement became a communal one by virtue of the way it was shaped and defined by the outside political world. Moreover, it had communal repercussions. The intervention of the Anjuman and the Mahasabha in Alwar triggered sympathetic and oppositional movements elsewhere. Over the next few years there were Hindu-Muslim clashes in Jind, Kapurthala, Bahawalpur, Jaipur (Sikar), Kashmir, and Hyderabad. Hitherto the princely states had been

largely free from communal conflict; after 1932 fewer and fewer remained immune.

Writing on the 'rise' of communalism in colonial India has tended,
as I have here, to emphasize change over continuity, to highlight
irruptions of communal violence at the expense of situations of peaceful
co-existence, even though there is much statistical and anecdotal evidence to suggest that, even in the twentieth century, the latter was the
prevailing norm in most places at most times. (As Bipan Chandra points
out, even in 1923–6, one of the peak periods for communal violence in
the provinces, there were 'only' 72 major riots, which is to say that on
19 out of every 20 days, there was no large-scale outbreak of violence.)[84] However one can argue that a potentially very fruitful alternative approach to the study of communalism is precisely to examine how
and why small communities in many parts of India (in most parts until
recent times) managed, generation after generation, to get along with
each other and to contain their disagreements and tensions short of
violence. Following Scott, the problem then becomes: why did these
self-regulating social units—these moral communities[85]—break apart?

In the literature on British India much is made of structural factors,
such as urbanization and industrialization, the market economy and the
advent of mass media of communication, which in various ways have
served to erode the autonomy of the locality and its customary, face-
to-face way of organizing production. Likewise, much is made in the
provincial literature of the political process. Politicians looking for
votes, it is argued, often found it convenient to couch their appeals in
cultural language which spoke to particular communities and which,
therefore, excluded other communities. Perhaps the relative 'backward-
ness' of the states in these respects explains why they took somewhat
longer to become communalized than the provinces, or, to put it another
way, why they were able, in most cases into the 1940s, to preserve
something of the older social ethic of peaceful co-existence, the ethic
of the moral community?

Translating these speculations into firm answers will require substantial research, and as yet, research into communalism in the context
of the princely states is still in its infancy. However if the Alwar
experience is any guide, the role of external agency will repay close
attention. The moral community of the Alwar Meo villages was destroyed not from within but from without.

Endnotes

1. T.S. Ashton and J. Sykes, *The Coal Industry of the Eighteenth Century*
   (Manchester, 1929), p. 131, quoted in E.P. Thompson, 'The Moral Economy

of the English Crowd in the Eighteenth Century', in *Past and Present*, no. 50 (February 1971), p. 77.

2. Quoted in Hamza Alavi, 'Peasants and Revolution', in Kathleen Gough and Hari P. Sharma (eds), *Imperialism and Revolution in South Asia* (New York, 1973), p. 291.

3. For Marx's disparaging views on the revolutionary potential of the peasantry see *The Eighteenth Brumaire of Louis Bonaparte* (1851-2), in *Karl Marx and Frederick Engels: Selected Works In Two Volumes* (Moscow, 1951), vol. 1, pp. 302-3; and 'The British Rule In India', *New York Daily Tribune*, 25 June 1853, reproduced in Shlomo Avineri (ed.), *Karl Marx On Colonialism and Modernization* (Garden City, N.Y., 1969), p. 94. Some scholars maintain, however, that these early Marxian works are not truly representative. See, e.g., Michael Duggett, 'Marx On Peasants', *Journal of Peasant Studies*, vol. 2 (January 1975), pp. 159-82.

4. Eric Wolf, *Peasant Wars of the Twentieth Century* (London, 1969), p. 291.

5. Neil Charlesworth, *Peasants and Imperial Rule: Agriculture and Agrarian Society in the Bombay Presidency, 1850-1933* (Cambridge, 1983), p. 269.

6. Wolf, *Peasant Wars*, p. 292.

7. This is substantially the thesis advanced in D.A. Low (ed.), *Congress and the Raj: Facets of the Indian Struggle 1917-47* (London, 1977). See Low's Introduction to the volume, especially pp. 20-4.

8. Charlesworth, *Peasants and Imperial Rule*, p. 225; Gyanendra Pandey, 'A Rural Base For Congress: The United Provinces, 1920-40', in Low (ed.), *Congress and the Raj*, p. 203; Christopher Baker, 'Debt and the Depression In Madras', in Clive Dewey and A.G. Hopkins (eds), *The Imperial Impact: Studies In the Economic History of Africa and India* (London, 1978), p. 235; Brian Stoddart, 'The Structure of Congress Politics in Coastal Andhra, 1925-37', in Low (ed.), *Congress and the Raj*, pp. 121, 123. Stoddart, examining Civil Disobedience in the Andhra delta region, found that the movement 'won most support amongst locally dominant groups which were most affected by falling grain prices, rising debt and the inheritance of fragmented holdings'. Elsewhere he identifies these groups as 'middle peasants'. The all-India index for foodgrain prices ($1873=100$) stood at ($1929=311$); by ($1930=217$), by ($1931=143$).

9. Interestingly, Hardiman distances himself from other contributors to the *Congress and the Raj* symposium by downplaying the depression as an explanation for peasant militancy in Gujarat in the first phase of Civil Disobedience in 1930. Prices in the area did not fall drastically, he points out, until late 1931, more than twelve months after the Patidars of Borsad had raised the flag of defiance against the government. He does, however, mount a case that the Patidars' actions in 1930 reflected a long-term decline in their prosperity. David Hardiman, 'The Crisis of the Lesser Patidars: Peasant Agitations in Kheda District, Gujarat, 1917-34', ibid., p. 63.

10. Sumit Sarkar, *The Swadeshi Movement In Bengal, 1905-8* (New Delhi, 1973), pp. 510-12.

11. Sarkar, 'Conditions and Nature', p. 277.

12. Eric Stokes in C.A. Bayly (ed.) *The Peasant Armed: The Indian Rebellion of 1857* (Oxford, 1986), p. 224. See also Bayly's appraisal of Stokes, ibid., pp. 231, 241. And similar conclusions have been reached, too, about Southeast Asia. Brocheaux, for example, thinks that the depression was only incidental to the political upheaval of 1930–1 in Vietnam. Pierre Brocheaux, 'Moral Economy or Political Economy? The Peasant Is Always Rational', in *Journal of Asian Studies*, vol. 42, no. 4 (August 1983), p. 796.

13. Thompson, 'Moral Economy', pp. 78–9.

14. James C. Scott, *The Moral Economy of the Peasant: Rebellion and Subsistence in Southeast Asia* (New Haven, 1976), pp. 170–4, 180–92.

15. For example, Amartya Sen, *Poverty and Famine: An Essay on Entitlement and Deprivation* (Delhi, 1982). For a discussion of some of this literature see Arjun Appadorai, 'How Moral Is South Asia's Economy?—A Review Article', in *Jounal of Asian Studies*, vol. 43, no. 3 (May 1984), pp. 481–97.

16. Paternalism need not be benevolent; it can also reflect self-interest. As Alavi graphically puts it, 'The master...must keep alive the animal on whose labor he thrives'. Alavi, 'Peasants and Revolution', p. 333.

17. The most eloquent attack along these lines was mounted by Samuel Popkin in *The Rational Peasant: The Political Economy of Rural Society in Vietnam* (Berkeley, 1979).

18. Paul R. Greenough, 'Indian Famines and Peasant Victims: The Case of Bengal in 1943–4', in *Modern Asian Studies*, vol. 14, no. 2 (1980), pp. 205–35; and 'Indulgence and Abundance as Asian Peasant Values: A Bengali Case in Point', in *Journal of Asian Studies*, vol. 42, no. 4 (August 1983), pp. 831–50.

19. This feature of pre-modern rural life is made much of by Louis Dumont in his seminal study of the caste system. He writes: the 'distribution on the threshing floor...takes place in virtue of the fact that everyone [in the village] is interdependent'. Louis Dumont, *Homo Hierarchicus* (Chicago, 1980), p. 105.

20. Quoted in Stanley J. Tambiah, *Levelling Crowds: Ethnonationalist Conflicts and Collective Violence in South Asia* (Berkeley, 1996), p. 313.

21. Sarkar, 'Conditions and Nature', p. 292.

22. Joseph W. Elder, 'Rural Landed Rights and Becoming Twice Born: Some Interrelations Between India's Secular and Sacred Hierarchies', in Robert Eric Frykenberg (ed.), *Land Tenure and Peasant in South Asia* (New Delhi, 1977), p. 198.

23. For example, Madhav Gadgil and Ramchandra Guha, 'State Forestry and Social Conflict in British India', in David Hardiman (ed.), *Peasant Resistance in India 1858–1914* (Delhi, 1992), pp. 257–95; and Ranajit Guha, *Elementary Aspects of Peasant Insurgency in Colonial India* (Delhi, 1983), pp. 18–19, 33. Guha suggests that in pre-modern times, the tradition of *bhakti*, devotional worship, was used by elites to inclucate an ethic of 'total dedication' to superior authority, human as well as divine.

24. Partha Chatterjee, 'Bengal Politics and the Muslim Masses, 1920–47', in *Journal of Commonwealth and Comparative Politics*, vol. 20 (1982), pp. 32–3.

25. Wood emphasizes the 'compensatory' role of the mosque, as well as the 'sanctioning' and/or leadership role of the ulama, in his study of the Moplah 'outrages' in Malabar. The Moplah revolts represent the most extreme case of Islamic-influenced peasant insurgencies in modern India, in that the killing of Hindu landlords seems to have been only a means to a greater end, namely the attainment of martyrdom and the status of shahid. Conrad Wood, 'Peasant Revolt: An Interpretation of Moplah Violence in the Nineteenth and Twentieth Centuries', in Dewey and Hopkins, *The Imperial Impact*, pp. 133, 142, 151. Wood's 'islamic' reading has been contested, however, by other scholars such as Dhanagare, who think that 'fanaticism' was 'only the symptom and not the disease'. D.N. Dhanagare, 'Agrarian Conflict, Religion and Politics: The Moplah Rebellions in Malabar in the Nineteenth and Twentieth Centuries', in *Past and Present*, 74 (July 1977), p. 141.

26. David Hardiman, for example, thinks that both the Kerala (Moplah) and Bengal evidence points to Islam helping the Muslim peasantry 'forge bonds of solidarity against largely Hindu landlords'. *Peasant Resistance*, p. 19. Likewise Sumit Sarkar asserts that 'Islam provided the key vehicle' for Muslim peasants to articulate 'their socio-economic grievances' in *swadeshi* Bengal Sarkar, 'Conditions and Nature', p. 282. However the primordialist position in the debate about Islam's role in the fashioning of political identity is most eloquently put by Francis Robinson. See his: 'Islam and Muslim Separatism', in David Taylor and Malcolm Yapp (eds), *Political Identity in South Asia* (London, 1979), especially, p. 104.

27. On the syncretism of convert communities see M. Mujeeb, *The Indian Muslims* (London, 1967), pp. 11–17; and K.S. Singh, 'Ethnography of Rajasthan', in N.K. Singh and Rajendra Joshi (eds), *Folk, Faith and Feudalism: Rajasthan Studies* (Jaipur, 1995), pp. 375–8.

28. Paul R. Brass, 'Elite Groups, Symbol Manipulation and Ethnic Identity Among the Muslims of South Asia', in Taylor and Yapp, *Political Identity*, p. 53.

29. Kalyan Kumar Sen Gupta, 'The Agrarian League of Pabna, 1973', in Hardiman, *Peasant Resistance*, p. 121.

30. Guha, *Elementary Aspects*, pp. 172–3.

31. According to Sarkar, the Rajputana peasants were subject to the 'grossest forms of feudal exploitation'. Sumit Sarkar, *Modern India 1885–1947* (Madras, 1983), p. 155. See also Rajat K. Ray, 'Mewar: The Breakdown of the Princely Order', in Robin Jeffrey (ed.), *People, Princes and Paramount Power: Society and Politics in the Indian Princely States* (New Delhi, 1979), pp. 218–19, 226–32.

32. Article in the *Daily Herald* (London), 14 January 1933, quoted in Majid Hayat Siddiqi, 'History and Society in a Popular Rebellion: Mewat, 1920–33', in *Comparative Studies in Society and History*, vol. 28 (1986), p. 442.

33. Iris Butler (ed.), *The Viceroy's Wife: Letters Of Alice, Countess Of Reading From India, 1921–5* (London, 1969), p. 54. [Entry of 16 November 1921].
34. Irwin to Lord Chelwood, 3 December 1926, Chelwood Papers, Add. Mss. 51084, British Library, London.
35. These days, regrettably, deviance is the only thing Alwar is remembered for. See, for example, Christopher Thomas, 'Dying Raj Protected Perverse Princes', *The Times* (London), 12 August 1997. Thomas alleges, inter alia, that Jey Singh 'routinely used village boys as bait on his tiger shoots'.
36. 'Resume of the Grievances of Alwar Muslims', appendix to Police Dept. note, March 1933, I[ndia] O[ffice] R[ecords], R/1/1/2325, British Library.
37. F.V. Wylie to P.A. Eastern Rajputana, 19 September 1933, IOR R/1/1/2366. One interesting measure of the Alwar darbar's orthodox orientation is the fact that the census consistently records a very low number of people professing butchering as their trade. Presumably the actual number was much higher, but was artificially depressed, either by Muslims deliberately concealing their occupation (for fear of attracting governmental attention), or by officials cooking the figures. Edward S. Haynes, 'Comparative Industrial Development in 19th- and 20th-Century India: Alwar State amd Gurgaon District', in *South Asia*, N.S., vol. 3, no. 2 (December 1980), p. 31.
38. And with less justification, since in all these states Hindus outnumbered the Muslim elite.
39. *Census of India 1931*, vol. XXVII, p. 120.
40. *The Times of India*, 5 January 1933.
41. Mujeeb, *Indian Muslims*, pp. 218–19; Partap C. Aggarwal, 'The Meos of Rajasthan and Haryana', in Imtiaz Ahmad (ed.), *Caste and Social Stratification Among the Muslims* (Delhi, 1973), pp. 22–6; Stokes, *The Peasant Armed*, p. 218.
42. *Census of India 1931*, vol. XXVII, p. 45.
43. A[gent-to-the-]G[overnor-]G[eneral] Rajasthan to Pol. Sec., G[overnment] of I[ndia] 21 February 1936, quoting report by F. Wylie dated 26 October 1934, IOR R/1/1/2815.
44. I.S. Marwah, 'Tabligh Among the Meos of Mewat', in M.S.A. Rao (ed.), *Social Movements in India*, vol. 2 (Delhi, 1979), pp. 82–3.
45. Nor did the Meos take kindly to acts of insubordination by the lower castes. When Partap Aggarwal was doing fieldwork in Alwar in the early 1970s a Meo informant told him: 'The Sakhas of our village [Chavandi Kalan] are a crafty bunch.... They are uppity. In order to acquire land thay are fraternizing [i.e. sexually] with a Meo family.... Before Partition we would have beaten them up and turned them out of the village'. Partap C. Aggarwal, 'Caste Hierarchy in a Meo Village', in Ahmad, *Caste and Social Stratification*, p. 85.
46. Siddiqi, 'History and Society', pp. 448–50. The results of the Nuh school experiment, however, did not match the hopes of its benefactor. As late as 1931, male literacy among Alwar's Meos was still only around 1 per cent. For a critical appraisal of Brayne's work see Clive Dewey, *Anglo-Indian Attitudes: The Mind of the India Civil Service* (London, 1993).

47. Michael O'Dwyer to the Political Agent, Alwar, 10 January 1901, quoted in Prime Minister Alwar to Political Agent, Eastern Rajputana, 7 July 1934, IOR R/1/1/2614.

48. Note by Political Secretary dated 27 October 1934, IOR R/1/1/2614.

49. 'Note on the Assessment of the Alwar State' prepared by the Revenue Minister, Alwar, enc. in AGG Rajputana to Political Secretary GoI 13 December 1932, N[ational] A[rchives of] I[ndia] Home/Pol. 43/3 of 1933.

50. Report by Special Commissioner, Meo Nizamats, dated 20 April 1933; G.D. Ogilvie, AGG Rajputana, to Maharaja of Alwar, 16 May and 14 August 1933, Jayakar Papers, National Archives of India, New Delhi, vol. 98; and Prime Minister Alwar to Political Agent, Eastern Rajputana, 7 July 1934, IOR R/1/1/2164.

51. Prime Minister Alwar to P[olitical] A[gent] Eastern Rajputana 7 July 1934, IOR R/1/1/2614.

52. The resultant standoff was settled by the authorities with brutal force: the village was surrounded by troops and systematically destroyed, with the loss of perhaps 50 lives. Pema Ram, *Agraraian Movement in Rajasthan, AD 1913–1947* (Jaipur, 1986), pp. 241–3.

53. Prime Minister Alwar to PA Eastern Rajputana 7 July 1934, IOR R/1/1/2641.

54. The contrast between Gurgaon and Alwar is a telling one. From 1928 to 1932 inclusive, the Punjab authorities remitted 30 lakhs of revenue due from Gurgaon and converted another 15 lakhs of *takavi* loans into gifts. In addition they spent seven lakhs in the district on famine relief works. Hearing how much better the situation was handled in British India fuelled the Alwar Meos' anger towards their own government. Note by Sir Charles Watson, Pol. Sec. GoI, on interview with the Commissioner of Ambala, dated 3 January 1933, NAI Home/Pol. 43/3 of 1933.

55. C.C. Garbett, Chief Secretary Punjab, to G. Wingate, Deputy Political Secretary, GoI, 26 November 1932, NAI Home/Pol. 43/3 of 1933.

56. Journalists at the time reckoned the number of Meo insurgents at 40,000; this is probably an overestimate. Moreover it is not certain how many of these were armed, and with what. As one newspaper cautiously remarked: 'How many firearms the Meo insurgents have is uncertain. There is a general belief that they possess a large number', *The Times of India* (Bombay), 5 January 1933. According to intelligence reports reaching the Punjab government, the Meos had some 1000 'modern weapons'. Report dated 28 December 1932, NAI Home/Pol. 43/3 of 1933.

57. *The Times*, 5 January, 6 January and 10 January 1933; *The Times of India*, 10 January 1933; PA Alwar to AGG Rajputana 28 December 1932, NAI, Home/Pol, 43/3 of 1933; and Ram, *Agrarian Movement*, pp. 249–50. For a few days there was even some apprehension that the Meos were 'contemplating an attack on Alwar City'. *The Times of India*, 4 January 1933.

58. The maharaja died in Paris in 1937. Jey Singh's embalmed body was brought back to Alwar and processed through the streets of the capital in

an open carriage, to the accompaniment of apparently spontaneous out-
pourings of mass grief and hysteria.

59. The details of the new revenue arrangements, which also included the
    cancellation of *begar*, the restoration of *biswardari* lands converted into
    jagir or state hunting preserves, and the reduction of the grazing tax, can
    be read in Ram, *Agrarian Movement*, pp. 252–7.

60. This, indeed, was the official British view. 'It is now generally admitted',
    wrote Francis Wylie, 'that the main...cause of the disturbances...was
    over-taxation and particularly the excessive pressure of the Land Revenue
    demand'. Prime Minister Alwar to PA Eastern Rajputana 7 July 1934, IOR
    R/1/1/2614.

61. The major difference being that the some of the Rajputs were privileged
    landholders—*jagirdar*s and *muafidar*s.

62. *The Times of India* 10 January 1933.

63. C.I.D. intelligence report dated 28 December 1932, Home/Pol. 43/3 of
    1933; and Senior Civil Officer, Alwar, to Political Secretary, 3 February
    1933, IOR R/1/1/2331.

64. See the Alwar government's statement of 1 January 1933, quoted in *The
    Times of India*, 2 January 1933. Interestingly, after discussing the commu-
    nal 'threat' with darbari officials, the paper's local correspondent went
    away persuaded that 'His Highness' advisers were convinced of its real-
    ity'. Ibid., 9 January 1933.

65. In particular, the Meos venerate Saiyyid Salar Masud Ghazi and Sheikh
    Muinuddin Chishti. Saiyyid Salar is reputedly the first Meo to have
    embraced Islam (in the 11th century). Sheikh Muinuddin was the founder
    of the Chishti sufi order; his tomb is at Ajmer in Rajasthan. Saiyyid
    Salar is memorialized throughout Mewat by square stone platforms,
    called *chabutras*; these are held to be sacred by Meos and at certain times
    of the year lighted lamps are placed upon them in remembrance of the
    saint.

66. Aggarwal, 'The Meos', pp. 33–7; Mujeeb, *Indian Muslims*, pp. 10–11
    M.A. Sherring, *The Tribes and Castes of Rajasthan* (reproduced in Delhi,
    1975), pp. 90–1.

67. Marwah, 'Tabligh', pp. 95–6. Shail Mayaram, who has looked at Maulana
    Ilyas' private correspondence, suggests that the Maulana was almost
    ready to give up on the Meos as a lost cause. Personal communication to
    the author, 5 August 1997.

68. Shail Mayaram, 'Speech, Silence and the Making of Partition Violence in
    Mewat', in *Subaltern Studies IX: Writings on South Asian History and
    Society* (eds. Shahid Amin and Dipesh Chakrabarty, Delhi, 1996), p. 130.

69. As we shall see, there *was* a serious communal riot in the state in May
    1932, but this took place in an urban neighbourhood of Alwar City, not in
    the countryside. I accept that the English language papers, which are the
    only ones I have surveyed, may have missed some incidents; but if there
    had been a riot in rural Alwar during the 1920s involving death or injury,
    it would certainly have come to the notice of the English press.

70. Note by the Political Department's Richard Wingate on an interview with a Meo ex-serviceman dated 12 January 1933, IOR R/1/1/2325.

71. Senior Civil Officer Alwar to Political Secretary, GoI (teleg.) 2 February 1933, IOR R/1/1/2331.

72. Alwar City in 1931 had a population of 47,900, of which about one-third were Muslims. The Sheikhs numbered just under 10,000 state-wide, and about half lived in the capital. The other important Muslim group in Alwar City were the Pathans, who numbered just under 3000. Male literacy among Muslims in Alwar City was 11.79 per cent, compared to around one per cent in the countryside. *Census of India 1931*, vol. XXVII, pp. 183, 202 and Appendix, p. 18 Table V.

73. The rioters included some people from the surounding villages, recruited to bolster the rival processions. Shail Mayaram has demonstrated convincingly, however, that Meo participation in, and support for, the May riot was minimal. The majority of the Alwar City Muslim crowd were evidently Julahas (weavers). Nor can we follow Ram when he suggests that the urban Muslims were behind the Meo agitation of November 1932. They made use of it (see below) but they did not start it. On 26 December a Hindu boy was knifed by a Muslim, but the incident does not appear to have been communally motivated. C.I.D. Intelligence reports dated 27 May, 28 December 1932, NAI Home/Pol. 43/3 of 1933; Ram, *Agrarian Movement*, p. 248; and Shail Mayaram, *Resisting Regimes: Myth, Memory and the Shaping of a Muslim Identity* (Delhi, 1997), pp. 74–5.

74. In July 1931 Muslims in Kashmir launched an agitation against the state's Hindu maharaja. The agitation was actively supported with men and money by Muslims in Punjab, particularly by members of the Ahrar party. By 1932 the insurgency had got so far out of control that the British were forced to send troops. Unlike Jey Singh, however, maharaja Hari Singh of Kashmir kept his throne. Note by Wingate dated 23 November 1932, IOR R/1/1/2314.

75. In a press statement on his departure he observed that the local Hindus 'generally did not appear...to be alive to their peril'. *The Times of India*, 9 January 1933.

76. Ganpat Rai, Gen. Sec. All-India Hindu Mahasabha to George Wingate, 17 February 1933, IOR R/1/1/2385; and Ganpat Rai to B.S. Moonje, President Hindu Mahasabha 10 July 1933, B.S. Moonje Papers, Nehru Memorial Library, New Delhi, subject file 34.

77. Ganpat Rai to Moonje 20 March 1933; and Dev Raj, Secretary Hindu Navajivak Samaj, Alwar to Moonje 13 April 1933, Moonje Papers, N[ehru] M[emorial] M[useum and L[ibrary], subject file 33.

78. The word 'state' may be a misnomer. Although discussed at several caste-councils over the winter of 1946–7, the idea remained nebulous. Nevertheless the Alwar and Bharatpur governments took it very seriously.

79. Dev Raj, Hindu Nawajivak Samaj, Alwar, to Moonje 13 April 1933, Moonje Papers, NMML, subject file 33.

80. The religious conflicts of the late 1930s and 1940s in Alwar are discussed at more length in my article, 'The Further Shores of Partition: Ethnic Cleansing in Rajasthan, India, 1947', in *Past and Present* (1998), pp. 203–39.

81. Scott, *Moral Economy*, p. 3.

82. Ibid., p. vii. Scott agrees that he has 'only scratched the surface' in regard to the cultural dimension in *The Moral Economy*. He has sought to remedy the deficiency in a second book, *Weapons of the Weak: Everyday Forms of Peasant Resistance* (New Haven, 1985).

83. Stanley J. Tambiah, *Leveling Crowds: Ethnonationalist Conflicts and Collective Violence in South Asia* (Berkeley, 1996), p. 323.

84. Bipan Chandra, *Communalism In Modern India* (Delhi, 1984), p. 4.

85. The term comes from Sarkar, 'Conditions and Nature', p. 306. It deserves a wider application.

7

Coexistence and Communalism

The Shrine of Pirana in Gujarat

DOMINIQUE-SILA KHAN AND ZAWAHIR MOIR[1]

In India, as elsewhere, Islam still tends to be perceived as a monolithic phenomenon. The study of its historical and contemporary aspects continues, more than often, to be restricted to 'legalistic' Sunnism which, as a result of the writings of both earlier Sunni theologians and orientalists, is considered to be its normative form viewed in isolation or in opposition to other religious movements.[2] The important part played by other Islamic traditions in the subcontinent, the various forms of interactions which existed and still exist between Islam and indigenous movements, the intricate issues of conversions and the emergence of clear-cut religious identities towards the end of the nineteenth century, have begun only recently to attract academic attention.

In particular, the role of Ismailism in its South Asian acculturated form has been considerably underplayed by scholars mainly concerned with the interface between Sufism and Hinduism, and the conflicts which have torn the 'rival religious communities', once more preconceived as two opposed monolithic blocks.

The *Imamshahi* tradition of Gujarat, centred on Pirana near Ahmedabad, which we have chosen to introduce here exemplifies in itself some of the complexities of the subject. This sect of Nizari Ismailism (itself a branch of Shia Islam) which emerged in the fifteenth century and survives to this day in spite of numerous crises, continues to play a part in contemporary Gujarat. Unfortunately the literature on the subject is rather scanty and does not fully comply with the requirements of modern scholarship. Besides, as no recent studies of the Imamshahis are available, the contemporary developments within the sect have not yet been analysed. This essay—part of our ongoing research project³—thus seeks to fill up a gap and, while challenging earlier perceptions of the subject, raises a number of issues. Their elucidation could help us to a better understanding of past and present South Asian society, especially by revealing the range of ambiguities and complexities that can underlie and thus call into question what seems like straightforward communal conflicts.

A Visit to Pirana

For a traveller or a pilgrim unaware of the intricacies of history, religion, and politics in western India, visiting the shrine of Imam Shah located at Pirana, about sixteen kilometres from Ahmedabad, can be a unique experience. Eager to see one of the famous *dargah*s (Muslim shrines) of Gujarat our visitor would hastily cross an enclosed courtyard and look around, searching for the entrance to the mausoleum complex. At first he would not know where to direct his steps but his attention being eventually attracted by an inscription on one of the side walls, he would most probably be confused, if not bewildered, after having read its contents: 'way to the *samadhi*', knowing that *samadhi* is a term commonly referring to a Hindu funerary monument.⁴

This would not be the only surprise in store. After having entered the precincts of the dargah one is confronted with another amazing fact; the priests who are in charge of the main tomb, that of Imam Shah and of his son Mohammed Shah, claim to be Hindus. When the pilgrim comes out after having bowed in front of the graves, a man clad in white puts on his forehead a *tilak* (religious mark) of saffron colour. Besides, by focusing one's attention on the open courtyard, a few more details become conspicuous—the Hindu syllable *Om* is painted at various places on the walls which do not, however, shelter any temple but a few more tombs and a big mosque.

Obviously, the visitor is confronted with one of the so called 'syncretistic' traditions of the subcontinent which have been described by various scholars since the last decades of the nineteenth century. From the religious message of the saints Kabir and Nanak to the sharing of festivals, cults, and sacred places between Hindus and Muslims, a whole range of interesting phenomena have been the focus of scholarly studies or the subject of articles published in Indian newspapers and magazines. As far as the latter are concerned, the case of Pirana has not failed to attract the attention of Gujarati journalists who chose to report on some recent events.⁵

The general tendency is to view this type of phenomenon either as the result of 'spontaneous' interactions between Hinduism and Islam (particularly Sufism), or as the conscious efforts of some religious figure to reconcile two opposite traditions. The historical context is seldom analysed, or even taken into account, as if it were not relevant for understanding the present situation. In this respect Pirana, as described by the journalists and even by some of its devotees, has been no exception. The coexistence of Hindu and Muslim elements, which one can observe within the shrine complex, are accounted for in the same simplistic terms—Imam Shah is portrayed as a tolerant Sufi saint of the fifteenth century who, 'fed up with the Islamic regidities',[6] created a sect where elements drawn from various Hindu traditions were associated with Sufi Islamic beliefs and practices. According to this version, the new order, referred to as *Satpanth* (true path), admitted among its members Hindus as well as Muslims without demanding conversion. Therefore Hindu *Satpanthi*s, who were by far the more numerous, would have retained through the centuries their religious and caste identities, while Muslims also continued to follow their previous customs.

Of course, such a naive point of view, common to so many ancient and modern hagiographes, leaves one essential question unanswered— what does one understand by 'conversion' and 'religious identities'? Undoubtedly, the past decades have shown how crucial this particular question can be, the recent developments at Pirana exemplifying its importance for the subject which occupies us.

However, without a proper knowledge of the historical context, totally ignored by the media as well as by the 'official' publications currently available at the Pirana shrine, it is not possible to grasp the issue in all its complexity nor to see all its implications.

The Nizari Ismaili Mission in South Asia

Historians have long been aware that the Imamshahi sect of Pirana is an offshoot of Nizari Ismailism, a branch of Shia Islam[7] and there is ample evidence to support this view.[8] In the eleventh century a quarrel of succession led to the formation of two mainstreams: Mustali and Nizari Ismailism. From Iran which has been its main seat,[9] the Nizari mission (*dawa*) penetrated into the Indian subcontinent some time during the twelfth or thirteenth century. There it was mainly known as Satpanth, a name which was a local equivalent of the Arabic *sirat-e-mustaqim* by which the Ismailis referred to their religion. Historically of course, the Satpanth must not be viewed as a different branch or sect of the Nizaris but rather as a South Asian acculturated form of their faith. Adaptation to the historical circumstances, as well as to the local environment has played a major part in the history of Ismailism. In the Muslim countries where it emerged and developed it had to face, for many centuries, the hostility of the Sunni or Twelver Shia rulers and of their theologians who considered its followers as heretics (*malahida*).[10]

The Ismailis have always struggled to survive their identity crisis and problems of fragmentation have been a constant threat in their history. When the Nizari missionaries reached the subcontinent they were confronted with the same problem, as the Sunnis from Central Asia had already established their rule in Delhi and elsewhere. But they had to respond to another challenge, of attempting to convert the non-Muslim population following various beliefs and practices which can globally be termed 'Hindu'. At this stage it is necessary to recall that the Sunni rulers of the subcontinent were less concerned with conversions than with conquests,[11] whereas conversion was an essential part of the idiom of the Ismaili dawa. Thus, in order to avoid persecution, the Nizaris resorted to the usual process of *taqiyya* (concealing one's identity and true faith in case of danger, which is a permitted Shia practice), they appeared outwardly as Hindu *yogi*s and saints or as Sunni Sufi pirs, according to the context in which they had to work,[12] never revealing their real identity to those who were not properly initiated. Besides, to attract the Hindus or the Jains they recast their doctrines and rituals in forms that were more familiar to the converts who were allowed to retain most of their customs whilst they themselves practised taqiyya, for which reason they came later on to be referred to as *Gupti*s (secret ones). Let us add that the experiences of the pirs and of their followers in practising taqiyya should be studied and understood separately, concealing one's true faith may have meant something different for the spiritual leaders and for the ordinary members of the *panth*. Be that as it may, among the achievements of the Nizari missionaries one must mention the ritual of the *ghat-pat*[13] and the religious poetry known as *ginans*[14] in which indigenous and Islamic elements are closely interwoven.

It was in fact a whole vision of history or rather of meta-and hierohistory[15] which was proposed to the new converts in a form which could be directly understood by them, for example, the figure of the Imam, so essential in Shia and, in particular, in Ismaili philosophy,[16] was associated with Vishnu and his ten main incarnations (*das avatar*). But while, in common Hindu belief, Vishnu's tenth *avatar* is expected only at the end of our era (*kali yuga*), in the new 'Hinduized' Nizari idiom his advent had already taken place; he was none other than Imam Ali, the Prophet Muhammad's son-in-law who became manifested in the successive line of Imams. The Ismaili belief in time cycles[17] was somewhat akin to the Hindu concept of yugas, so that Vishnu's previous incarnations could be made to fit into an already existing conceptual framework. The centrality of this idea is attested by the fact that, till recently, a ginan entitled 'Das avatar' was a part of the regular prayer session in the Nizari *jamat-khana*s where the Khojas (one of the names used to refer to the Nizari community of the subcontinent) gathered three times a day.[18] Ultimately it is the whole Islamic concept of successive revelations completing and superseding each other which was retained, in the same way as Judaism and Christianity had been accepted in the Quran as successive phases of the sacred history, the past as reflected in Vedic and Brahmanical mythology was integrated in a form modified to suit the requirements of Ismaili ideology. Therefore, it is not only as a result of taqiyya (precautionary dissimulation) but also as a expression of this idea, that Nizari Ismailism, conceived as the latest Revelation, was referred to, in its South Asian context, as the *Athar* (sometimes Arharva) or fifth Veda, following the Brahmanical Artharva Veda.[19]

To conclude this brief survey it will not out of place to add a few words about the subsequent evolution of this branch of Islam in the subcontinent. A few historical records[20] supplemented by traditional oral sources tell us of the setback suffered by the dawa, mainly in the fifteenth century, when various groups seceded from the parent body. Among these one should mention the Imamshahi sect of Pirana,[21] and most probably various groups in Rajasthan and other parts of north India.[22] The weakening of the central authority represented by the Imam residing in Iran, who most of the time had to live in concealment, allowed various religious bodies to attract the Nizari convert into their orbit. The influence of British power and ideology associated with the arrival of the Aga Khans (the living Imams) in the subcontinent in the nineteenth century led to a re-evaluation of the identity of the Khoja community,[23] best illustrated by the famous Aga Khan court case of Bombay (1866). The spiritual leader of the Nizaris forced them to choose between these alternatives—either follow him and pay the customary tithe (*dasondh*) or integrate into another community, Sunni, Twelver Shia, or Hindu.[24] The British concern for clear-cut categories, mirrored in the census operations of that period, as well as the activities of some local revivalist movements which were a response to the colonial challenge, created a pressure which made it more and more difficult for social groups to retain intermediary or 'liminal' religious identities.[25]

In this way the Nizaris who remained faithful to the Aga Khans were gradually, through various fluctuant phases, led to re-Islamize their tradition to suit the requirements of a particular policy aimed at a rapprochement between Ismailis and their former rivals in the Muslim world.[26] Meanwhile those who had chosen to adopt a different religious identity followed their own way.

To sum up, the main features of Nizari Ismailism, in its South Asian form, should be stressed once more: acculturation, shifting of identities according to the historical and local contexts, and the practice of taqiyya reflected by the existence of Gupti communities. These are specific phenomena the extreme significance of which needs to be emphasized.

A Crisis of Identities

Scholarly literature on the Imamshahi sect is rather scanty.[27] The only extensive study was conducted by W. Ivanow, a well-known specialist of Ismaili studies.[28] In his article published some sixty years ago, the historical link of the Pirana Satpanth with Nizari Ismailism is fully acknowledged although, in the absence of any documentary evidence, the exact way in which the whole process of secession and dissidence occurred can be only conjectured. A reason why the historical role of Ismailism in the subcontinent has been greatly under-estimated is precisely the scarcity of written documents, a fact which can find its natural explanation in the necessity of taqiyya.

We will not dwell at length on the history of the sect as reconstructed by Ismaili sources, since this essay deals only with one particular aspect of the subject. It will suffice here to mention its principal phases and its most salient features. Imam Shah was the son of Hasan Kabiruddin (d. 1470), one of the main pirs or local leaders of the Nizari mission, the centre of which was located at Ucch-Multan (in present Pakistan). It is said that, at his father's death:

> ...he failed to win the Imam's nomination or the support of the Khojas of Sind and...went east to Kachchh and Gujarat, where he succeeded in converting many Hindus from the Kunbi peasant caste. He eventually established his headquarters at Pirana near Ahmedabad where he was buried.[29]

One tradition has it that his son Sayyid Nar Muhammad Shah (d. 1533) declared that Imam Shah was not merely a pir but the real Imam of the time.[30] His breakaway would have led to the emergence of the Imamshahis of Gujarat and Khandesh as a distinct group, separate from the Khojas and the term Satpanthi or 'followers of the true path', used in the ginans to describe all Ismailis came to be particularly reserved for the Imamshahis.[31]

The subsequent history of the sect is complicated by inner schisms which led to the formation of three other branches, respectively known as Athias, Satias, and Panchias,[32] not to mention the attempts of the various rulers of Gujarat and the Mughal governors to 'Islamize' these groups which had often fragmented the community. As a result, a separate mosque was created within the complex to accommodate changes to Sunni and Shia followers.[33] It is further believed that during the eighteenth, and perhaps the nineteenth century, the two groups attempted to win followers from each other's communities.[34] The Imamshahis have their centre at Pirana, as has been said above, and their own versions of the ginans.[35]

More than half a century having elapsed since Ivanow's study, it will be interesting to compare his valuable data with our preliminary research. For instance, according to his inquiries, Imamshahis do not acknowledge any historical connection with the Nizari Ismailis. Each branch attributes a different origin to the founder pirs, for example, those who appear now with a Ithna Ashari Shia identity will link the pirs with a Twelver Shia Imam.[36] The same author also alludes to the fact that 'many Hindu bodies are making efforts to reconvert the Satpanthis to Hinduism'.[37] However, among these, he mentions only the Arya Samaj.[38] Before going further it will be necessary to specify here that at the time of Ivanow's research as well as at the present time the members of the same sect, which is historically known as Imamshahi, appear with at least three distinct identities: the majority of disciples are Hindus from various castes, in particular from a section of the agricultural Kunbi community that now refer to themselves as Patels or Patidars,[39] while the remaining ones define themselves as Muslims, both Sunnis and Twelver Shias.[40] We will see that this interesting phenomenon is accounted for in various ways according to our informants. For the moment, suffice it to say that the efforts of the 'Hindu bodies' as mentioned by Ivanow were clearly aimed at those who termed themselves Hindus although they followed, in conformity with the Satpanthi ideal, a good many Muslim customs, such as the practice of burial and the erection of graves (*mazars*) in the Islamic fashion. For the sake of comparison it must be added that a similar campaign was launched at the beginning of our century by the Arya Samaj with its *suddhi* programme, among various other groups with 'liminal' identities.[41]

It is clear that, from the last decades of the nineteenth century onwards, defining or redefining one's identity as a group within the Indian society had become a crucial issue, where economical and political factors played a much more important role than religious considerations.[42] Questions which had never been raised in the past grew more and more significant and 'syncretic' or 'composite' traditions less and less acceptable, unless, as in the case of the Sikhs, they chose to proclaim themselves as religious movements outside the pale of Hinduism and Islam, which tended to be represented as hostile blocks. For centuries the Satpanthis, whether appearing outwardly as Sunnis, Shias, or Hindus, had more or less peacefully shared a sacred space.[43] In the new context which arose before and after Partition, a major split emerged within the community over questions of religious identity, which, once more, could not be dissociated from issues of power and money.

DIVIDING THE SACRED SPACE: CONFLICTING VOICES

A major event occurred in 1939 when, at the conclusion of a long court case (civil suit no. 168 filed in the court of the F.C. sub-judge at Ahmedabad on 13 February 1931), a Trust was created to resolve various disputes about the management of the dargah and the use of land and funds pertaining to the shrine. In this suit, a number of Patels lodged a complaint against the Hindu *guru* of the sect, Kaka Ramji Laxman, then supported by a few Muslim Sayyids.[44] The resultant Imam Shah Bawa Rauza Sansthan Committee consists of ten members, three Sayyids from different constituencies and seven Kacchi Patels—this ratio being calculated according to the proportion of Satpanthi followers (at present it is claimed about nine hundred thousand of which perhaps 85 per cent register themselves as Hindus and 15 per cent as Muslims). Later on the Trust was registered by the charity commissioner according to the Bombay Public Trust Act of 1950, under category E which is defined as 'cosmopolitan'.[45] The composition of the Trust was to ensure a fair management of the shrine, while the cosmopolitan nature of the sect was to be guaranteed by its registration under category E.[46]

However, in contemporary Indian the existence of a majority of Hindu members within a sect recognizing a Muslim pir as its founder could not but pose a serious challenge to all those who were eager to re-evaluate caste and religious identities. On the other hand, the sanctity of tradition, coupled with the legal protective framework, does not usually allow total freedom to the followers who wish to introduce certain changes. It is interesting to study the different responses which have been made to this challenge by various Indian communities, organizations, or sects over time.[47] Reconstructing one's own history according to the new ideology seems to be a universal strategy which has been widely resorted to through the centuries.

Let us now return to Pirana. Our first impression, undoubtedly a superficial one, when we first visited the shrine in January 1999, was that we were confronted with a Hindu versus Muslim conflict—the space, we felt at that time, was divided rather than shared. The large open courtyard, with its various sacred structures and pattern of square stones, conjured up the image of a huge chessboard at both ends of which the rival players, while seemingly ignoring each other, were engaged in a silent game. In front of the main tomb sat the white-clad Patels who had told us the 'true version of the story' that is the Hindu identity of the shrine, the best evidence of which was that the perpetual light (*akhand jyot*) burning in the samadhi was made of *ghi* (clarified butter) and not of oil which would have been the case if the shrine were a 'real' Muslim dargah. Just opposite the dark-clothed Sayyids, descendants of Imam Shah Bawa, sitting in front of the saint's *gaddi* (throne), a more modest structure, claimed that their tradition has been shamefully distorted; to prove this they had proudly stood up at the end of our conversation to recite the whole sacred genealogy in which, nobody could question it, only Muslim names appeared. When we had started our visit, even before reaching the main place of worship, our attention had been attracted by a model standing on a low platform, inside the enclosed courtyard. It represented various buildings, including what was visibly a temple topped by the classical *shikhara* superstructure. The Patels told us that it was the model of a new complex under construction not far from the village. It would include a *gurukul* school and a majestic temple referred to as *Jyoti mandir* or *Niskalanki Narayan ka Mandir*. Niskalanki, it was specified, was their main deity (*aradya dev*), the tenth incarnation of Vishnu whose cult was a essential part of the Satpanth. A similar place of worship already existed, opening on the same courtyard. It had been arranged inside the former resting place of Imam Shah (*dholia*) and was used for the daily *arati* (Hindu offering cult) as well as for the specifically Satpanthi ritual of holy water or ghat-pat. It was really breathtaking to see, so close to the Muslim dargah (even it has been renamed samadhi by the Patel worshippers) what strikingly looked like a Hindu *mandir*. If the walls depicted the miracles of Imam Shah and his life, the ceiling was entirely covered by colourful representations of the ten avatars of Vishnu and of other gods and goddesses. In the recess, which could have corresponded to the inner sanctum (*garbhagrha*) of a temple (but which was oriented towards the West as the *mihrab* in a mosque or a tomb) we could see a mural depicting the Hindu trinity, Vishnu, *Mahesh* (Shiva), and Brahma. On the gate one could read the words *puja khand* (prayer hall). The Patels added:

If you want more information you must see our Guru, the supreme leader of our Panth, Kaka Acharya Karsan Das Maharaj.... Then you must see the books we are selling at our small bookshop (these are our own publications) and please do no believe other people and do not read any other books since they are not genuine....

We promised to buy all the books and the shrine being closed for some time, went to partake of the common meal served in the community's *langar*, in the company of numerous Patels and, to our surprise, a family of Agakhani Ismaili Khojas. But when the shrine reopened, instead of going immediately to see the supreme Guru, we re-entered the open courtyard with the intention of drawing a map of the various sacred structures. And there, unexpectedly, we were captured by the 'enemy'. Under the shelter of the *chajja* covered by a white cloth upon which shone words of protestation in bright red paint, sat a few young and middle-aged men, most of them wearing dark-coloured clothes, some of them ostentatiously displaying their Muslim identity by wearing the usual laced cap, whereas, curiously enough, all the custodians of the various tombs (*mujavars*), whether Hindus or Muslims, were wearing exactly the same white cloths and 'Nehru' cap. When we reached the spot the Sayyid players had been sitting regularly on this side of the chessboard for about two hundred and eighty days in *dharna*. In order to protest, they had created the Imamshahi Sadat Committee headed by M.M. Sayyid and Nuruddin Sayyid.

'Our heritage (indeed they are descendants of the large Imam Shah family) has been hijacked,' they explained, giving us a tract which we carefully read. It began with the following words: 'this shrine is a symbol of secularism and national integration...now this shrine has become a place of communalism and fascism'. And then we had to listen to another version of the Pirana tradition—Imam Shah, as we were told, was the son of the Sufi pir Hasan Kabiruddin who came to Gujarat from Multan. He traced his descent back to Imam Jaffar al-Sadiq and his son Ismail, and that is why he himself and all his descendants, including the present Sayyids, are known as 'Jaffri Ismailis'. At first we silently triumphed, tempted to conclude that our informant admitted, directly or indirectly, the Shia Ismaili origin of the sect. But we were soon disillusioned—Ismaili? Did it mean that that Imam Shah was a Shia? The reply came immediately—he was a Sufi, neither a Sunni nor a Shia, a detail which overthrew all our former convictions.[48] And, as if the blow were not mighty enough to shatter the rest of our illusions, one of the men added: 'we are Sunnis'. And he pointed to the mosque where he and his brothers offered regular prayers (*namaz*) five times a day. After this interruption he went on with the story of Imam Shah.

According to him, the saint converted many Hindus, and entrusted to one of them the custody of the dargah. These people, who are celibate, are referred to as kakas which means 'servant' in Persian. Why should a mere servant entitle himself 'Guru', 'Acharya' and 'Maharaj'? Karsan Das, we were told, had undertaken a series of changes which were not in conformity with the Satpanth—painting the Om sign everywhere, publishing a revised version of the traditional literature, transforming the dholia into a temple with idols, while image worship is strictly prohibited in this religion, changing the name of the place into 'Pirana Prena Pith' and, still worse, the founder of the movement into a Hindu pir.[49] If these Patels were converted by Imam Shah, we enquired, why do they do that? The answer came unhesitatingly—these people are Guptis... they look outwardly as Hindus, in reality they still follow (yes, even now) a number of Muslim customs which are a part of the Satpanth.

This declaration comes as a most exciting revelation, although it sounds strangely familiar to us—the Gupti phenomenon is well-known in the history of the Nizaris of the subcontinent and till recently many Khojas concealed themselves under the guise of Hindus. Thus, according to the Sayyids the present identity of the Patels was essentially a form of taqiyya. Conversion to Islam 'really' took place. Now what happens is that, under the influence of fundamentalist Hindu bodies, they want to revert to a full-fledged form of Hinduism, a fact which we must acknowledge, had already been noted by Ivanow. According to Sayyid:

> The Kaka is a life member of the VHP. This fundamentalist organization is attempting to take over the shrine. Our opinion on the subject is clear: if himself and his supporters want to introduce changes of this type they had better abandon the place and go somewhere else to follow their new religion.

These words had led us to formulate an interesting hypothesis—if the Hindu members of the Panth were in reality crypto-Muslims (the Patels), was not the Sayyid Sunnism originally also a form of taqiyya? Imam Shah himself had married the daughter of a (Sunni Sufi) Suhrawardi saint, and one of the wives of his son, Muhammad Shah, was the daughter of the equally Sunni Sultan of Ahmedabad. Would these marital links have been possible at that period if both pirs had openly acknowledged their Shia Ismaili identity?

One can surmise that in the course of time, what was now happening to the Patels had earlier taken place with these Sayyids; from a kind of Gupti Sunnism they had passed into a state of more overt Sunnism. Later, looking across the chessboard at the white Patels who stared blankly at us, we were reminded of our promise and took leave of our informants. And ultimately we went upstairs to the Kaka's 'retreat'. There we bowed in front of an imposing character wearing a flowing white beard, a ochre-coloured turban and displaying a red tilak proudly on his forehead. The Maharaj was quietly sitting on a bed near a window, in a modern room equipped with a cooler and a telephone. He greeted us with a smile, which made it difficult to believe that he was a 'Hindu hardliner'.

If we had not studied the historical background of the Imamshahi sect and had no knowledge of the Ismaili tradition, we would have been in the same position as our imaginary visitor or pilgrim, that is to say in a state of total confusion. But the main elements of the Satpanth were already familiar to us, owing to the fact that they were basically the same as in the Nizari Khoja tradition. Niskalank, Atharva Veda, ginans and many other names and concepts reminded us of one essential factor— the acculturation of the Ismaili idiom in South Asia. It was clear that, if one chose to stress these 'Hinduized' patterns and to play down or leave out the Islamic themes, the sect had a decidedly 'orthodox' Hindu appearance.

Imam Shah, according to Karsan Das, was 'a Sufi saint' (a definition which also occurs occasionally in the official literature of the Patels). When we asked 'what do you mean by Sufi'?, and with the dim hope that he would after all acknowledge some sort of Islamic connection, the Acharya rejoined: ' Sufi like Kabir, Nanak, the nine Nath yogis...' However original this definition of Sufism sounded to us (who had always naively believed that Sufism was the 'mystical dimension' of Sunni, and to a lesser extent, of Shia Islam) we had to accept it as one of the major moves of the invisible chess game, one which enabled the Hindu side to reconstruct history. The Kaka then continued: 'Sufism means brotherhood, absence of any discrimination, call these Sufic ideas or Vedic ideas, this is all the same...'. However, to our great relief, he spontaneously admitted that Imam Shah's father was Hasan Kabiruddin from Multan (another Muslim name) and that he had married Fatima, the daughter of a Sufi saint but added, as if he wished to underplay these well-known historical facts, that the saint was to be viewed as an avatar of the god Brahma, an idea which, we knew, perfectly coincide with the Nizari Ismaili 'patterns of transformation',[50] equating the Imam with Vishnu and his representatives, the pirs with Brahma. The Acharya's discourse was, after all, reassuring—Imam Shah had had, among his disciples, not only Hindus, such as Bhabha Ram, Kiki Bai, Naya Kaka, but also the Persian Hazar Beg; the shrine was referred to by Hindus as samadhi or mandir, by Muslims as *rauza* or dargah, the Guru could be equally called pir or *Bawa*. The main *mantra* of the sect was '*Om Niskalanki Naranaya namaha*' but, concluded Karsan Das, it was also possible to use the words '*Pir Shah*' (as, we both silently remembered, in the Nizari tradition), and even to recite the Kalma. Gratified by these revelations, we started to think that, after all, the chief accusations levied by the Sayyids from across the Pirana chessboard were a little too far-fetched—the Kaka was not at all appearing as a fundamentalist, a fierce exponent of Hindutva.

During the following days, however, we started to read the 'official' Satpanthi literature sold at Pirana. It was amazingly different from what the Kaka had told us, except the name of Imam Shah himself and the adjective 'Sufi' (but again in the sense used by the Acharya) Islamic characters and elements were totally absent. Imam Shah had become 'Satguru Sri Imam Shah Maharaj' portrayed in the pictures available at the bookshop as a saint with a long black beard, holding a rosary in his right hand and displaying the same red tilak which decorated the forehead of Karsan Das (also Maharaj). His ancestors, and even his father, were mentioned nowhere, as if he had directly fallen from Heaven. There was not even the slightest allusion to the existence of Sayyids, or other Muslim disciples.

We had been told by the Patels to ignore all the other books which were not sold here. Thanks to this precious advice we had learned of the existence of rival publications. The Sayyids had their own books telling the same stories in their own way, and to make matters worse, we learned of the existence of a secret locked chamber at Pirana sheltering heaps of dusty books and manuscripts containing a third version of the same story, the oldest one. The key to this 'archive' was carefully kept by a third party who presided, invisible, over this silent game of chess, the man who claimed to be the legitimate *sajjada-nishin*, the physical and spiritual heir of Imam Shah, although he was not recognized as such by all Satpanthi followers, whether Hindus or Sayyids. However, we had to meet him to try to harmonize the disturbing cacophony of all these conflicting voices.

THE INVISIBLE PIR: A CONTEMPORARY CASE OF TAQIYYA

In the end, when the clouds of ignorance were dispersed we saw clearly that, as in many other cases, the Pirana dispute was not exactly a Hindu versus Muslim conflict. According to the Hindu nationalist reconstruction of Indian history (curiously initiated by the British author James Tod), Maharana Pratap, the Hindu ruler of Mewar (present Rajasthan), was fighting a battle against the Mughal emperor Akbar for the liberation of the Hindu nation from the tyranny of Muslim rule.[51] Although this version is still unfortunately the most popular, the facts, as recorded by non-sectarian historians, are somewhat different. On one side we have the rebellious Pratap helped by an army of equally rebellious Muslim Pathans (Afghans), on the other the ambitious Hindu *Raja* of Amber sent by the none less ambitious Akbar. Instead of this supposedly eternal Hindu–Muslim enmity, we have thus a battle for territory and power between two coalitions whose religious identity is of little concern. Somewhat similarly, the following facts were gradually revealed to us after a few meetings with the above-mentioned 'third power'—there were Muslim Sayyids siding with the Hindu Patels and their elected Kaka, and Hindu Patels supporting the protesting Sayyids. So it was not a game opposing the 'white' Patels to the 'black' Sayyids.

If we had not known earlier of the existence of the 'invisible Guru' we would probably never had met him, as neither the Patels, nor the Kaka, and not even the Sayyids had made the slightest allusions to him. His photograph did not appear anywhere, contrary to the ubiquitous picture of the Hindu Acharya, and there was no trace of his existence either in the new 'official' literature. The Sayyids had finally acknowledged his existence when answering, rather reluctantly, our question: 'and what about Pirzada Shamsuddin (the heir of Imamshah who claims to be the sajjada-nishin)? They preferred not to talk about him as he had treacherously 'passed over to the enemy'.

This was not at all surprising if one knew, as we later discovered, that the ignored Pirzada had supported Karsan Das, the present Kaka, during the 1987 election to the *gaddi* while the opposing Sayyids, who had proposed another man, Pachan Kaka as their candidate, had been defeated. So after all, if Karsan Das had behind him an invisible Sayyid the rebellious Sayyids had their hidden Kaka.

The Pirzada's address and phone numbers had been supplied to one of us by one Ismaili informant. We called, started to talk in Hindi and were answered in flawless English: 'you can come tomorrow at one o'clock...' His office (the seat of the Pirana Gurukul Education Trust) was located in a lane near one of the main streets of Ahmedabad, crowded with smaller and bigger shops, bustling with incessant traffic. We were ushered into a tiny room where we were welcomed by a neat late middle-aged man wearing a coat and a shirt in the Western fashion, sitting behind a desk like a businessman or the manager of a modern company. We were to meet him three more times and these sessions would extend over long hours. He was like the director of a theatre who would reveal to us the secret mechanisms behind the stage.

His father, Sayyid Ahmad Ali Kakhi, has been a prominent writer of the Satpanth and most of the copies of his works which had not been sold or given to the Satpanthi disciples were piled up in the famous locked chamber of Pirana, waiting for better times. Luckily for us, we were able to acquire a few of them which the Pirzada kept in his own store, at Ahmedabad. Shamsuddin said:

> My father was fighting to rescue the Satpanth, and his battle was fought with the pen...I am continuing his work, but according to the necessity of the time, I have to do it through politics. Karsan Das, who was my candidate for the election to the gaddi, could win only thanks to my power, but his main rival, Pachan Kaka, and the Sayyid party who supported him could not accept their defeat and started to create trouble. The protest of these Sayyids is not dictated by religious but political considerations: what they want ultimately is simply to overthrow Karsan and replace him by their own man, Pachan.

However, our informant admitted that the greatest danger was coming from the various fundamentalist bodies which attempted to draw the members of the sect into the orbit of Hindutva. Some villagers had already, under their influence, started to abandon the 'True Path', taken over a portion of the land attached to the original shrine and started their own temples with idol worship. The dividing line between the cult of the specifically Satpanthi Niskalanki Narayan (the tenth incarnation of Vishnu) performed in the *nirgun* way without the presence of an image[52] and the worship of Lakshminarayan, who was a pan-Hindu modern form of the Brahmanical Vishnu, represented by an idol, could be wafer thin. But a greater peril was looming ahead. Karsan Das was ambitious. There was no denying that he had made a hazardous rapprochement with the Vishwa Hindu Parishad (VHP) and its allies, although it had been allegedly done for taqiyya purposes, that is to protect his followers and prevent the eventual dissolution of the Satpanthi. Being thus recognized and approved, in its new revised version, by the exponents of Hindutva, the sect founded by Imamshah could survive and its 'humble servant' (kaka in Persian) would be promoted to the rank of a real Acharya Maharaj, in other words one of the leading sants of the VHP. But now the enemy was within. 'I had told him not to go so far...' declared the Pirzada. But he himself never intervened directly, for fear of communal riots. He thought it wise to sit here, silently pulling the strings through letters, phone calls, and meetings with the various personalities of the political world who were his friends. He went to Pirana only three times a year. In other words he was himself obliged to practise taqiyya.

Shamsuddin was perfectly aware of the historical link of his sect with the Nizari branch of Ismailism which developed in the subcontinent. The pirs who are also revered by the Khojas, such as Shams or Sadruddin, he explained, were all Satpanthis. After Kabiruddin there had been a split; according to him those who were to be known as

Aghakhani Khojas drifted away from the 'True Path' while Imam Shah's line remained faithful to the original religious message. What was amazing, though, was that the Pirzada insisted on the fact that he, also, was a Sunni, that the tradition was a Sunni (Sufi) one, and that the influence of Shiism came much later.

Karsan Das, he explained, was a Guru only in the sense of religious teacher, he was not like a real pir,[53] which only a physical and spiritual heir of Imam Shah could be. However, he knew all the secrets of the Satpanth, including its Muslim elements, perfectly well. In the Satpanth and its very conception of meta-history (as, we thought in the Nizari Khoja tradition) Islam and Hinduism were closely interwoven. For instance, among the descendants of Krishna (the Imam of the time in the *Dwapar Yuga* in Hindustan) who went to Arabia were Muhammad, Ali, and all their sons and grandsons. 'Most of my Hindu *murid*s', said Shamsuddin, as if he wished to account, in another way, for the publication of revised versions of the former literature expurgated from Muslim elements, 'do not read texts with Islamic contents, they would not understand. But those who long for the true spiritual knowledge can have access to these things, first through a *mukhi* (an important functionary of the sect at the local level, the one who also leads the ghat-pat ritual) then through Karsan Das and eventually, for the final and total initiation, they have to come to me only...'.

So there were various stages of initiation—from the basic ritual through which each Satpanthi child was integrated into his community, to these more esoteric phases which enabled him to obtain the 'ultimate' knowledge. But even the murid who had gone successfully through these stages kept his earlier appearance, his customs, his Hindu name etc.

These words, as we almost immediately realized, were of exceptional importance. In fact it amounted to acknowledging the fact that these Hindu murids were Guptis (a term which had been used by the Sayyids as well). However, it must be stressed that Shamsuddin denied that the process could be called 'conversion'—embracing the Satpanth and acceding to its ultimate revelation did not amount to being 'converted'. One remained Hindu, Sunni, or Shia nonetheless.

Shamsuddin, the 'invisible pir', had decided to let the players go on without interfering directly:

See, for example, the fate of an important book written by my father, *Yogya vidhi*...the Patels of Pirana has issued another expurgated version of it which they sell openly at their bookshop, while the original *Yogya vidhi* (which is no more distributed) is with me only. Now the rival Sayyid party, the supporters of the defeated Pachan Kaka, have published their version and recently filed a suit; they are showing that the new 'official' book has drifted away so much from the Satpanthi tenets that it is in fact another religion which is reflected in it...Karsan Das, of course was embarrassed, so to protect himself he was obliged to produce my father's version and to declare that the book sold at Pirana had been released without his permission.... The original version, no one could deny, was representing the ideas of our tradition. The Kala could no longer be accused of having betrayed the Satpanth. So, in the long run, the old Satpanthi truths, which have been concealed, do surface once more... I have always believed it would be so. I have dedicated my life to this purpose....

FACING THE SAFFRON BRIGADE: HINDUS REINVENT TAQIYYA FOR THEIR OWN PURPOSE

Should the alliance struck by Karsan Kaka with the Sangh Parivar and his active membership in the VHP be seriously considered as a modern form of taqiyya? One has to remember only the legendary Ismaili pirs of Hindustan concealing themselves under the guise of yogis (some of them may have even become members of the Nath sect) or Sufis, in the latter case even taking formal initiation into some 'orthodox' *tariqa* to see that this may not be so absurd as it seems.[54]

Whatever the truth, one cannot deny that the 'Saffron Brigade', on its side, has set for itself very clear goals. Having produced another version of the earlier Aryasamaji suddhi,[55] the *dharm parivatran*, it continues to function as a 'factory for conversions of various communities to (their form of) Hinduism'.[56] According to the protesting Sayyid Party, the events which took place at Ayodhya on 6 December 1992 were like a starting signal for the Hindu hardliners; they would not (or could not after the destruction of the Babri Masjid) demolish the mosque at Pirana, instead, they began a slower process of undermining. They prompted the Kaka to cut its electricity and water supply and to forbid the Sayyids to have access to the common kitchen, forcing them to start their own separate langar. The Sayyids also started to perform the ghat-pat ritual separately. Since the Bharatiya Janata party (BJP) had formed the government in Gujarat, the Sangh Parivar could act much more freely. If one believes the representatives of the Sadaat Committee, it was also in 1992 that the Akhil Bharatya Sant Parishad, an organization within the VHP, met at Sarsa Gurugadi, district Kheda.

Karsan Kaka had become the president of the Parishad (henceforth ABSP) for the Western zone. It is said that the committee decided at that time to expurgate Islamic symbols and traditions from the Satpanth. The next meeting of the ABSP which was the ninth one, took place in Jaipur and for the venue of the tenth one, Pirana was selected. In 1995 another extraordinary event occurred, the Bharatiya Vedic Dharm Samelan which met near Mumbai. There the ambitious Kaka, who decidedly emerged as a powerful exponent of the Hindutva ideology, was seen, in a photograph, nearly hand in hand with none other than the working president of the VHP himself, Ashok Singhal. There the triumph of the Acharya of Pirana was total when 'a number of doubts concerning the sect were cleared up' and the Satpanth tradition was declared to be one of the many 'Vedic *sampradayas*' (religious traditions) of India. To celebrate the victory of Hinduism there was a magnificent procession where the Guru of the Satpanthis was seen majestically seated on an elephant. Eventually in May 1997 in the Gujarati province of Kutch, the thirteenth session of the ABSP commemorated as a grand event the tenth anniversary of the election of Karsan Das. This event as well as the Vedic Samelan are the subject of a special issue of the magazine *Satpanth Jyoti* and of a commemorative volume issued at Pirana. Both the volume and the magazine are abundantly illustrated and among the religious leaders and political personalities one can identify prominent members of the Saffron Brigade.[57] In the light of these events it is easier to understand the project of the temple cum gurukul, the transformation of the dholia of Imam Shah into a puja khand, the release of expurgated and revised versions of the Satpanthi literature and so on.

Actually, it is possible to view the whole issue in more than one light. The VHP and its supporters may think that they have drawn back those 'syncretic Hindus' into the fold of Hinduism by forcing them to eliminate the Islamic elements or persuading them that their tradition had always been Hindu but had been distorted and misconstrued by the Muslims.[58] A leader of the Swami Narayan sect linked to the VHP,[59] for example, goes as far as to declare that, every doubt should be dispelled. Imam Shah was never a Muslim, he was born in a Hindu Brahmin family[60] but had to conceal his identity under an Islamic guise for fear of persecution. Here it will not be out of place of mention a similar phenomenon. The re-Hinduized followers of the Nizar panth in Rajasthan, faced with the difficult problem of revering a Muslim pir named Shams reconstructed his story explaining that he was in reality a Brahmin saint who dressed as a *fakir* to avoid being killed by the Muslims![61] One cannot help thinking that this 'inverted' case of taqiyya has been inspired by the original tradition of Ismaili taqiyya.

Ultimately it is difficult to decide who among the 'Hindu' Satpanthi followers who have joined the ranks of the VHP sincerely performs the Ismaili taqiyya as a faithful defender of the Imamshahi sect. Some 'Hindu' members of the sect claim to have on the contrary always concealed their identity to save Hinduism from the maltreatment of earlier Muslim rulers. Actually, the younger generations may not be aware of their Islamic roots and of the meaning of taqiyya.

THE SANDAL CEREMONY AT PIRANA

Sharing a Sacred Space

Each year, on the twenty-fifth day of the month of Ramzan, the sandal ceremony or sacred bathing of the tomb of Imam Shah is celebrated with much solemnity on the occasion of the death anniversary of the saint, also referred to as *Urs*. When we arrived in the morning the open courtyard was already bustling with activities. But in the late afternoon the crowd became thicker, as the time for the sandalwood ceremony (*chandan vidhi*) was nearing. The formal members of the Satpanth are far from being the only visitors to the dargah. If the opposing parties had decided to engage in a relentless war, the ordinary devotees had firmly resolved to celebrate the Urs as usual. Clad in white drapery, a Hindu worshipper of Imam Shah who was not a follower of the Panth (he was from the Rabari caste) was repeatedly circumambulating the main shrine. He explained to one of us that he had been cured of a certain disease by the grace of the pir and was coming regularly to the dargah after his vow had been fulfilled. Sunnis from the nearby villages were devotedly offering chaddars (ornate clothes laid on the graves of Sufi saints), incense, and flowers to the grave of Hazar Beg, the Persian disciple of Imam Shah. As I approached the huge flagstaff on the top of which an immaculate white flag was fluttering in the breeze (was it white because of the Suhrawardi connection or because it was the colour of the Atharva Veda?), I caught sight of a group of women sitting on its platform and reading the Quran. They invited us to join them and seen revealed themselves to be Twelver Shias from the Nurshahi Momin Jamat.[62] When we came back to Imam Shah's tomb, which was the main centre of attraction, we saw a saffron-clad *sadhu* standing near the gate, rosary in hand, murmuring some mantras, while a fakir wearing black clothes and a black turban was performing a similar exercise.

This was the striking, reassuring image of a peacefully shared space. Early in the afternoon the Kaka had come to perform certain rituals before returning to the first floor where he quietly sat on a chair in front of his room. In the sacred enclosure the white Nanak Das Patel, the *karbhari* (religious functionary in charge of the shrine) was standing in front of the gate to the samadhi in the golden light shed by the last rays of the sun, while the dark Nuruddin Sayyid, one of the leaders of the

Sadat Committee, was thoughtfully pacing the platform in the shade, behind the shrine.

Strange as it may seem, the Pirzada had not come to honour the ceremony. However, we could feel his invisible presence everywhere, as when he had told us, during our last interview: '*zamana kharab hai...*' (we are living in a dark age), 'but it will be soon the end of the Kali Yuga and the time will change....'

Endnotes

1. Our thanks are due to our respective husbands, A.S. Khan and Martin Moir, who accompanied us on our various trips to Gujarat and fully and fruitfully participated in our research work.
2. F. Daftary, *The Isma'ilis, Their History and Doctrines* (Cambridge, Delhi, 1990), p. 22.
3. The authors are currently preparing a comprehensive study of the Imamshahi sect.
4. It would be interesting to note that at the shrine of the goddess Ai Mata at Bilara, in Rajasthan, the case is exactly the reverse. A Hindu devotee visiting the temple would be surprised to read the following words engraved on a marble slab: dargah of Ai Mata. For more details see D.S. Khan, *Conversions and Shifting Identities* (Delhi, 1997), pp. 175–86.
5. See for example 'Distorting a Tradition', *Rashtriya Sahara*, (May 1988), pp. 24–5 and 'The Pirana Shrine becomes a Bone of Contention', *Indian Express*, Ahmedabad, 19 April 1998.
6. In 'Distorting a Tradition', p. 24, article mentioned in note 5 above.
7. S. Nanjiani, *Khoja Vrttant* (Ahmedabad, 1892, reproduced 1918); J.M. Campbell (ed.), *Gazetteer of the Bombay Presidency, Gujarat Population: Musulmans and Parsis*, vol. IX, pt. II (Guragon, 1988, reproduced 1990), pp. 66–7; W. Ivanow, 'The Sect of Imamshah in Gujarat', *JBBRS*, vol. 12 (1936), pp. 19–70; F. Daftary, *The Isma'ilis*; J.N. Hollister, *The Shi'a of India* (Delhi, 1953, reproduced 1979); A Nanji, *The Nizari Ismaili Tradition in the Indo-Pakistan Subcontinent* (Delmar-New York, 1978); C. Shackle and Z. Moir, *Ismaili Hymns of South Asia: An Introduction to the Ginans* (London, 1992).
8. Unfortunately, this is not the case for other probable offshoots of Nizari Ismailism, such as the Nizar Panth, the Bishnoi Panth etc. See D.S. Khan, *Conversions*.
9. B. Lewis, *The Assassins, a Radical Sect in Islam* (London, 1967, reproduced 1985).
10. Daftary, *The Isma'ilis*, p. 5.
11. D. N. Maclean *Religion and Society in Arab Sind* (Leiden, 1989), pp. 22–36.
12. Nanji, *The Nizari Ismaili Tradition*, p. 68.

13. A. Nanji, 'Ritual and Symbolic Aspects of Islam in African Context', in R.C. Martin (ed.) *Islam in Local Contexts* (Leiden, E.J. Brill, 1982).

14. Shackle and Moir, *Ismaili Hymns of South Asia*.

15. For the concept of meta-history in Shia and Ismaili philosophies, see H. Corbin, *Histoire de la philosophie islamique* (Paris, 1986), pp. 98–107.

16. Corbin, ibid., pp. 78–85.

17. F. Daftray, *A Short History of the Ismailis* (Edinburgh, 1992), pp. 139–40, 394.

18. Shackle and Moir, *Ismaili Hymns of South Asia*, pp. 157–9.

19. Ibid., p. 186.

20. Ibid., pp. 5–8.

21. Ivanow, 'The Sect of Imamshah'.

22. Khan, *Conversions*.

23. J.C. Masselos, 'The Khojas of Bombay: The Defining of Formal Membership Criteria During the Nineteenth Century', in Imtiaz Ahmad (ed.), *Caste and Social Stratification Among Muslims in India* (Delhi, 1978).

24. Masselos, 'The Khojas of Bombay, and H.A. Rose, *A Glossary of the Tribes and Castes of the Punjab and North-West Frontier Province*. 3 vols (Delhi, 1919, reprinted 1990), p. 403.

25. S. Mayaram, *Resisting Regimes: Myth, Memory and the shaping of a Muslim Identity* (New Delhi, 1997), pp. 36–52.

26. On this fascinating issue see M. Boivin, 'The Reform of Islam in Ismaili Shi'ism from 1885 to 1957' in Delvoye F. Nalini (ed.), *Confluences of Culture* (Delhi, 1994).

27. There are the odd references in various publications, but the only study devoted entirely to this subject is Ivanow, 'The Sect of Imamshah'.

28. Ivanow, ibid.

29. Shackle and Moir, *Ismaili Hymns of South Asia*, pp. 7–8.

30. Ibid.

31. Ibid.

32. Ivanow, 'The Sect of Imamshah', p. 48.

33. The mosque which is located within the dargah complex was probably built during Aurangzeb's rule. The issue connected with the Islamization of the Nizari Khojas during the medieval Muslim rule has not been studied till now.

34. Ivanow, 'The Sect of Imamshah'.

35. Ibid.

36. Ibid., p. 25.

37. Ibid., p. 20.

38. Ibid., p. 59.

39. Campbell, *Gazetteer*, pp. 66–7, and R.E. Enthoven, *The Tribes and Castes and Bombay* (Delhi, 1920, reproduced 1990), pp. 150–5.

40. However it is necessary to add that these Muslim followers were also originally Hindus who had embraced the Imamshahi faith before adopting the Sunni or Twelver Shia identity, probably in the seventeenth century, and later on, built the mosque. (Ivanow, 'The Sect of Imamshah', *passim*).

41. Ram Narayan Contractor, the author of a book heavily criticizing the Imamshahi sect, was himself a Satpanthi who became a member of the Arya Samaj, underwent *suddhi*, and later on came close to the Swami Narayan religious reformist movement.

42. As suggested by the history of the Imamshahi sect, land disputes have always been crucial in this respect. Besides, one should not forget the role played by a British officer, Alexander Forbes who, as Tod had done for Rajasthan, sought to reconstruct the glorious part of Gujarat in order to give a distinct identity to this region. Forbes worked with the Gujarat poet Dalpatram Daya who edited an important journal called *Buddhi Prakash* in which an article on the Imamshahis was published in 1871.

43. It seems that in the past 'communal' conflicts occurred between Sunnis and Shias.

44. The term *kaka* which means 'servant' in Persian is used to refer to the Hindu leader of the sect. It is interesting to note that in the case of the recent conflict which we will examine further, most Sayyids are opposing the Kaka.

45. Category A applies to Hindu, Jain, and Sikh institutions, B to Muslim ones etc.

46. According to one of our informants, the registration under this category is being questioned as a result of a recent civil suit in which it has been proposed to register the shrine of Pirana under the *waqf* board which takes care of all Islamic places of worship.

47. Khan (1996) and (1997), *op. cit.*

48. With the exception maybe of the *be-sharia* Qalandars, wandering dervishes who do not follow the Islamic law or sharia. The Sufis generally belong to a particular order of *tariqat*, whether Sunni or Shia. For Indian Sufism see for example S.A.A. Rizvi, *A History of Suffis; in India*, 2 vols (Delhi, 1978, reproduced 1986).

49. It will be interesting to compare these facts with those found in the Rajasthani traditions of the Bisnoi and the Ramdev sects: the mausoleum of the saint Jambha, originally referred to only as *Mukam* (a word which usually refers to a Muslim graveyard) has been now re-Hinduized into 'Mutkidham Mukam' (from *mukti*, liberation, salvation and *dham*, sacred pilgrimage centre). Similarly, Baba Ramdev is traditionally called 'Hindu pir'.

50. T. Kassam, 'Syncretism on the model of the figure-ground: A Study of Pir Shams' Brahma Prakasa', in K.K. Young (ed.), *Hermeneutical Paths to the Sacred Worlds of India—Essays in Honour of Robert W. Stevension* (Atlanta, 1994), pp. 231–41.

51. J. Tod, *Annals and Antiquities of Rajasthan* (Delhi, 1829–32, reproduced 1983), pp. 253–64.

52. In the Indian devotional tradition (*bhakti*) the Nirgun or non-qualified God is opposed to the Sagun (qualified) Deity who can incarnate himself and be represented in the form of a sacred image.

53. Although, as we learned recently, before the re-Hinduization of the tradition, Karsan Das had been given the title of 'Pir Karim Kaka'.

54. Nanji, *The Nizari Ismaili Tradition*, p. 68 and D.S. Khan, *Conversions*, p. 34.

55. K.W. Jones, *The New Cambridge History of India*, Vol. III, pt. 1 (Cambridge, Cambridge University Press, 1989), pp. 100–3.

56. We are paraphrasing here the Arya Samajists who, on the contrary, once accused the Satpanth of being 'a factory fort converting the Hindus to Islam'.

57. We thank Christophe Jaffrelot for helping us to identify these characters and for his precious information on the Lakshiminarayan temples.

58. The case of the Ramdev sect is strikingly similar.

59. This Vaishnava sect, to which many Gujarati Hindus are affiliated, was founded by Swami Narayan in 1875. Curiously enough, according to an Imamshahi oral tradition, the founder had become a Satpanthi whose role was to collect the *dasondh* (obligatory tithe) from the members of the community. One day he is said to have run away with the money and eventually created his own religious movement. See A. Khaki, *Satpanth Yagya* Viddi (Pirana, 2nd ed.), p. 57. Be it as it may, many Patels who were previously affiliated to the Satpanth became followers of Swami Narayan.

60. After the non-sectarian movements founded by Kabir and Dadu (fifteenth and sixteenth centuries) became full-fledged Hindu Panths, a Hindu Brahmin origin was attributed to both saints.

61. Khan, *Conversions*, p. 69.

62. The members of the Nurshahi Momin Jamat seem to have been only recently converted to Twelver Shia Islam (Ithna Aharis), whereas the Sayyidkhanis represent the main the 'original' Ithna-Ashari stream within the Imamshahi tradition: while the former are 'faithful to the main shrine of Imamshahi' but have given up all Satpanthi rituals, the latter are connected with the Athia branch and have their own sajjada-nishin.

8

Sikhs and Muslims in the Punjab

W.H. McLeod

The migrations which took place between India and Pakistan in 1947–8 were accompanied by massacres on both sides of the border. No one knows how many were killed or kidnapped, but a moderate Sikh account gives the following figures. Ajit Singh Sarhadi in his *Punjabi Suba* writes:

> There could not be any estimate of those killed in this unprecedented civil war between the peoples of the two partitioned parts of the country, nor is there any estimate. But [the] assessment of those who saw the conditions is that six lakh people must have been killed on both sides of the border. There is no doubt, however, that five million Hindus and Sikhs, which included the entire Sikh population of the area, migrated from West Pakistan and a large number of Muslims left India. A modest estimate of the Sikhs killed in the massacre can be stated as nearly two lakhs, about two and a half percent of the entire Sikh population. About Rs 700 crores' worth of property was left in Pakistan. About a lakh of girls on both sides were kidnapped and converted.[1]

Sarhadi is an Akali and for that reason his figures would have to be regarded as suspect. Opinions concerning the number who died range from the official estimate of approximately a quarter of a million up to those of other eye-witness observers who put the figure at more than a million. Overall, however, Sarhadi's views are not dramatically out of alignment with the more cautious observers and for that reason it seems appropriate that we can accept him as at least a rough guide to the results of this episode in the history of the Punjab. His description does, at least, capture something of the horror associated with Partition.

The purpose of this essay is to examine relations between Sikhs and Muslims in the Punjab during the period prior to the partition of India in 1947. In particular, it is to seek an explanation for the pronounced hostility between the two, a hostility which was plainly evident at the time of Partition in 1947 and which has continued in the years which have followed. The subject is approached chiefly from the Sikh perspective and for that reason it may be held to represent a partial point of view. That risk is certainly present and every effort must be made to avoid it. Whether the attempt has been successful each reader must judge for himself or herself. The justification for making the attempt is that a distinctively Sikh point of view is all too often overlooked.

Everyone with any knowledge of India knows that immediately prior to Partition, relations between the Sikhs and the Muslims were manifestly strained. Likewise everyone with any knowledge of the Partition is aware of the slaughter which took place on either side. Muslims killed Sikhs and Hindus during the winter of 1947–8, Sikhs and Hindus killed Muslims. How are such extreme feelings and their resultant actions to be explained? To attribute them to the events leading up to Partition is not enough. Any explanation must go deeper than this.

Each side claims that the killings were started by the other side, and to this day there is no agreement concerning the issue. This particular question we shall not be considering in this essay. Instead, we shall focus on the causes of the enmity which separated the two and do our best to disentangle them. At first sight this seems to be not as easy as we had hoped. Try to find evidence of the post-Partition massacres and one runs into immediate difficulty. Only rarely will one find anything like a frank account of the episode, for with rare exceptions neither side has been prepared to speak openly about the experience. There is, however, no need to seek the causes by concentrating on the events of 1947–8. The real causes are much older than that.

The reasons for the enmity separating Hindu and Muslim have been well explored. The subject is a complex one and it arouses all the usual prejudices on both sides, but at least the attempt has been made many times. There is, it is true, much ground to be covered before agreement is reached. Is primary blame to be attached to the fundamental differences between the two cultural patterns? Was it not rather the intentions of Jinnah which lay at the root of the division? Should Gandhi or Nehru or Patel bear the primary blame? Or was it a mixture of these factors plus several more? We are still far from agreement, but at least the issue continues to be argued.

But what of the Sikhs? They, like the Muslims whom they confronted, were true Punjabis. This surely served to draw the two closer together. And the distinctive religion of the Sikhs had certainly evolved well beyond its Hindu roots, bringing it closer to Islam. The Sikhs worship the one Akal Purakh just as the Muslims worship the one Allah. The two religions certainly are not the same, but nor are they as different as the gap separating Muslims from most Hindus. In the *Adi Granth* the fifth Guru of the Sikhs, Arjan, preserved the works of two Muslims and to one of these, Baba Farid, later generations of Sikhs have given considerable prominence, acclaiming him as a person truly inspired. The Sikhs are indeed a people of the Book. The *Adi Granth* may not be the same book as the Quran but there are certainly resemblances to be found in them.

Moreover, the Sikhs had only recently emerged from the Singh Sabha movement, that period of radical religious change which included amongst its prime features the insistent emphasis of the Sikh reformers that Sikhs are 'not' Hindus. *Ham Hindu Nahin*, that highly significant booklet by a leading Singh Sabha figure Kahn Singh Nabha, had become a rallying call for all who regarded themselves as true followers of the ten Gurus.[2] Out of the confrontation between Sikhs which marked the Singh Sabha movement, one of the contending groups, the Tat Khalsa, emerged as the clear victor and from the time when it achieved supremacy within the Sikh Panth the message that Sikhs should not be regarded as Hindus became accepted as an article of faith.[3]

There were also caste similarities which seemed to link the two. A substantial majority of Sikhs are Jats by caste. In the Indian Punjab of today virtually all Jats are Sikhs, but this was not the case in undivided India. Many of the Jats were actually Muslim, all of this variety now living in Pakistan. Much of the land in Punjab was owned by the Jats and amongst the large land-owners there was support by both Muslims and Sikhs for the Unionist Party.[4] Until Partition was very near the multi-communal Unionist Party appeared to both varieties of land-owner to be the best guarantor of their position in the society of the Punjab. It appealed to both Muslim and Sikh land-owners as well as to the Hindu Jat land-owners of the Haryana area of the Punjab.[5]

So how do we explain the pronounced hostility towards Muslims felt by the Sikhs, and likewise the equally pronounced hostility of the Muslims towards the Sikhs? Obviously the feeling ran deep, for otherwise the pooling of their economic concerns in the Unionist Party would have been sufficient to hold Muslim and Sikh together, at least precariously. This, it is true, applied only to the wealthy rural Jats, but they after all wielded considerable authority within the community. Given the other factors involved in the independence dispute we can assume that the Hindu would have been excluded. The Muslim and the Sikh, however, should have been able to reach agreement. But they did not reach agreement. Quite the reverse was the case and so we must look for causes.

If we go back to the early Gurus (the first four Gurus who led the Sikh Panth or community during the sixteenth century) we find little evidence of any hostility. The Panth was too small to be noticed by the Muslim rulers (who were at this time the Mughals), and in the Sikh sacred scripture (the *Adi Granth*) there is no condemnation of those whom the Gurus regarded as 'true' Muslims.[6] There certainly is criticism of the conventional Muslim, but so too is there criticism of the conventional Hindu. The Muslim (or the Hindu) who ceased to observe the outward trappings of faith and instead looked for inner truth within his or her own heart was bound for spiritual liberation and met with the Gurus' unqualified approval without ever ceasing to be a Muslim or a Hindu.[7]

During the time of Guru Arjan, the fifth Guru (1581–1606), the activities of this hitherto unknown community were unfavourably noticed by the Mughal emperor, Jahangir. He observed how Guru Arjan was having some success in converting Muslims as well as Hindus and vowed to put an end to his works. Arjan was arrested and in 1606 he died while in Mughal hands.[8] Sikhs regard Arjan as the first martyr Guru, yet the contemporary Sikh feeling against the Muslim community or against Islam as such was scarcely pronounced. Although Arjan's successor, Guru Hargobind, was later involved in a series of skirmishes with Mughal forces he served a *faujdar* of the emperor for a brief period.[9] There was indeed opposition towards the Mughals under Hargobind, but it seems clear that this was opposition directed against the governors and the landed interests of the time.[10] It did not represent strong feelings against the Muslim people.

We have moved now into the seventeenth century and the period of the later Gurus. When Aurangzeb became emperor in 1658 the Sikhs were again targeted and the ninth Guru, Tegh Bahadur, was arrested and executed in 1675. His execution is regarded by the Sikhs as a part of Aurangzeb's concern that India should become increasingly Muslim. Sikhs look up to Tegh Bahadur as the second martyr Guru and as one who strove to prevent Aurangzeb's purpose. Yet even so the feeling is directed against what is seen as the evil intention of Aurangzeb rather than against the beliefs of Muslims as such. Sikhs were certainly opposed to such beliefs and modern interpretations encourage such convictions, yet their outrage was not directed against Islam. It was directed against the actions of the Mughal emperor Aurangzeb.[11]

The same also applies to the period of the tenth and last of the Sikh Gurus, Gobind Singh.[12] Certainly he believed that evil had emerged in strength and that he had been called by Akal Purakh to fight for what was just in order to restore balance to human affairs. This was what lies behind his decision to create the Khalsa. Certainly also Aurangzeb was seen as the supreme symbol of all that was evil, and he was indeed a Muslim. Vazir Khan, the subedar of Sirhind, figures very prominently in the list of the Guru's opponents and adds weight to the fact that the principal enemies were Muslims. Yet in his defence of Anandpur in 1704 Guru Gobind Singh was not merely confronted by a Mughal army. These alone were not the enemies of the Guru. In defending Anandpur he was also confronted by the Hindu armies of other neighbouring hill states.[13]

As yet the Sikhs do not seem to have identified all Muslims as their sworn enemies or as their irreconcilable foes. Aurangzeb, as the symbol of injustice, may have been typed in this manner; and Vazir Khan, the supreme emblem of treachery, was certainly so regarded. In the years immediately following the death of Guru Gobind Singh in 1708 this seems to have been still the case. The first notable event in the Punjab following his death was the rebellion led by the Sikh leader Banda from 1710 until his capture by the Mughals in 1715. Banda made one of his primary objectives the death of the hated Vazir Khan, a purpose which he accomplished at the battle of Sirhind early in the rebellion in 1710. Vazir Khan was indeed slain, but so too was the equally hated Suchanand, the Hindu in Vazir Khan's retinue who was evidently responsible for persuading his employer to brick up alive the two younger sons of Guru Gobind Singh. Zoravar Singh and Fateh Singh had been captured with their mother following the evacuation of Anandpur in 1704 and Suchanand was blamed for their cruel deaths which followed. Both men were symbols and representatives of the kind of inhumane opposition which had confronted the Guru, the one Muslim and the other Hindu. And both received the same punishment at the hands of Banda.[14]

The career of Banda does, however, seem to mark a shift in the attitude of the Sikhs. Banda was leading a rebellion against the rulers of the Punjab and there was no doubt that these rulers were Muslims. It was a situation which became even more marked when Abdus Samad Khan became governor of Lahore, and when he was transferred to Multan in 1726 his son Zakariya Khan, who succeeded him in Lahore, continued the same policy. Abdus Samad Khan waged a particularly fierce campaign against the bearded Khalsa Sikhs during the first five years of his governorship, killing many of them and driving most of the remainder into hiding in the hills and wastelands of the Punjab. Zakariya Khan followed the same method, harrying the Khalsa for periods of his rule and relaxing his efforts only when he was satisfied that they were no threat to his authority.[15]

To this day the names of those two Mughal governors are remembered with loathing and abomination in Sikh tradition, and when the
central government took measures against the Sikhs from 1984 onwards the names of Abdus Samad Khan and particularly of Zakariya
Khan were freely applied to them. It was during one of Zakariya Khan's
periods of relaxation that Kapur Singh rose to prominence amongst the
Khalsa. Zakariya Khan offered the rank of nawab to any member of the
Khalsa if they would agree to unite peaceably under that chosen leader
and cease to trouble the state. According to tradition the offer was
received by Khalsa leaders hiding in the wilderness, and although the
idea had its attractions they were unable to decide who would be their
chosen leader. Eventually they elected the person who was fanning the
assembly and in this manner Kapur Singh acquired the title of nawab.[16]

The period of peace was, however, only a temporary one and again
the Khalsa were driven into hiding. Attitudes were now hardening. The
intermittent campaigns are represented by the Sikhs as a determination
to exterminate them (or at least the Khalsa Sikhs), and martyrdom
became the supreme example of noble heroism. Always the martyr was
killed because of his opposition to the rulers of the Punjab; and although
their deputies might occasionally be Hindus the rulers were always
Muslims.[17] The Mughal governors gave way in the mid-eighteenth
century to the invading armies of the Afghan ruler Ahmad Shah Abdali,
but still the claimants to authority were Muslims.[18]

George Forster, in a series of letters published in London in 1798 as
A Journey from Bengal to England, passed through the Punjab in 1783
and devoted considerable attention to the Sikhs. He writes of the sixth
invasion of Ahmad Shah Abdali in 1762:

> The Sicques, in their day of success, having defiled and destroyed the places
> of the Mahometans, compelling also many of them newly converted to
> embrace the faith of Nanock, now felt the savage vengeance of their
> enemies. Amrut Sir was razed to the ground, and the sacred waters choked
> up with its ruins. Pyramids were erected, and covered with the heads of
> slaughtered Sicques; and it is mentioned, that Ahmed Shah caused the walls
> of the principal mosques which had been polluted by the Sicques, to be
> washed with their blood, that the contamination might be removed, and the
> ignominy offered to the religion of Mahomet, expiated.[19]

This was the incident known as the *Vadda Ghallughara* or 'Great
Holocaust'. Forster reports that after Ahmad Shah Abdali withdrew to
Afghanistan at the end of 1762 the Sikhs assaulted Lahore,

> ... where wildly indulging the enmity that had never ceased to inflame them
> against these severe scourges of their nation, they committed violent outrages.

The mosques that had been rebuilt on Hindu shrines or restored to use by the Mahometans, were demolished with every mark of contempt and indignation: and the Afghans, in chains, washed the foundations with the blood of hogs.[20]

Forster may not have been entirely accurate in his reporting, but he was certainly well placed to gauge the feelings of the Sikhs towards the Muslims and vice versa.

It is out of this eighteenth-century situation that the Sikh attitude towards the Muslims took shape, and although one can never refer to any attitude remaining permanent for all time the hostility of the Sikhs towards Muslims (or at least their marked suspicion of them) has certainly had a long history, continuing to the present day. It embraced all Muslims (not just those who were rulers), largely because those who were rulers from time to time appealed to the communal loyalty of those who shared the Muslim faith. In his *Memoir on Historical and Political Transactions in the Punjab*, recorded in 1830, Captain William Murray writes of the same invasion by Ahmad Shah Abdali:

> With a conscientious zeal for the precepts inculcated by the Arabian Lawgiver, directing the extirpation of all idolators and the demolition of their temples, the Shah on reaching Umrutsur acquired the merit and received the applause of all true Moosulmans by blowing up the Hur Mundur and destroying the sacred reservoir which with bigotted frenzy was polluted with the blood and entrails of the bovine species an act perhaps more shocking to the feelings and sacreligious in the estimation of the schismatic disciple of Govind than it would be to the orthodox Hindoo.[21]

This attitude found its clearest expression in the *rahit-namas* (the Sikh codes of belief and conduct) which date from the middle of the eighteenth century or its later portion. The *Chaupa Singh Rahit-nama* is the earliest extant example of a rahit-nama and the list of offences which it provides is explicit. The following illustrate its attitude:

> Never associate with a Muslim nor trust his word.
> Never drink water from a Muslim's hands, never eat his food, and never sleep in his company.
> Do not be influenced by anything which a Muslim may say.
> Never touch a Muslim woman.
> Never eat meat from animals killed according to Muslim rites.
> Do not distribute or eat karah prasad in the company of Muslims.
> Never eat sweets or any other food offered as an oblation by a Muslim official.
> Do not hold religious discourse with Muslims.
> A Sikh should never entrust the management of his household affairs to a Muslim.

A Sikh should never entrust his sword to a Muslim and then walk ahead unarmed.
Never attend the mourning ceremony for a deceased Muslim.
Never touch the feet of a Mughal nor eat food which he leaves.[22]

For many of the prohibitions the implication is clearly that the presence of Muslims or dealings with them will involve pollution. The Muslims have demonstrated that they are on the side of the evil-doers and their participation in anything which involves a Sikh will therefore result in contamination of the Sikh.

One interesting feature of this analysis concerns the reason for the firm Khalsa prohibition of smoking or rather (in its original form) the use of the *huqqa*. One possible reason for the introduction of this prohibition into the evolving Khalsa Rahit was that the huqqa was associated with Muslims and smoking the huqqa was seen in the seventeenth century to be a Muslim practice. The suggestion is attractive, but it needs to be remembered that the prohibition of the huqqa was one of the features of the early Rahit, introduced into it by the end of the seventeenth century. If it was indeed introduced because it was anti-Muslim it may mean that the feeling against Muslims should perhaps be pushed back further than we have allowed.[23]

Under Maharaja Ranjit Singh the strength of feelings against Muslims persisted. It is true that Ranjit Singh had some important Muslims as court servants, but the treatment accorded to Muslims during his reign showed that the feeling was certainly alive.[24] After the fall of the Punjab kingdom in 1849 the British moved into the Punjab and were soon promulgating their western understanding through government schools and support for those operated by the Christian missions. This understanding played down the more extreme views of inter-communal rivalry. It seems highly likely that many of the Tat Khalsa sector of the Singh Sabha reform movement were influenced by these ideals,[25] and when a new rahit-nama was eventually issued by the successful Tat Khalsa reformers (the *Sikh Rahit Maryada*) many of the more explicit prohibitions were dropped or amended as altogether too overt in their attitude towards Muslims.

Anti-Muslim features were, however, retained as two of the four *kurahit*s (major infractions of the Rahit), one of them unchanged and the other amended. The one which was retained unchanged was the ban on *kutha* (on meat which was prepared in the approved Muslim manner and was thereby rendered halal). The amended one was the prohibition against touching Muslim women which in the modern rahit-nama emerged as an injunction to avoid extra-marital sex.[26] *Sikh Rahit Maryada* was not issued until 1950, but the substance of the rahit-nama had been drawn up during the early 1930s and it was only the political uncertainty of the intervening years which prevented an earlier appearance. During the early decades of the twentieth century feeling against the Muslims was more subdued, but it certainly was not absent.

It was under these circumstances that the Punjab was plunged into the rapidly mounting demand for Pakistan and the Sikhs were soon driven to the conclusion that they would be compelled to opt either for the Pakistan of Jinnah or for the Bharat of the Congress Party. The leader of the Sikhs during this period was unquestionably Master Tara Singh. Baldev Singh was commonly their representative on ministries formed during the Second World War, but there was no doubt who commanded the allegiance of most Sikhs during this period. It was Tara Singh.

Tara Singh's attitude was interesting. On the one hand, a search through the written material of the Second World War period and immediately after (published and unpublished), can give the impression that he was, on the whole, unbiassed with regard to Muslims and Islam. It is true that feelings against the Muslims can be read, for example, into his response to the Cabinet Mission's plan of 1946:

> The Cabinet Mission recognizes the genuine and acute anxiety among the Sikhs lest they should find themsleves subjected to a perpetual Muslim majority rule. If the British government is not aware of Sikh feelings, the Sikhs will have to resort to some measures to convince everybody of the Sikh anxiety in case they are subjected to perpetual Muslim domination.[27]

It is also true that Tara Singh was very much the centre of events when on 3 March 1947, he unsheathed his sword on the steps of the Assembly Chamber of Lahore and cried '*Pakistan murdabad*' (death to Pakistan).

Such incidents can be treated as essentially political, however, and the sword-waving incident occurred when the political temperature was running at an unprecedented height. Rather less political was the intention of one of Tara Singh's relatives (a Keshdhari Sikh) to marry a Muslim girl. Tara Singh did not forbid the marriage, but made it clear that the girl would have to become a Sikh.[28] On the face of it Tara Singh must remain something of an enigma, possibly a result of his overwhelming passion for politics. The attitude of a large number of Sikhs was, however, writ large. Similarly the attitude of a substantial number of both Punjabi Muslims and Punjabi Hindus was writ large in the over-heated conditions which followed the announcement of the Radcliffe Award. The migration and the massacres of 1947–8 were the result.

We return to the point at which we began. Feelings as deep as those
which surfaced in the months following Partition cannot be explained
simply by reference to the immediate past. They must have origins
which lie further back in time. The eighteenth century, it is submitted,
was the period to which we must look when we seek an understanding
of those attitudes.

Endnotes

1. Ajit Singh Sarhadi, *Punjabi Suba: the story of the struggle* (Delhi, 1970),
   p. 131.
2. Kahon Singh Nabha, *Ham Hindu Nahin* (Amritsar, 1899).
3. For the division in the Singh Sabha movement between the conservative
   Sanatan Sikhs and the radical Tat Khalsa see Harjot Oberoi, *The Construction of Religious Boundaries: culture, identity and diversity in the Sikh
   tradition* (New Delhi, 1994; Chicago, 1994).
4. Stephen Oren, 'The Sikhs, Congress, and the Unionists in British Punjab,
   1937–45', *Modern Asian Studies*, vol. 8, no. 3 (1974), p. 399.
5. J. S. Grewal, *The Sikhs of the Punjab* (The New Cambridge History of
   India, Cambridge, 1990), pp. 167–8.
6. A large portion of the Sikh sacred scripture was recorded under the
   direction of the third Guru, Amar Das (1552–74). This was the scripture
   contained in the Goindval or Mohan *pothi*s (volumes). The work was
   supplemented by the fifth Guru, Arjan, in 1603–4, principally by the
   addition of the fourth Guru's compositions and his own. To this substantial
   collection a few works by the ninth Guru, Tegh Bahadur, were subsequently added and the scripture came to be known as the *Adi Granth*
   to distinguish it from the eighteenth-century *Dasam Granth*.
7. Guru Nanak, *Var Majh* 7:1, 7:3, 8:1, *Adi Granth*, pp. 140–1. Harbans Singh,
   The Heritage of the Sikhs (New Delhi, rev. ed. 1994), p. 16; W. H. McLeod,
   Guru Nanak and the Sikh Religion (Oxford, 1968), pp. 212–13.
8. Grewal, *The Sikhs of the Punjab*, pp. 63–4.
9. *Dabistan-i-Mazahib*, quoted in English translation by Ganda Singh in
   Panjab Past and Present, vol. I, part 1 (April 1967), p. 62. *Dabistan-i-
   Mazahib* is an anonymous Persian work of the mid-seventeenth century by
   a writer who personally knew Guru Hargobind.
10. Chetan Singh, *Region and Empire: Panjab in the seventeenth century*
    (New Delhi, 1991), pp. 271–2.
11. Fauja Singh in Fauja Singh and Gurbachan Singh Talib, *Guru Tegh
    Bahadur: martyr and teacher* (Patiala, 1975), pp. 65–6. Anil Chandra
    Banerjee, 'Inter-religious relations during Muslim rule in India', in Gurbachan
    Singh Talib (ed.), *Guru Tegh Bahadur: background and the supreme
    sacrifice* (Patiala, 1976), p. 93.
12. *Akal Ustat* 15:85–17:87. *Dasam Granth*, pp. 19–20.

13. J.S. Grewal and S.S. Bal, *Guru Gobind Singh* (Chandigarh, 1967), pp. 129 ff, 174–6.

14. Ganda Singh, *Banda Bahadur* (Amritsar, 1935), pp. 55–74. Muzaffar Alam, *The Crisis of Empire in Mughal North India: Awadh and the Punjab, 1707–48* (New Delhi, 1986), pp. 134–47.

15. Alam, *The Crisis of Empire*, pp. 176–85.

16. Teja Singh and Ganda Singh, *A Short History of the Sikhs* (Bombay, 1950), p. 121.

17. For a very interesting study of martyrdom amongst the Sikhs see Louis Fenech's Ph.D thesis 'Playing the Game of Love: the Sikh tradition of martyrdom' (Ph.D, University of Toronto, 1994), particularly the introduction.

18. Ganda Singh, *Ahmad Shah Durrani: father of modern Afghanistan* (Bombay, 1959), pp. 40 ff.

19. H.S. Bhatia (ed.), *Rare Documents on Sikhs and their Rule in the Punjab* (New Delhi, 1981), pp. 26–7.

20. Ibid., p. 27.

21. Ibid., p. 53.

22. W.H. McLeod (trans.), *The Chaupa Singh Rahit-nama* (Dunedin, 1987), p. 42.

23. Another possible explanation for banning the huqqa was that it was much too cumbersome to be used by the armed horsemen of the Khalsa. This explanation seems less likely.

24. 'A Tour to Lahore' (1808) by an officer of the Bengal Army, in the *Asiatic Annual Register*, vol. XI, 1809, reproduced in *Panjab Past and Present*, vol. I, part 1, p. 120; Alexander Burnes, *Travels into Bokhara*, vol. III (London, 1834), p. 118. Charles Masson, *Narrative of Various Journeys in Balochistan, Afghanistan, and the Panjab*, vol. 1, (London, 1842), pp. 409–10, 419–21. G.T. Vigne, *Travels in Kashmir, Ladak, Iskardo, &c*, vol. 1 (London, 1844), p. 184; Leopold von Orlich, *Travels in India*, vol. 1 (London, 1845), p. 164. Charles von Hugel, *Travels in Kashmir and the Punjab*, (London, 1845, reproduced in Patiala, 1970), pp. 190–1, 238.

25. The Singh Sabha was founded in 1873.

26. *Sikh Rahit Maryada* (Amritsar: SGPC, 16th ed. 1983), p. 26.

27. Master Tara Singh's letter of 25 May 1946 to the Secretary of State for India. Gurmit Singh (ed.), *History of Sikh Struggles*, vol. 1, documents for period 1946–66 (New Delhi, 1989), p. 249.

28. Personal communication from other relatives of Master Tara Singh.

9

Ethnicity, Islam, and National Identity in Pakistan

ADEEL KHAN*

Since its creation in 1947, Pakistan has been confronted with the self-assertion of one ethnic group or another. Although all of these groups are Muslim and they have never questioned the Muslim identity of the state, they have serious reservations about the state's overarching definition of Muslim-Pakistani identity at the expense of regional ethnic identities. This essay proposes to analyse the issue of Pakistan's national identity by looking at the state-society relationship in that country as well as the use and abuse of Islam as an ideology.

The areas that were to form the state of Pakistan, after the Partition of British India, had five major ethnic groups, namely, Bengalis, Punjabis, Pakhtuns, Sindhis, and Baloch—each with its own distinct language and culture. To that, another group, Muhajir (literally meaning migrant), was added in the shape of Indian Muslim migrants, predominantly from Muslim minority provinces of north India.[1] There are a few points about the creation of Pakistan that need to be noted at the outset.

PAKISTAN MOVEMENT

Pakistan did not come into being as a result of an overt mass struggle[2] but through, what the official Pakistani version calls, 'constitutional means'.[3] The party that created Pakistan, the All-India Muslim League, was an elitist group of the aristocratic Muslim families predominantly

* I would like to thank the Sociology Program and School of Social Change and Critical Inquiry, University of Wollongong, for contributing to my travel expenses for carrying out fieldwork for this paper.

from Muslim minority provinces of India with a very few members from the future Pakistan areas.[4] As late as 1937, the Muslim League support in the future Pakistan areas was so meagre that the only province where it could win a respectable number of provincial assembly seats, thirty-nine, was Bengal. Otherwise it won only one seat in Punjab and none in Sindh and the North-West Frontier Province (NWFP).[5] It was only in the 1946 elections, one year before the creation of Pakistan, that the Muslim League emerged as a major force in most of the Muslim majority provinces. Still, at the time of Partition none of the Muslim majority provinces which were to form the state of Pakistan had a pro-Pakistan provincial government.[6]

The demand for Pakistan was a secular nationalist demand of a section of Muslims who felt threatened, not religiously but economically, by the Hindu majority. Had the treat been religious, Muslim religious groups would have been the first to demand a separate homeland. But 'the Pakistan movement was not a movement of Islam but of Muslims'.[7] The Pakistan Resolution of 1940, which was to become the basis for Pakistan, 'can be explained *without reference to Islam* [emphasis original], though not without reference to Muslims'.[8] Understandably, almost every Muslim religious group was opposed to the Muslim League, its leader Mohammad Ali Jinnah, and its demand for Pakistan.[9] But there is no denying that the rhetoric and slogans for the demand were couched in religious symbolism.

The Muslim League was fighting for a better deal for Muslims within the federation of India and it was only one year before Partition that it opted for an independent state.[10] In 1946, the Muslim League accepted the Cabinet Mission Plan for a confederal India with a greater autonomy for the provinces.[11]

JINNAH AND STATE-BUILDING

All these factors had a serious bearing upon the future politics of Pakistan. But before Pakistan could evolve a political system for itself through deliberations in the constituent assembly, the founder of the new state, M.A. Jinnah, had already determined what course the politics of Pakistan should take. By his words and deeds during the one year that he lived after Partition, Jinnah had made it clear that Pakistan would have a highly centralized political system. By becoming the all-powerful first governor-general of Pakistan, Jinnah founded a unitary political system that retarded the growth of the parliamentary system, which was more suitable for the multi-ethnic society of Pakistan. By holding three most important positions of governor-general, president of the constituent assembly, and president of the Muslim League at the same time to himself, Jinnah laid a tradition in which a powerful individual came to be more important than the institutionalized distribution of state power. 'No constitutional ruler and few autocrats have possessed such a plenitude of power'.[12]

While continuing with the colonial Government of India Act 1935, Jinnah[13] amended it to make it more authoritarian and less federal by increasing the powers of the governor-general and by removing the sales tax from the provincial list and putting it on the central government list. Within two weeks after Partition, he dismissed the elected government of Pakhtun nationalist, Dr Khan Saheb, in the North-West Frontier Province, replacing it with his own party man. He then dismissed the elected government of M.A. Khuhro in Sindh province. Jinnah also contributed to the future confusion on the ideological basis of the Pakistani state by making contradictory statements, which emphasized democracy and secularism at one time and the role of Islam at another.

Furthermore, when the Bengali majority expressed their unwillingness to accept the north Indian Muslims' language, Urdu, as the national language of Pakistan, Jinnah, in an authoritarian manner, declared that Urdu alone would be the national language. He claimed that it embodied the best in Islamic culture and Muslim tradition,[14] thus denigrating the value of Bengali and other regional languages. But the most disastrous contribution of Jinnah, to the future of Pakistan, perhaps, was 'a demotion of the political leadership in favour of the bureaucracy'.[15]

He created the post of secretary-general for one of his lieutenants, Chaudhri Mohammad Ali, to run the government single-handedly through the central and provincial bureaucracy.[16] As a consequence the British-trained civil servants assumed prominence in the state system at the expense of political leadership. On the other hand, Pakistan's insecure leadership which, in the face of the Indian propaganda that the new state could not survive very long, was not sure about the viability of the Pakistani state, diverted national resources to the build-up of a strong military force. This set the Pakistani state on a path that was soon to lead to a military-bureaucratic authoritarianism, which continues to plague Pakistan's political system till today.

The predominance of the civil and military bureaucracy not only retarded the political system but also adversely affected the ethnic composition of the state managers. For the civilian state administrators were predominantly Punjabis and Muhajirs from Muslim minority provinces of British India, and the army was overwhelmingly from one province, Punjab. Therefore, Pakistan came to be ruled by minority ethnic groups, Muhajir and Punjabis, whereas the majority group, Bengalis, had neither adequate representation in the civil bureaucracy nor in the military. In 1948, East Pakistan (now Bangladesh), which had 54 per cent of Pakistan's total population, had only 11.1 per cent share in the civil service and the rest of the personnel, 88.9 per cent, were from West Pakistan.[17]

PUNJABI-MUHAJIR DOMINATION

It is instructive to note here that the two dominant groups, Muhajirs and Punjabis, had been the most favourably placed communities under the colonial rule. The reason for that was the colonial administration's dependence on the loyalty of the big landlords for the maintenance of its control system. The United Provinces (UP) of India, from where these Urdu-speaking Muhajirs had migrated, was the traditional power base of the Muslim landed gentry and they continued with their privileges even after the colonial takeover. For instance, in 1913 Muslims were only 14 per cent of the UP population but they occupied 35 per cent of the most important jobs.[18] And it was, in fact, the Muslim elite of UP who first started thinking in terms of communal politics and launched the Muslim League, with the support of British government, to counter the Indian National Congress' influence. The Muslim elite had felt that the Congress' demands for representation in the government would unfavourably affect their privileges and later demanded the creation of Pakistan for they feared that in an independent and democratic India the Hindu majority would rule. On the other hand, although not the traditional elite like UPites, Punjabis endeared themselves to the British authorities by helping them to put down the armed resistance movement of 1857. The British showered their favours on Punjab through the irrigation schemes that led to the reclamation of large areas of West Punjab.[19] Thus came into being a large class of Punjabi land-owners who played an important role in strengthening the colonial system of control by providing men for army service. During the First World War, the number of Punjabis in the army was as large as over 75 per cent of the total Indian Muslims recruited.[20] This led to the militarization of the bureaucratic structure of the province, 'as nearly all aspects of its activities were geared towards the provision of men and material for the war effort'.[21] As mentioned above, Punjab had initially little support for the Muslim League and its demand for Pakistan, but later when the appeal for Pakistan captured the imagination of the people the 'Muslim landed elite chose to use the League as its vehicle for carrying over its authority into the post-colonial period.[22]

Another peculiarity in the Pakistani case was that it inherited those parts of India which had little or no industrial base. People in most of these agrarian areas were immobile and illiterate. These were not the people who had struggled for a separate homeland: they had succumbed to the idea of the new state only because they were given the choice between a Hindu majority state and a separate Muslim state. Hence the movement for Pakistan was the movement of a small literate class from the urban areas who were aspirants for state employment and who believed that in the new state, where they would not have to face the Hindu majority, the jobs would be theirs only. But the dream did not come true for all ethnic groups.

The Muhajir-Punjabi dominated state system of Pakistan was heavily biased in favour of particular regions and particular ethnic groups. When regional discontent was growing, the central government, instead of addressing regional grievances, resorted to the methods of cultural imperialism with its centralizing and homogenizing strategies. Urdu, the language of 3.7 per cent of the population, was imposed as a national language. Bengali legislators were warned that if they used their own language they would be tried for treason. Bengali poet Rabindranath Tagore's songs on Radio Pakistan were banned. During the first two decades of Pakistan, the central government's bias against the east wing turned the comparatively more educated Bengalis into less educated and then their lower representation in the civil services was rationalized on that basis.[23] In Sindh, the Sindhi language was replaced by Urdu as the medium of instruction. Though these discriminatory policies triggered ethnic and regional protest, in a state being run without any democratic channels the voices of disaffection carried little weight.

For almost a decade the country had no constitution. And even when a constitution was worked out in 1956, it was abrogated in 1958 before becoming operative. A scheme of One Unit was devised in 1955 for the western part of the country to arbitrarily amalgamate the four provinces and turn them into one administrative unit, West Pakistan, for the mere purpose of countering the majority of the eastern wing. When the first elections were due to be held under the new constitution, martial law was imposed and elections were indefinitely postponed. After more than two decades of Partition, when elections were held in 1970, the results were not honoured for that would have meant the transfer of power from the Muhajir-Punjabi oligarchy to the Bengali majority. A civil war ensued that resulted in the dismemberment of Pakistan and the creation of an independent state, Bangladesh.

In the truncated Pakistan, Punjabis became the majority ethnic group. Although Pakistan had the first elected government in 1972, the political system continued to be intolerant and authoritarian. The first elected prime minister, Zulfiqar Ali Bhutto, had little patience for opposition and when the Balochistan government asserted its authority, Bhutto unceremoniously dismissed it. The NWFP government, in protest against the arbitrary decision, resigned. The central government's repression of the nationalist groups in Balochistan led to underground activities that soon culminated in a guerilla war with the armed forces that claimed thousand of lives.[24] In less than half a decade the Pakistan army was fighting its second war against an ethnic group.

Just when Pakistan had its second general elections in 1977, and it was hoped that the days of military dictatorship had become history, the opposition parties' refusal to accept the elections results that they thought were rigged by the ruling party, led to a mass agitation against the government. After days of unrest, right at the time when the government and opposition had agreed on another election, the generals struck once again. The elected government of prime minister Bhutto was deposed and martial law was imposed for the third time. Within two years after a dubious trial[25] Bhutto was hanged.

The execution of Bhutto, who was a Sindhi, created deep feelings of anger among the Sindhis. In 1983, when the opposition alliance, Movement for Restoration of Democracy (MRD), launched a mass movement against the military government it looked as if Sindhis were waiting for the moment. The movement got out of the leadership's control and turned into street battles with the armed forces, resulting in the death and imprisonment of thousands of Sindhis.[26]

In 1984, yet another ethnic movement was launched. This time it was the creators, and for a long time virtual rulers, of Pakistan, the Muhajirs, who felt that they had lost their privileges to the Punjabi majority. In 1986, the Muhajir Quami Movement (MQM) had violent clashes with Pakhtun settlers in Karachi, which marked the beginning of a protracted ethnic strife in Sindh province that continues till this day.[27]

Pakistan's predicament has been explained by one sociologist,[28] Hamza Alavi, as a conflict between the state and civil society. He says that Pakistan suffers from the tension between an 'overdeveloped' state and underdeveloped society, defining the 'overdeveloped' state as one where 'the excessive enlargement of powers of control and regulation that the state acquires, extend far beyond the logic of what is necessary in the interests of orderly functioning of the peripheral capitalist class'. On the surface, this explanation may seem plausible but a little in-depth investigation would reveal that such a one-to-one linkage fails to explicate the intricacies of a society where the interactions and contradictions of various classes are not well defined.

Another important point is that a state that depends solely on coercion and violence betrays weakness rather than strength. Resort to frequent violence indicates a lack of legitimacy on the part of the state, whereas the lack of legitimacy points to the ideological frailty of the state. For instance, if democratic states do not resort to frequent violence the reason lies in the development of sophisticated networks of surveillance coupled with a high level of ideological production and distribution. In the absence of modern techniques of domination through surveillance and ideology, a state like Pakistan suffers from the inability to expand its writ. As a result, violence is the last resort. Such a state might be called 'fierce' rather than strong because the expression of interests here is direct, not mediated, and relations between the state and society are contradictory rather than complementary.[29]

In a 'fierce' state like Pakistan, any voice of disaffection from the ethnic and regional groups is treated by the ruling elite as a challenge to the stability and sovereignty of the state from which their privileges emanate. This siege mentality of the power elite forces them to strengthen the state's security agencies at the expense of social and economic sectors. What further exacerbated the situation in Pakistan was the fact that it had a territorial dispute with India over Kashmir. Soon the two states' tense relations turned into an open hostility. Consequently, nearly 30 per cent of the central government's expenditure went to defence and still remains at that level, making it the highest in the less developed world.[30] and well beyond the needs of the state for normal security purposes. Naturally, when such a large portion of the national budget is allocated to a non-productive sector like defence, the productive and social sectors get neglected. Thus only five countries in the world spend less than Pakistan on health. Pakistan's spending on education is well below the average for less developed countries.[31] According to a recent UNESCO report, of the nine countries surveyed, Pakistan is the only one where military expenditure exceeds spending on education.[32]

So far this essay has dealt mostly with the material side of the history of Pakistan. The remaining part will look at the ideological aspect of the national identity. A country that was created in the name of religion has not even after over fifty years of its existence been able to determine what role religion should play in the affairs of the state.[33] Also contentious is the very definition of the Pakistan culture that has sparked debates on whether Pakistani culture is different from Indian culture and if so what makes it different. First, let us deal with Islam as an ideology.

ISLAM AND THE IDEOLOGY OF PAKISTAN

Pakistan was created in a moment of history, but then it had to face the reality. The irony, however, is that the reality of the state conflicts with its ideology.[34] The reality of the Pakistani state is that it is a composite of various regional and ethnic cultures, which cannot be defined as Islamic or un-Islamic. Islam is a very important part but is not the basis of these cultures. The ideology of the state, however, is based on rationalist Islam and Urdu language, both imported from elsewhere. The role of Islam in all regional cultures of Pakistan cannot be over-emphasized. In fact it is difficult to imagine these cultures without Islam. But that is an Islam which the people live and breathe—it is a belief system that has become part of everyday life. It is an Islam based on the syncretic Sufi traditions. In contrast, the Islam that is projected by the state, is an ideology, an instrument to deny diversity and differ-ence. It is a tactical Islam strategically deployed by the rulers to legitimize their misconduct and to cover their failings. As far as Urdu is concerned, by now an established *lingua franca*, it has not been able to become as natural a part of the ethnic psyche as Islam. It has been imposed from the top to serve the nation-state's need for a national language. Thus the idea of a nation based on ideological Islam and the Urdu language is more of a fiction than reality.[35]

The tactical use of Islam and the confusion about its role in the affairs of the state, too, owes much to the founder of Pakistan. Evidence suggests that Jinnah's use of Islam as a rallying force was a political tactic, not a conviction and that is why his 'appeal to religion was always ambiguous'.[36] Jinnah based his demand for Pakistan on the premise that Hindus and Muslims were two different people who could never be-come one nation. In 1940, he said that Islam and Hinduism:

> ...are not religions in the strict sense of the word, but are, in fact, different and distinct social orders and it is a dream that the Hindus and Muslims can ever evolve a common nationality...[37]

In his famous presidential address to the constituent assembly of Pakistan on August 1947, however, he claimed exactly the opposite of his words above. He said:

> You may belong to any religion or caste or creed—that has nothing to do with the business of the state...you will find that in [the] course of time Hindus would cease to be Hindus and Muslims would cease to be Muslims, not in the religious sense, because that is the personal faith of each individual, but in the political sense as citizens of the State.[38]

No wonder, even today those who want to prove Jinnah's religious credentials quote the former statement and those who try to present him as a secularist quote the latter.

After Jinnah, although some of the early rulers categorically denied links between religion and politics, almost all used Islam to justify their coercive and authoritarian methods in dealing with ethnic, regional, and economic discontent. The leadership's inability to provide a coherent ideological basis for the new state, confronted with not just diverse but conflicting ethnic and regional interests obliged them to present Islam as symbol of unity. The hypocritical use of Islam plunged the country in an ideological wilderness that further widened the divisions and ruptures in the polity of an already confused nation.

Despite Jinnah's secular leaning, his exhortation that the foundations of Pakistan's democracy must be laid on the basis of Islamic ideals and principles tilted the political discourse in Pakistan towards the vague, confusing, and contradictory interpretations of Islam. Moreover, in March 1949, the first prime minister of Pakistan, Liaquat Ali Khan, moved the Objectives Resolution in the assembly, which said that 'sovereignty belonged to God, and that the authority He had delegated to the state of Pakistan, "through its people" would be exercised "within the limits prescribed by Him"; that the state would fully observe the principles of democracy, freedom, equality, tolerance, and social justice as enunciated by Islam; and that it would enable Muslims to order their individual and collective lives according to the teachings and requirements of Islam as set forth in the Quran and *Sunnah*'.[39]

Significantly, Liaquat did not stop there and went on to declare that as Pakistan was created for the Muslims to live by Islamic teachings and traditions, '(t)he state would therefore *do more than merely leave them free* [emphasis added] to profess and practice their faith'.[40] This was an obvious declaration of the government's intention to interfere with the life of the people on the pretext of Islamic teachings. To pacify the liberals and Hindus, however, Liaquat concluded by saying that the goal before Pakistan was 'to build up a truly liberal Government where the greatest amount of freedom...(would) be given to all its members'.[41] With such self-contradictory claims of intending to do more than merely leaving the citizens free to profess and practise their faith and at the same time claiming to build up a 'truly liberal government' with the 'greatest amount of freedom' was obviously to set in motion an unending debate on the actual role of Islam in the affairs of the state and society.

To further obscure the already blurred picture, the governor-general, Ghulam Muhammad, declared that 'Pakistan is a secular, democratic and not a theocratic state'.[42] His interior minister, Iskander Mirza, who would later become the first president of Pakistan, went so far as to warn that 'religion and politics should be kept apart otherwise there will be chaos'.[43] Ironically, one of the prime minister, H.S. Suhrawady, in 1956, even declared that the two-nation theory, on the basis of which Pakistan was created, had 'ceased to be valid as soon as Pakistan was established', thus calling 'the often-repeated Islamic bond between East and West Pakistan fatuous'.[44] Despite these occasional references to secularism and democracy, however, the Objectives Resolution proved to be a preamble to the three constitutions that Pakistan would see in making and breaking during the next three decades.

The first constitution of Pakistan, which is known as the 1956 Constitution, declared the state to be an Islamic republic where no law repugnant to Quran and *Sunnah* could be enacted. But interestingly, Islam was not declared the official religion of the 'Islamic Republic' of Pakistan. Another amusing feature of the constitution was that the head of state was to be a Muslim, but the speaker of the assembly need not be a Muslim, though he was to assume the office of the head of state under certain circumstances. According to the constitution, the president was to appoint a commission, which would recommend measures to bring the existing laws in conformity with the Islamic injunctions. But the president, major-general Iskander Mirza, who had once said that the mixing of religion and politics would create chaos, understandably, never appointed that commission. Anyway, in the chaotic political culture of Pakistan the constitution was not going to last long. In 1958, Mirza imposed martial law and abrogated the constitution to ensure that there were no elections, which according to the constitution were to be held in February 1959.[45]

After four years, the regime of general Ayub Khan promulgated another constitution in 1962. Although the new constitution was not much different from the previous one, the role of Islam was significantly diminished in the first draft. The preamble started with the same 'sovereignty of the entire universe belongs to Almighty Allah alone and the authority exercisable by the people is a sacred trust', but it was circumscribed by the words 'within the limits prescribed by God',[46] an obvious indication that the regime did not intend to limit its powers by such ambiguous words. Unlike the previous constitution, Pakistan was not declared an Islamic republic, but just 'Republic of Pakistan', and there was no provision to suggest that the laws of the country would be brought in conformity with the principles of Islam. The words 'in accordance with the Holy *Quran* and *Sunnah*' were substituted with 'in accordance with the fundamental principles and basic concepts of Islam.'[47] Naturally, the orthodox sections took great exception to the diminished role of Islam, and the regime easily gave in. The first amendment to the constitution added the dropped word Islamic to the republic of Pakistan, and stated that 'all existing laws shall be brought in conformity with the Holy *Quran* and *Sunnah*'.[48] Islam was still not declared the official religion of the state. In 1969, Ayub violated his own constitution by inviting general Yahya Khan to take over and thus came to an end the second constitution of the country.

In 1973, Zulfiquar Ali Bhutto gave a third constitution to the remaining Pakistan (after the creation of Bangladesh). It was, in fact, the first unanimous constitution of Pakistan, signed by the elected representatives, including the religious ones. The 1973 Constitution may not have been different from the previous two constitutions in many respects, but as far as Islamic symbols are concerned, it was overflowing with them. For the first time, Islam was declared as the official religion of the state. Freedom of speech and the press were made subject to, among other things, considerations of national security and the 'glory of Islam'.[49] The head of state as well as the head of government were required to have 'a belief in the unity of God, the finality of Muhammad's prophethood, the *Quran* as the last of the holy books, and the day of judgement' and 'strive to preserve the Islamic ideology which is the basis for the creation of Pakistan'.[50] It was made incumbent upon the government to Islamize the laws within nine years.

During Bhutto's rule for the first time in Pakistan's history, the post of minister for religious affairs was created in the central cabinet. High class hotels were asked to have a copy of the Quran placed in every room. Among the most disastrous actions of Bhutto, however, were the ones in which, under the pressure of the religious lobby, he declared the Ahmedi sect of Islam non-Muslim, shut down nightclubs and banned gambling and liquor for Muslims, and made Friday (Muslim prayers' day), instead of Sunday, the weekly holiday.[51] Ironically, the man who was by all standards the most westernized of all the rulers of Pakistan after Jinnah and the first elected prime minister of the country, used Islam the most. But still none of his actions endeared Bhutto to the religious lobby. In fact, never before in the history of Pakistan, had the conservative sections of society, whether religious or otherwise, hated and dreaded anyone as much as they did Bhutto. Though Bhutto talked about change more than anyone else, his desire to keep the existing system intact was no less than anyone else's. He was feared not because he did, or intended to, bring a revolutionary change, but as the one who had the ability to do so if he desired.

Bhutto's unintentional contribution to the politics of Pakistan was to alert the forces of reaction against a change that he had no intention of bringing about. His intentional contribution was to alienate those who really wanted a change. By the end of his term in office, whether it were religionists, secularists, or democrats, all were united by their fear and hatred of Bhutto under the banner of the Pakistan National Alliance (PNA), which launched a camaign of Islamic fervour with the slogan of 'Nizam-i-Mustafa' (the system of the prophet).

In the dark of night, on the 4 July 1977, the army stepped in, deposed Bhutto, and two years later executed him. During his trial, Bhutto once said: 'I appointed a Chief of Staff (general Zia-ul-Haq) belonging to the Jamaat-i-Islami (a fundamentalist Islamic group) and the result is before all of us'.[52] Unfortunately, it was not only Bhutto who had to pay with his life for his misdeeds, but the whole country was to experience the worst crimes of political coercion, social repression, widespread corruption, and religious bigotry during the more than a decade long dictatorial rule of Zia.

Zia's period (1977–88), might have been the darkest in the otherwise not so bright history of Pakistan. It was marred by public hanging, widespread flogging, sexism, and the worst kind of religious bigotry and intolerance, all in the name of Islam. Zia did not abrogate the constitution, instead he suspended it and then brought in such drastic changes which facilitated a justificatioin for his rule and a constitutional role for the army, all for the 'glory of Islam'. He declared:

> Pakistan was achieved in the name of Islam, and Islam alone could provide the basis to run the government of the country and sustain its integrity... The present government would provide opportunity to others to serve the country after it *achieved its objective* [emphasis added]...(but) no un-Islamic government would be allowed to succeed the present regime.[53]

The brutal 'Islamic' rule of Zia continues to haunt Pakistan in the shape of ethnic and sectarian violence and endemic corruption.

Zia's military dictatorship, imbued with Islamic fundamentalism, brutalized the society and 'increased the divisions, ruptures and bitterness within an insecure nation'.[54] Consequently, Pakistan, today, is a less tolerant and more aggressive society. Its biggest city and industrial center, Karachi, has for the last one and a half decades been one of the most dangerous cities in Asia due to ethnic violence and other crime. Its biggest province, Punjab, has for over a decade been under the spell of sectarian violence. And the country on the whole is plagued with lawlessness, corruption, and drug and arms trade.

CONCLUSION

What emerges from the politics of Pakistan is that every ruler, whether military or civilian, has used Islam to justify and legitimize their repression and coercion. As far as national integration is concerned, Islam has been projected to obscure the ethnic and regional divisions in society. In the absence of a coherent national ideology, Islam has been cynically used to suppress the voices of regional and ethnic discontent. That is why at different stages in Pakistan's history there have been many different kinds of Islam that have been projected according to the demands of the times. For instance, there were the 'liberal-modernist Islam' of the early rulers, Ayub Khan's 'developmental Islam', Yahya Khan's 'nationalist Islam', Bhutto's 'socialist-populist Islam, and Zia's 'revivalist-fundamentalist Islam'.[55]

These were different faces of political Islam. The cultural Islam, however, had no resemblance to this. That Islam is a belief, a way of life, and a source of identity for the people. That Islam thrives on the spiritual and emotional insecurities of the people. Political Islam plays upon these insecurities and exploits them. This has caused a rather ambiguous and confusing interaction between political and cultural Islam. As a result of this confusion, the Pakistani intelligentsia has yet to agree on a broadly acceptable definition of Pakistani culture. As it is, there are at least three main interpretations. One school of thought believes that Pakistani culture came into existence with the creation of the state. Another claims that it began with the Arab invasion of Sindh and flourished during the more than a thousand years of Muslim rule in India. A third view holds that Pakistani culture is 5000 years old and that the ruins of ancient civilizations which have been excavated in various parts of Pakistan should be owned as a national heritage. The first two views emphasize Muslim nationhood and Islam as the basis of culture at the expense of regional and ethnic cultures, whereas the third view assigns greater importance to geographical and historical factors and regards religion as an important but secondary part of the culture.[56] Understandably, the first two views are more acceptable to the state whose ideological engineering requires, on the one hand, to disown the subcontinental identity, and on the other, to discourage indigenous identities.[57] Indigenous identities become problematic when they assert their local and ethnic characters, demand regional autonomy, and resist the homogenizing project of the territorially demarcated and officially constructed and imposed national identity of the state based on Urdu-Islam ideology.

In conclusion, it is instructive to take a look at the findings of a survey conducted by *Herald* magazine (January, 1977) on the fiftieth anniversary of Pakistan. According to the survey, if given the choice 82 per cent Pakistanis would prefer to leave for another country. Only 56 per cent believed that Muslims of the subcontinent are better off now than before

Partition. Despite the official propaganda, 47 per cent of Pakistanis held politicians and army responsible for the breakup of Pakistan in 1971. On the issue whether Pakistan was intended to be a religious state or a modern democracy, Pakistanis seem to be as confused as the state managers. Thus 52 per cent thought that their country was meant to be a religious state whereas 47 per cent believed it to be a modern democracy. As far as mixing of religion with politics is concerned 72 per cent thought that religious parties have done more harm than good and even a bigger number, 81 per cent, were in favour of Imams (priests) of the mosque not politicizing their sermons.

The gap between the perceptions of the Pakistani state and society; between the officially constructed reality and the lived is self-explanatory.

Endnotes

1. It was only the Urdu-speaking Muslim migrants from the United Provinces and Bihar who were to form a distinct ethnic group, Muhajir, whereas the migrants from East Punjab merged with the people of West Punjab as they spoke the same language and shared the same ethnic origins.

2. In an interview with this writer in 1997, Sindhi historian, Ibrahim Joyo, said: 'Masses had nothing to do with Pakistan movement, nowhere in India and at no stage of the movement. It was purely and exclusively a movement of the elite'.

3. During the turbulent years of the independence movement, Mohammad Ali Jinnah, the founder of Pakistan and the president of the Muslim League party, was the only top-ranking Indian leader who was never imprisoned by the British government. Iftikhar H. Malik, 'Ethnic Politics in Sindh', in Rasui Bakhsh Rais (ed.), *State, Society and Democratic Change in Pakistan* (Karachi, 1997), p. 158.

4. At the Simla deputation of 1905, which led to the formation of the All-India Muslim League in 1906, out of 35 members only 11 were not titled and only 8 out of 35 members nominated by the Muslim League were from the future Pakistan areas. Mohammad Waseem, *Politics and the State in Pakistan* (Lahore, 1989), p. 64.

5. Ian Talbot, *Provincial Politics and the Pakistan Movement: The Growth of the Muslim League in North-West and North-East India, 1937–47* (Karachi, 1988), p. 61.

6. Keith Callard, *Pakistan: A Political Study* (London, 1957), p. 14.

7. Hamza Alavi, 'Ethnicity, Muslim Society and the Pakistan Ideology', in Anita M. Weiss (ed.), *Islamic Reassertion in Pakistan: The Application of Islamic Laws in a Modern State* (New York, 1986), p. 22.

8. Omer Norman, *Pakistan: A Political and Economic History Since 1947* (London, 1990, revised edition), p. 4.

9. Alavi, 'Ethnicity, Muslim Society and the Pakistan Ideology', p. 21.
10. For a detailed account of this view, see Ayesha Jalal (1992). During General Zia ul-Haq's military rule (1977–88), with a greater emphasis on Islam and Pakistan ideology, this book was banned and therefore when reprinted after the general's death, it certified that: 'Permission to reprint this title in Pakistan under the Publications of Books (Reprint) Ordinance 1969 was obtained from the Department of Public Relations, Ministry of Information, Government of Punjab, Lahore'.
11. 'Some of Jinnah's followers, were bewildered by his acceptance of a plan which explicitly rejected Pakistan in its preamble'. Norman, *Pakistan*, p. 23, n. 18.
12. Callard, *Pakistan: A Political Study*, p. 20.
13. Ironically in the 23 March 1940 presidential address at the All-India Muslim League session at Lahore. Jinnah had termed this Act as a 'dangerous scheme' that was not acceptable to him and therefore 'the Act of 1935 must go once and for all'. Mohammad Ali Jinnah, *Quaid-i-Azam Speaks: His Vision of Pakistan* (Karachi, 1991), pp. 3, 6.
14. Chaudhri Mohammad Ali, *The Emergence of Pakistan* (Lahore, Research Society of Pakistan, University of the Punjab, 1967), p. 366.
15. Hamza Alavi, 'Class and State', in Hassan Gardezi and Jamil Rashid (eds), *Pakistan, the Roots of Dictatorship: The Political Economy of a Praetorian State* (London, 1983), p. 78.
16. Talking about his job. Chaudhri Mohammad Ali says, 'On my recommendations...the central government decided to amalgamate the various provincial cadres into a single cadre that would meet the needs of the provinces and of the nation as a whole. It was my responsibility as Secretary-General to keep every front supplied as well as I could and to maintain its morale'. C. Ali, *The Emergence of Pakistan*, pp. 357, 360.
17. Although the new recruitment policy was geared towards increasing the Bengali share and by 1958 it came up to 41.7 per cent, the key positions were still controlled by senior bureaucrats from West Pakistan. In 1955, of the 19 secretaries in the federal government, none was a Bengali. Of the total 41 joint secretaries only three were from East Pakistan. Likewise, out of 133 deputy secretaries and 548 undersecretaries only 10 and 38, respectively, were from the east wing. In the military elite, out of 894 army officers, 593 navy officers, and 640 air force officers only 14, 7, and 60, respectively, were from East Pakistan. Rounaq Jahan, *Pakistan: Failure in National Integration* (New York, 1972), pp. 25, 26.
18. David Page, *Prelude to Partition: The Indian Muslims and the Imperial System of Control 1920–32* (Karachi, 1987), p. 8.
19. Ibid., p. 9.
20. Stephen Cohen, *The Pakistan Army* (Karachi, 1984), p. 42.
21. Tan Tai Yong, 'Punjab and the Making of Pakistan: The Roots of a Civil-Military State' in D.A. Low and H. Brasted (eds), *Freedom, Trauma, Continuities: Northern India and Independence* (New Delhi, 1998), p. 202.

22. Imran Ali, 'Punjab and the Retardation of Nationalism', in D.A. Low (ed.), *The Political Inheritance of Pakistan* (London, 1991), p. 47.

23. Feroz Ahmed, *Ethnicity and Politics in Pakistan* (Karachi, 1998), pp. 26, 27.

24. For a detailed account of the Baloch movement, see Selig S.S. Harison, *In Afghanistan's Shadow: Baluch Nationalism and Soviet Temptations* (New York, 1981).

25. One of the judges on Bhutto trial case, Justice Qaiser Khan, who had resigned from the bench, in an interview with me in 1998, said: 'The whole trial was a sham and legally untenable, for Bhutto was not presented as a murderer but the one who connived in the murder and therefore there was no legal justification for Bhutto to be tried as a principal accused'.

26. For a detailed account of Sindhi grievances, see Ahmed, *Ethnicity of Politics in Pakistan*.

27. Ibid.

28. Alavi, 'Ethnicity, Muslim Society and the Pakistan Ideology', p. 42.

29. Nazi Ayubi, *Over-stating the Arab State: Politics and Society in the Middle East* (London, 1995), pp. 399–400.

30. Norman, *Pakistan*, p. 178.

31. Ibid., pp. 177–8.

32. The other eight countries are: Bangladesh, Brazil, China, Egypt, India, Indonesia, Mexico, and Nigeria. Pakistan's military expenditure is 7.7 per cent of GNP and education expenditure 2.7 per cent. *Dawn*, 29 September 1998. According to *The London Economist*, 22 May 1999, Pakistan's defence budget is US$ 3.2 billion.

33. On 28 August 1998 the Nawaz Sharif government announced that changes would be made to the constitution to make it truly Islamic. Why would a constitution that says Islam is the religion of the state and that law repugnant to the Quran and *Sunnah* shall be passed needs further Islamization? For detailed report and comments see *Newsline* (Karachi, September 1998).

34. I owe this point to Arif Hassan, Town Planner and writer, Karachi, 1997.

35. Interview with I. A. Rehman, Director, Human Rights Commission of Pakistan, Lahore, 1997.

36. Ayesha Jalal, *The Sole Spokesman: Jinnah, the Muslim League and the Demand for Pakistan* (Lahore, 1992), p. 5.

37. Jinnah, *Quaid-i-Azam Speaks*, p. 18.

38. Ibid., pp. 36–7. Interestingly, this speech, according to M.A. Zuberi (ed.), *The Business Recorder*, was held back by the early managers of Pakistan without the knowledge of Jinnah and was released to the media only after midnight for fear of Jinnah's wrath. I owe this information to A.R. Siddiqui, a journalist in Karachi, 1998. It should also be noted that general Zia ul Haq's military regime (1977–88), which had an added emphasis on Islam and the ideology of Pakistan, removed this portion of the speech from text books.

Commenting on this statement, Shahid Javed Burki in *Pakistan: A Nation in the Making* (Boulder, 1986), p. 42, asks: 'How could Muslims cease to be Muslims and Hindus cease to be Hindus in the political sense when the religions to which they belong were, in Jinnah's passionately held belief, so utterly different from one another? Was Jinnah giving up the two-nation theory, the ideological foundation of the state of Pakistan, once the new state had come into existence? Was the speech a clear signal to the people of Pakistan that the new state, though founded to preserve Islam in South Asia, was to be run on secular grounds? Was Jinnah providing a confirmation of the view shared by many of his opponents that he had cynically exploited the issue of religion to divide India?'

39. Anwar Syed, *Pakistan, Islam, Politics and National Solidarity* (Lahore, 1984), p. 80.
40. Ibid., p. 80.
41. Ayesha Jalal, *The State of Martial Rule: The Origins of Pakistan's Political Economy of Defence* (Lahore, 1991), p. 285.
42. Norman, *Pakistan*, p. 8.
43. Ibid., p. 8.
44. Khalid B. Sayeed, *The Political System of Pakistan* (Karachi, 1987), pp. 170, 171.
45. G. W. Choudhury, *Constitutional Development in Pakistan* (London, 1969, rev. ed.).
46. Ibid., pp. 179–80.
47. Ibid., p. 181.
48. Ibid., p. 184.
49. Syed, *Pakistan, Islam, Politics*, pp. 145, 146.
50. Ibid., p. 146.
51. Ibid., pp. 149–50.
52. Syed Vali Reza Nasr, *The Vanguard of the Islamic Revolution: The Jama'at-i-Islami of Pakistan* (Berkeley, 1994), p. 172.
53. Mumtaz Ahmad, 'The Politics of War: Islamic Fundamentalisms in Pakistan, in James Piscatori (ed.), *Islamic Fundamentalisms and the Gulf Crisis* (Chicago, 1988), p. 232.
54. Norman, *Pakistan*, p. 214.
55. Ahmad, *op. cit.*, p. 231.
56. For discussions on Pakistani culture, see Faiz, *op. cit.* Laeeq Babree, *Culture of Pakistan* (Lahore, 1997) and Jameel Jalibi, *Pakistan: The Identity of Culture* (Karachi, 1984).
57. I owe this insight to Zulfiqar Gilani of Peshwar University.

10

Islamization and Democratization in Pakistan

Implications for Women and Religious Minorities

SAMINA YASMEEN

The notion of citizenship has come under increased scrutiny in the 1990s. What is meant by citizenship? Who is a citizen? What are the rights and responsibilities of citizens and what spheres do they operate in? These and other similar questions are being asked and answered by analysts the world over.[1] Against the backdrop of the end of the Cold War, emergence of different forms of democracies in eastern Europe and religious revivalism in different parts of the world, the linkages between citizenship, democratization, and religion is also emerging as an area of concern. This essay attempts to explore these linkages with reference to the situation in Pakistan. To this end, it begins by outlining the assumptions about the notion of citizenship which form the matrix within which the analysis is undertaken. Then it focuses on the context of Islamization in Pakistan initiated in the late 1970s, and the extent to which it affected women and religious minorities as citizens. The last part investigates if the process of democratization has changed the position of these two groups in the country.

CITIZENSHIP: A MULTIDIMENSIONAL AND EVOLUTIONARY CONCEPT

Citizenship is more than the mere political act of voting and/or participating in the political organs of the state. As elaborated in T.H.Marshall's famous work entitled *Citizenship and Social Class,* citizenship finds expression in civil, political, and social spheres.[2] But the concept is even wider in scope than suggested by him.[3] The idea of citizenship includes an emotional and psychological aspect; the sense of belonging and the feeling that the citizen is not just part of a system but is acknowledged and respected in this system. The psychological dimension also involves a feeling that a citizen can express ideas and explore one's individuality without fear or concern of being denied this right. It involves a written and/or unwritten claim to human equality in economic, political, social, and psychological arenas.

The claims to equality notwithstanding, not all citizens are equal. The relationship between the individual, the society, and the state can be structured in a manner that creates classes of citizens. Some citizens are more equal than others. At the same time, other citizens can be reduced to the status of 'lesser citizens' by rendering them unable to operate freely and openly in spheres of their choice. Effectively, therefore, the philosophical notion of equality coexists with a visible or invisible inequality and hierarchy of citizens which is often either encouraged or sanctioned by the state.

The notions of citizenship and the right and responsibilities of citizens, however, are not static. Instead they are evolutionary concepts which change with a change in the nature of a state, regime, and/or society. The evolution is not necessarily linear and can be cyclical in nature. A change in regime, for example, can set in motion societal processes that lead to a redefinition of rights and responsibilities of citizens. The pressures thus created, in turn, can force the state to either question or condone the redefinition of what and who is a citizen. At the same time, the state can also introduce change in a society's attitudes which facilitate a further redefinition of the concept of citizenship. The manner in which Islamization and the return to democracy have determined the status of women and religious minorities in Pakistan is a vivid example of this non-linear evolution.

ISLAMIZATION IN PAKISTAN: THE CONTEXT

Since Pakistan's independence in August 1947, Islam has occupied a central place in the country's mass consciousness. That the movement for its creation was triggered and spurred on by the need for Muslims to find a separate state has not been an issue. Nonetheless, the question of the relationship between Islam and state has attracted opposing views. On one end of the spectrum have been the 'modernists' who led the independence movement and subsequently propagated the idea of

200 Islam in History and Politics

a secular state while accepting the centrality of Islam in the Pakistani society. This separation of the state and societal religious values effectively translated into a notion of a Pakistani state for Muslims but not an Islamic state. The corollary to this view was the notion of equality of citizens irrespective of their gender, race, or religion. At the other end of the spectrum have been the 'traditionalists' who were initially opposed to the creation of Pakistan on the grounds that the concept of an Islamic *Ummah* was not bound by or could be restricted to artificially created boundaries. Since Pakistan's independence, however, these traditionalists have argued for and viewed the relationship between the state and Islam as non-negotiable. Pakistan is seen as having been created for Muslims and, therefore, by implication and necessity accorded an Islamic identity. Pakistan is not merely seen as a *state for Muslims* but as an *Islamic state*. For the traditionalists, not only does sovereignty lie with Allah but the sharia provides the only source of knowledge for mediating the relations between individuals and the Pakistani state. While such a view does not necessarily entail inequality of citizens, their patriarchal and narrow Islamic interpretations of sharia do open the way for creating hierarchies of citizens based on their gender, race, and religion.[4]

In this struggle of opposing notions of the Pakistani state, modernists held sway for nearly two-thirds of the country's existence. Pakistan's first governor-general, Mohammad Ali Jinnah, categorically stated that Pakistan was a state for Muslims but one where followers of other religions could also be sure of their equal rights as citizens.[5] That such claims were supported by actions was obvious from the fact that the first meeting of the National Assembly of the nascent state was chaired by a non-Muslim, Mr Mandal. Soon, Mr Mandal, a Hindu, was inducted into the country's first cabinet as the law minister. At the same time Pakistan's first foreign minister was chosen from the Ahmadiyya community— a heretic sect in Islam whose founder claimed prophethood, thus questioning the basic foundations of the religion which is based on the belief that Prophet Mohammad is the last messenger of God. The dominance of the modernists continued as the military took over the reins of the country. The chief martial law administrator and later the president of Pakistan, Ayub Khan, stressed the modern and secular character of the state by allowing a number of Ahmadis to rise to the top echelons of government. In the late 1960s and the 1970s, the mantle of modernism was taken over by Zulfiqar Ali Bhutto. The 1973 constitution of Pakistan, which was unanimously passed during Z.A.Bhutto's rule therefore, clearly articulated the principle of equality of its citizens irrespective of their gender and/or religion.[6]

The modernists, it is important to note, maintained their relative preponderance in Pakistan by carefully negotiating and incorporating some of the ideas presented by the traditionalists into the construction of Pakistani statehood. The second draft constitution of 1952, for instance, introduced the idea of a board of ulama who 'would examine if any Pakistani law was repugnant to Quran and Sunnah'.[7] Similarly, while adhering to the notion of a state for Muslims, Ayub Khan was amenable to declaring Pakistan an Islamic Republic in the 1962 constitution. His successor, General Yahya Khan, also indirectly supported the main Islamic party, Jamaat-i-Islami during the 1970 general elections. More importantly, during the mid-1960s, Z.A. Bhutto introduced the discourse of Islamic Socialism in Pakistan. By claiming to bring alive the real socialist spirit of Islam through the Pakistan People's Party (PPP), he acknowledged the need to incorporate some of the ideas presented by the traditionalists in a modern form.

While this trend continued during Bhutto's rule (1971–7), the early 1970s marked the beginning of the traditionalists' moves to assert their ideas. Against the background of Pakistan's defeat in the 1971 Indo-Pakistan War, the emergence of an educated middle class and quick social mobility resulting from mass migration of labour force into the Middle East, Islamic political parties began identifying 'fertile grounds' for their ideas. Educational institutions, especially colleges and universities, provided such a venue with student wings of Islamic parties emerging as major contenders for power. Islam came to occupy a special position in the political discourse in these institutions. It was, however, not until the 1977 elections that Islam emerged at the centre of national political discourse. The Pakistan National Alliance (PNA) which consisted of anti-Bhutto parties including the Jamaat-i-Islami, argued for introducing *Nizam-i-Mustafa* and, by implication, projected the PPP as a less-Islamic regime. The rigging in the 1977 elections which denied the PNA direct access to power paradoxically strengthened their position.

The traditionalists gained preponderance in Pakistan as a result of the military coup in July 1977. General Zia ul-Haq had initially seized power for ninety days with the declared promise of holding elections. Soon he shelved these promises and planned to rule Pakistan indefinitely. To legitimize this shift and balance the appeal of the PPP, General Zia forged a de facto alliance with conservative elements in the country. The traditionalists were the main beneficiaries of this change. Maulana Maududi of the Jamaat-i-Islami, who had emerged as the main opponent of Bhutto during the 1977 elections, was courted by the military regime. For the first time in the country's history, his ideas were given prominence by the government controlled media.[8] References to the need for Islamizing Pakistan became frequent with General Zia often taking the lead in the process. The traditionalists, however, demanded more than mere pronouncements. If they were to provide the necessary political legitimacy to a military regime, they expected real moves towards establishing an Islamic state in Pakistan. To appease the traditionalists, therefore, Zia embarked on a policy of tokenism; Islam was introduced in the country but only in a piecemeal fashion. The emphasis was on symbolic changes that gave the impression of a state-sponsored move towards Islamization rather than on implementing the real spirit of Islam.

ISLAMIZATION, WOMEN, AND RELIGIOUS MINORITIES

At a general level, Zia's tokenism found expression in the introduction of Islamic banking in Pakistan, establishing a Federal Shariat Court and identifying the Parliament as the *Majlis-i-Shura*. The military regime also tinkered with the penal code; previously accepted punishments for robbery and prohibition of alcohol were dressed in Islamic garb to appease the traditionalists. Specifically, however, Zia's Islamization process targeted weaker elements in the society, women, and religious minorities.

The military had traditionally been the harbinger of modernity in Pakistan. It had introduced laws that protected weaker elements in the society. Ayub Khan, for instance, had introduced the Family Law ordinance in 1961 which regulated marriage, divorces, and controlled polygamy.[9] In marked contrast to this trend, General Zia reverted to a conservative and traditional interpretation of Islam. The notion of purdah supported by Mawdudi was propagated in terms of *chador aur chardevari*. Women were increasingly reminded of their role as nurturers within the confines of home—the private sphere—with the explicit and implicit admission that the public sphere was to be left to men only. To stress the need for such segregation, women appearing on national television were ordered to cover their heads and behave modestly. In line with the principles supported by the Jamaat-i-Islami, schemes were floated for separate women's educational institutions, including women's universities.

This symbolism was parallelled by changes in the legal system with serious ramifications for women.[10] In February 1979, the Hudood ordinance was promulgated which dealt with crimes of 'theft, drunkenness, adultery, rape, and bearing false witness'. The clauses dealing with adultery (*zina*) and rape (*zina-bil-jibr*) were apparently introduced to tackle with the problem of moral decay. The manner in which they were introduced, however, contained the possibility of their exploitation for abuse, and not protection, of women. Zina, according to the ordinance, was classified as a crime against the state and not the husband as was the case in the penal code inherited from the British system. Specifically, in line with the Islamic principles, it required four witnesses who could testify that zina had taken place. Based on the testimony of these witnesses, the ordinance provided for maximum punishment under *hadd* of stoning to death for married people and one hundred lashes for unmarried individuals. In cases where four witnesses were not available, the ordinance provided for the lesser punishment under *tazir* consisting of 'imprisonment for upto 10 years, and flogging of up to 30 strips and/or a fine'.

In 1980, the Council of Islamic Ideology (CII) drafted a law dealing with *qisas*, or retribution for harm done, and *diyat*, blood money in lieu of a murder or bodily harm. The draft bill, which was passed by the Majlis-i-Shura in August 1984, relegated women to a secondary status; it provided for blood money equivalent to the value of 30.63 kg of silver for a man and half that amount for a woman murdered. The provision was defended on grounds that while men are the breadwinners, women remain dependent on men. The clauses related to qisas also discriminated against women. They required two male witnesses for a murder to be proven. By excluding women, they provided for situations where testimony of women could go unnoticed. Two years later, in April 1982, the CII proposed a new Law of Evidence. Designed to replace the Evidence Act of 1872, this law originally aimed at literally halving the value of testimony by women. It argued that two women witnesses equalled one man! Faced with opposition from women's organizations, the draft law was modified and made applicable to financial cases only. For other cases, determining the value of a single woman's testimony was left to the concerned judge.

Together, the symbolic and legal changes reduced women to the status of 'lesser citizens' in Pakistan. They were not only denied the protection of the state but the door was opened to increasing their exploitation. The Hudood ordinance, for instance, failed to distinguish between rape and adultery by setting similar requirements for witnesses. The witnesses had to be male and needed to have witnessed the act of zina or zina-bil-jibr. Not only did the provision regarding gender of the witnesses deny women the right to accuse rapists of rape, but by implying that a child born out of a wedlock was a proof of a crime committed, it put women in an unwinnable position. Even if they were raped, bearing a child as a result of the rape could be considered 'their' crime against the state while the rapists could walk freely for want of four witnesses. The problem with the ordinance further stemmed from its failure to establish clear linkages with previous laws of the country. For example, it did not clearly distinguish between zina, which is a sexual relationship outside a marriage, and the failure to report a second marriage. In a patriarchal system, where women are equated with the notion of *izzat* (honour), these loopholes were easily exploited by interested parties. Often men accused their divorced women who chose to remarry of committing zina and led them to being imprisoned until the case was dismissed by the courts. On other occasions, rape went unpunished while the victim was punished because she gave birth to a child as a result of the rape.

Religious minorities became the other major target of the symbolic Islamization in Pakistan. According to the 1981 census, 2.8 million non-Muslims constituted 3.3 per cent of Pakistan's total population. Of these, Christians and Hindus formed the two major groups accounting for nearly 89 per cent of the total non-Muslim population. Ahmadis, who were declared non-Muslim by virtue of a decision by the Parliament in 1974, formed the next biggest group with 104,244 members. Most of these communities had settled in Punjab and Sindh.[11] The 1973 constitution of Pakistan granted them equal rights as citizens. Although the fourth amendment to the constitution introduced special seats for religious minorities and women, it did not deny them the right to participate politically in the system on equal footing. Soon after coming to power, General Zia ul-Haq ended this equality. In September 1978 he introduced an amendment to the electoral system altering the 1973 constitution which created separate electorates for non-Muslims in national and provincial assemblies. Not only could non-Muslims not vote for Muslim candidates, but they also had to elect their own representatives from across the country and/or the provinces. For this purpose, Christians and Hindus were given four seats each in the national assembly, while Sikhs, Buddhists, and Parsi communities and other non-Muslims were given one seat. Ahmadis were given one seat as well. At the provincial level, the minorities were allocated twenty-three seats with Sindh and Punjab accounting for seventeen of the seats.

The change in the electoral system was prompted by a need to please the traditional elements in Pakistan. Maududi's notion of citizenship in an Islamic state, for instance, had included a dichotomy between Muslims and *dhimmis* (protected subjects).[12] An interest in reducing the chances of progressive groups, especially the PPP, to win support of religious minorities, provided the other incentive. Interestingly, it was also supported by some non-Muslim Pakistanis, such as Julius Salik, as well.[13]

The net result of the change was an alteration in the rights of non-Muslim Pakistanis as citizens. While the constitution invoked principles of equality irrespective of gender, race, and religion, the amendment relegated non-Muslims to the status of lesser citizens. No longer could they operate in political space as equals.

The process of Islamization resulted in other legal changes which also restricted the psychological space for non-Muslims as Pakistani citizens. Blasphemy laws were added to Pakistan's penal code which was amended to make defiling of the Holy Quran punishable with life imprisonment (295-B), of the name of the Holy Prophet with death (295-C), and of any other personage revered in Islam with three years imprisonment (298-A).[14] Equally discriminatory was the promulgation of Ordinance No. 20 which barred Ahmadis from calling their places of worship mosques, reciting *azaan*, and directly or indirectly passing themselves as Muslims or referring to their religion as Islam. Given that Ahmadis had consistently identified themselves as Muslims and viewed themselves as a sect of Islam, rather than a religious minority, the ordinance directly targeted their sense of identity and made it difficult for them to practise their religion.

The legal injunctions affecting women and religious minorities came under heavy criticism from domestic human rights groups and women's organizations. Internationally, Amnesty International, the United Nations, and the US Congress urged General Zia to end the discrimination of the weaker groups of Pakistani society.[15] The pressures were faced and absorbed by a regime which was confident of its usefulness to the west. Aware of the American need to rely on Pakistan as a front-line state against the Soviet incursions into Afghanistan, General Zia studiously avoided giving in to the pressure. Combining Islamization and military dictatorship, therefore, General Zia was directly and indirectly able to maintain a hierarchy of citizens in Pakistan until his death in August 1988. To what extent did his death, and the introduction of democracy, rectify this categorization of Pakistani citizens? The answer to this question necessitates an understanding of the societal implications of Zia's policy of Islamization and an appreciation of the context in which democratization in Pakistan has proceeded since late 1988.

DEMOCRATIZATION AND SOCIETAL ISLAM

The state-sponsored Islamization triggered a societal change in Pakistan. Until Zia's use of Islam for political purposes, religion was considered a personal rather than a state issue. The attitude was partly due to the influence of sufi tradition in South Asia which survived despite the presence of more orthodox approaches to Islam. Once the military regime deployed governmental resources, especially the government controlled print and electronic media, the relative balance changed. Pakistani people were regularly exposed to the traditional interpretation of Islam, as well as the notion of Pakistan as an Islamic state. This gradually altered the dominant notions of identity. While in the past, Islam was primarily used to distinguish Pakistani Muslims from Indian Hindus, the general public now began to use Islam to construct their national/domestic identity. People came to be identified in terms of good and bad, practising and non-practising Muslims. Just as Islam had moved to the centre-stage of political reality, it also came to occupy a special position in the social discourse and construction of social identities.

The process was aided by the Zia regime's policies on education. Within the context of privatization of education and support for privately funded institutions, the military regime embarked on a process of supporting religious educational institutions (*din-I madrasa*). The number of these institutions increased exponentially from 868 in 1975 to more than 1644 during Zia's rule. Not only were these schools allowed to receive financial assistance from foreign sources, but the government also met approximately 36 per cent of their costs through the Zakat Fund. The policy was not restricted to any one religious denomination. Instead followers of all schools and views, such as Deobandis, Brelvis, Ahl-i Hadith, and Ahl-i Tasih, received such assistance. By the 1990s, the number of such religious educational institutions had reached 2512 in Punjab alone with a total number of 218,939 resident and non-resident students.[16]

The cumulative effect of these policies has been the creation of groups of educated citizens who subscribe to different, and often contradictory, interpretations of Islam. The state-sponsored Islamization of the 1980s, in other words, has led to a situation where Islam dominates social discourse.

Parallel to this trend has been the introduction of controlled democracy in Pakistan. The process started in 1985 when General Zia, as a quid pro quo for lifting martial law, secured an amendment to the 1973 constitution by the Parliament elected on a non-party basis in 1985. Known as the eighth amendment, the change in the constitution altered the balance of power between the president and the prime minister. While the prime minister was elected by the National Assembly and retained executive powers, the president acquired the right to nominate the prime minister and dismiss him if he deemed it appropriate. The president acquired the powers to appoint judges of the Supreme Court and the High Courts, provincial governors, chiefs of the army, and other senior bureaucrats. Most importantly, Article 58–2(b) of the constitution inserted via the eighth amendment gave the president the discretionary power to dissolve the national assembly if the considered that the federation was not functioning appropriately. These alterations to the constitution effectively changed the nature of Pakistan's political system; instead of being a parliamentary system, it came to include elements of the presidential system as well.

Given that General Zia was both the president and the chief of army staff (COAS), the eighth amendment resulted in a dyarchy, with the balance of power favouring General Zia against the prime minister, Junejo. That this anomaly was fraught with dangers for the country's political stability became apparent as General Zia summarily dismissed Junejo's government in May 1988 due to personal differences. Three months later when Zia was killed in a plane crash in August 1988, the situation changed, albeit slightly. The November 1988 elections were held on a party basis and Benazir Bhutto became the first democratically elected prime minister. The structural inequalities in the political system, however, persisted. The dyarchy of 1985–8 was replaced by a troika consisting of the president, the COAS and the prime minister. With the military and the president holding most of the actual and real power, Benazir Bhutto was forced to focus on managing this triangular relationship as a prerequisite for her political survival. The pervasiveness of corruption in the society, government, and political circles, as well as personal and institutional interests of the president and the military, however, made management of the troika difficult for Bhutto and her government was dismissed by the president in August 1990. Nawaz Sharif's rise to power in 1990 did not change the situation. Instead, the trend set in 1985 continued resulting in nine governments in as many years!

The political instability, massive corruption, and the imbalance between presidential and prime ministerial powers, which have been the hallmark of Pakistani political system from 1988 to 1997, have contributed to each government's failure to address pressing social and political problems. Interested in ensuring their political survival, these governments have shied away from tackling issues that are either too divisive or risky. Questioning the implications of Zia's Islamization policies falls in the second category of too risky a business. Given that Islam has come to occupy a special place in social discourse, and traditionalists have been able to mobilize masses in the name of Islam (evidenced in the case of demonstrations against Salman Rushdie in 1990), no government has attempted to seriously alter the hierarchy of citizenship created by General Zia. Instead, they have resorted to a policy of tokenism aimed at placating critical elements in the society.

The policies pursued by Benazir Bhutto during her two terms as the prime minister (1988–90 and 1993–6) are a vivid example of such tokenism. During her first term, she upgraded the women's division established by General Zia to the status of a ministry. She also established a women's bank operated by women only.[17] During her second term, she introduced the idea of police stations managed by women only. The initiative was taken on the grounds that often women intending to complain avoided visiting police stations for fear of more harassment by male police. Similarly, the idea of lady health visitors was introduced with the avowed belief in increasing women's ability to earn incomes and disseminate knowledge about health issues to other women. At the same time, the government controlled electronic media, especially television, was used to alter the commonly held images of women's role in private and public spheres. Beyond these symbolic and token gestures, however, no real progress was made to improve the condition of women in Pakistan. So obvious was the need to restrict oneself to tokenism that the issue of reviving reserved seats for women (introduced in 1973 and lapsed in 1990) became a hostage to political wrangling. Instead of unilaterally declaring that the PPP would issue tickets to more women in the next elections, Bhutto's government insisted on tackling the issue on a bilateral platform with the Pakistan Muslim League.[18] The record of Nawaz Sharif's first term as the prime minister was equally flawed. Instead of attempting to repeal the legal changes introduced during Zia's period, his government got the Sharia Bill passed which indirectly strengthened the hands of the traditionalists in the country.

The state's inability to protect its citizens and correct imbalances in the status of different members of the system has had serious repercussions for women and religious minorities in the 1990s. The society has generally tended to translate and evaluate issues in terms of good and bad practices, and attempted to find Islamic answers to even previously accepted practices with negative connotations for women. The question of *halala* (remarrying the ex-wife after her marriage to someone else) raised in January 1996 as a result of the Sindh High Court's decision is a case in point. In this decision, the judge condemned the practice of halala and of divorcing a woman by three simultaneous pronouncements of *talaq* (divorce). Soon afterwards ulama differed on the notion of halala.[19] The controversy raised doubts about the divorces resulting from simultaneous pronouncements and/or the remarriages of divorced women. The controversy surrounding Saima Waheed's marriage of her own choice and her father's opposition on grounds of the right of the *wali* (guardian) in a marriage is another example of the negative implications of unreflected references to and rigid interpretations of Islamic principle. That the country was divided on the merits of the case until it was settled by judiciary is an example of how piecemeal Islamization has affected women's rights in the country.

Apart from the general notions of a woman's role, justified on erroneous notions of Islam, Zia's policy of Islamization has continued to have a negative impact on women. The abuse of the Hudood ordinance, which was obvious during the military regime, has continued in the 1990s. According to the Human Rights Commission of Pakistan, for instance, of the more than a thousand women jailed in 1995, a majority were imprisoned under this ordinance.[20] The increased recourse to these laws is obvious from the fact that recently men from the middle and upper middle class have also come to use the Hudood ordinance to take revenge from their divorced wives. The frequency of dowry deaths, a phenomenon where brides are accidentally killed if they do not bring enough dowry, has also been on the rise.

The implications of the interplay between Islamization and controlled democratization have been equally, if not more, devastating for religious minorities. The policy of separate electorates for non-Muslims has introduced a de facto apartheid in Pakistan in which the inequality of citizens is condoned and supported. While this inequality was less obvious during the Zia regime, it has become apparent during the 1990s when frequent elections have been held in Pakistan. The boundaries of the electorate are determined by the state boundaries in case of the National Assembly, and the provincial boundaries for provincial assemblies. Such a delimitation imposes severe pressures on those willing to represent their respective communities. A Christian candidate for the National Assembly, for instance, has to canvass across the country, whereas a candidate for the Punjab Assembly needs to do the same across the province. Not only is the cost prohibitive for the candidates but it also adds to the overall expenditures incurred by the Election Commission.[21] More importantly, such a policy limits the rights of non-Muslim citizens in securing appropriate representation at national and provincial levels. If faced with any problem, the non-Muslim citizens cannot approach their Muslim members of the Parliament as they do not play a part in electing these representatives. The problem becomes significant when the religious minorities are harassed on religious grounds and denied access to jobs.[22] To put it differently, the system of separate electorates not only restricts the political space but also constricts the economic and social space for Pakistan's religious minorities.

The Islamization started during the Zia regime and its societal implications in the 1990s also restricts the psychological space available to non-Muslim Pakistani citizens. With the possibility of being accused of blasphemy in the background, religious minorities find themselves under a constant threat of undue victimization. Not that such threat does not exist for Muslim Pakistanis as well, but non-Muslims have been suffering more than their Muslim counterparts from the effects of the blasphemy laws of the Zia regime. The internationally publicized case of Salamat Masih (1993–5),[23] in which a thirteen-year old boy was accused alongside two other Christians of blaspheming, is an example of the negativity created by these laws. As the High Court heard the case and released the accused, religious parties and groups announced prizes for those who would kill Salamat and Rahmat Masih.

THE FUTURE FOR *LESSER* CITIZENS

Faced with the continuation of their secondary status as citizens, a number of women and members of the religious minority groups have established organizations aimed at rectifying the situation.[24] The moves, however, are unlikely to bear results without an active role played by the state. While the Muslim League Government of Nawaz Sharif repealed parts of the eighth amendment dealing with presidential powers, the other discriminatory laws that were introduced by General Zia and made sacrosanct through the eighth amendment remain. Without such a bold action, which is bound to irk the traditionalists, women, and religious minorities will remain lesser citizens in Pakistan.

Endnotes

1. See, for example, Michael Hill and Lian Kwen Fee, *The Politics of Nation Building and Citizenship in Singapore* (New York, 1995); and David Prior, John Stewart and Kieron Walsh, *Citizenship: Rights, Community and Participation* (London, 1995).
2. T.H. Marshall, *Citizenship and Social Class, and Other Essays* (Cambridge, 1950); see also, Martin Bulmer and Anthony M. Rees (eds), *Citizenship Today: The Contemporary Relevance of T.H. Marshall* (London, 1996).
3. Hill and Fee, *Politics of Nation Building*, pp. 27–35
4. Ishtiaq Ahmed, *The Concept of An Islamic State* (Stockholm, 1987).
5. G.W. Choudhury (ed.), *Documents and Speeches on the Constitution of Pakistan* (Dhaka, 1967), pp. 21–2.

6. *The Constitution of the Islamic Republic of Pakistan*, as modified upto 27 July 1994 (Islamabad, National Assembly of Pakistan, January 1997), Articles 25 and 26.

7. Hamza Alavi, *Pakistan and Islam: Ethnicity and Ideology*, in Fred Halliday and Hamza Alavi (eds), *State and Ideology in the Middle East and Pakistan* (London, 1988), pp. 106–7.

8. Seyyed Vali Reza Nasr, *Mawdudi & The Making of Islamic Revivalism* (Oxford, 1996), pp. 41–6.

9. Khawar Mumtaz and Farida Shaheed, *Women of Pakistan: Two Steps Forward, One Step Back?* (Lahore, 1987), pp. 57–61.

10. The following discussion of the legal changes draws heavily upon: Khawar Mumtaz and Farida Shaheed, *Women of Pakistan*, chapter 7; and Anita M. Weiss, 'The Consequences of State Policies for Women in Pakistan', in Myron Weiner and Ali Banuazizi (eds), *The Politics of Social Transformation in Afghanistan, Iran and Pakistan* (New York, 1994), pp. 412–44.

11. *Report on The General Elections 1988*, vol. I, Election Commission of Pakistan, pp. 205–7.

12. Nasr, *Mawdudi and the Making of Islamic Revivalism*, pp. 99–102.

13. Personal interview with a leader of a religious minority group, 1 July 1996.

14. *State of Human Rights in 1995* (Lahore, Human Rights Commission of Pakistan), pp. 104–5.

15. Mohammad Waseem, *Politics and the State in Pakistan* (Islamabad, 1994), pp. 379–86.

16. Tanveer Kureshi, 'Madariss fanning sectarian hatred', *The Friday Times*, 22–8 February 1996, pp. 6–7.

17. Weiss, 'The Consequences of State Politics, pp. 438–44.

18. Personal interview with a member of the Bhutto government, August 1996.

19. Khaled Ahmed, 'Halala', anyone?, *The Friday Times*, 8–14 February 1996, p. 9.

20. *State of Human Rights in 1995* (Lahore, Human Rights Commission of Pakistan), p. 141. The other major cause of women's imprisonment was illegal immigration.

21. Personal interview with a leader of a religious minority community, July 1996; see also, Khaled Ahmed, 'Unbearable irony of separate electorates', *The Friday Times*, 14–20 March 1996, p. 9.

22. C.M. Naim, 'The Second Tyranny of Religious Minorities', *South Asia Bulletin*, vol. XIV, no. 2, 1994, pp. 104–5.

23. *State of Human Rights in 1995* (Lahore, Human Rights Commission of Pakistan), pp. 104–7; *State of Human Rights in 1993* (Lahore, Human Rights Commission of Pakistan), pp. 40–3.

24. Najma Babar, 'Ready for Action: Minorities', *The Herald, Election Special 1993*, pp. 42–4.

11

Salience of Islam
in South Asian Politics
Pakistan and Bangladesh

ASIM ROY

There are some general misconceptions and wrong assumptions underlying popular non-Muslim perceptions of the Islamic world, especially
in the West. First, there is a tendency to regard the 'real' world of Islam
as coextensive with the 'Middle East' and almost synonymous with the
Arab world. This pervasive misconception would seem extraordinarily
intriguing in the light of the fact that Arab Muslims constitute no more
than a quarter of the total Muslim population in the world, and nearly
two-third of the world's Muslims are to be found east of the Persian
Gulf. For our purposes here, it is even of greater interest that out of
the four countries with the highest Muslim population today, namely
Indonesia, Bangladesh, India, and Pakistan, the last three are located
in South Asia. Secondly, there has been the most persistent stereo-
typification of Islam as militant, violent, puritanical, and fundamentalist
in inspiration as well as anti-modernistic and anti-Western in orientation. For these non-Muslim critics, Muslim opposition to separation
between religion and state as well as to the very basic political concept
of sovereignty of the nation-state overridden by the primacy of the
concept of the *umma* (community of believers), Islamic socio-religious
practices like polygamy, seclusion of women, and harsh inhumane
physical punishment under the sharia (Islamic religious law) courts all
testify to their 'conservative anti-modernistic' minds. Examples of this
nature, taken together with other expressions of their 'anti-Westernism'
as well as their 'militant, violent, puritanical, and fanatical' predispo-
sitions have been noted with some avidity by these critics in their

coverage of what has been seen and interpreted as the upsurge of militant Islam, particularly since the 1970s.[1]

I

A very large part of the Muslim world appeared indeed, particularly since the last two decades of the last century, in severe ferment.[2] The South Asian world of Islam, which is our particular concern here, not only found reverberations of such well-publicized developments, but itself contributed in some important respects to the totality of the phenomena. In conformity with the global trends since 1970s, the South Asian Muslim world also seemed to have been revolving a great deal around the axle of what was seen as an integral part of the global phenomenon of a resurgent Islam. We shall return to these South Asian developments later.

In the light of such pervasive developments in the Muslim world, one would be tempted, and justifiably so, to read religious meaning and significance in them, as has generally been the case with sundry observers. Islamic resurgence, to most, is what it says to be—religious in its origin, inspiration, and expression. Our concern here is not so much to reject totally this popular perception of the centrality of Islam in Muslim developments as to reveal its inadequacies and simplistic nature in particular reference to the two dominant Muslim countries of South Asia—Pakistan and Bangladesh.

There are some major problems with this predominantly religious interpretation of events in the Muslim world, with special reference to South Asia. First, such a perception is necessarily grounded on a both monolithic and normative view of Islam which is found totally inadequate in any empirical or historical analysis of Islamic development in a regional-cultural setting.[3] Until fairly recently we had very little social-scientific knowledge of the regional varieties and formulations of Islam.[4] Secondly, even within this limited validity of the religious explanation, this view fails to differentiate between the 'appearance' and the 'reality'—the 'symbol' and the 'substance'. Religion in South Asia, as elsewhere, is so often found to conceal secular concerns. Transcendental symbols were, in reality, nothing more than convenient covers for not so elevated mundane interests. Clever, and often cynical manipulation of religious symbols for the purposes of social mobilization by both religious and secular elites has been a dominant feature of Muslim politics in South Asia as with other communities there or elsewhere. One could so easily be misled by the apparent 'religious' symbolism of the contemporary 'Islamic resurgence'.

There is a further, and even more contentious problem, generally speaking, in studying politics in relation to Islam, the field being 'strewn', as rather succinctly put by a commentator, 'with ancient potholes and modern mines', the traditional Islamic theological orthodoxy constituting the 'ancient potholes', and the Western academic orthodoxy of 'orientalism' forming the 'modern mines'.[5] Both have tended to view the relationship between Islam and politics in purely scriptural or canonical terms, in total disregard of the historical realities, and hence underlined the unique absence of separation between religion and politics in Islam. In a broad general sense of a linkage between the civil society and the institutions of power, no major religion would allow this separation. One has only to look around the contemporary developments in Judaism in West Asia, Hinduism and Sikhism in India, Buddhism in both South and Southeast Asia, and the fundamentalist Christianity in the USA, Latin America, and elsewhere. To attribute to Muslims a unique and exclusive disposition towards politics of religion seems, therefore, not merely unwarranted but somewhat tendentious. Besides, the separation between Islam and politics, in the more specific sense of a hiatus between the religion and state power, has remained a dominant feature of Islamic history for nearly a millennium. The unity of the temporal and spiritual in Islam is thought, even by many pious Muslim believers, to have ended, for all effective purposes, with the advent of the dynastic rule in Islam in AD 661.

And yet, it is unquestionable that there is a remarkable nexus in Islam of the faith, community, power, and history. A total identity of the faith, its social ideal, and the community is a special genius of Islam. The centrality of the faith and its social ideal in Islam stems from the basic belief that man alone was given a choice and responsibility which he accepted and must act upon, both individually and collectively. There is both gravity and urgency of the Islamic mission not only in the sense that there is a day of reckoning and judgment, but also because it is God's last warning and the last chance given to mankind, after the repeated failures of the earlier prophets, to redeem themselves not merely by individual piety but through actualization of the Islamic social ideal in history. The intertwining of the temporal and the spiritual in Islam is also facilitated by the very nature of historical development of Islam. While the church represented the organized community in Christendom, it fought the state for religious freedom or autonomy until their domains were separated on secular lines. Islam has no 'church', and in its absence the 'community' came to identify itself with the 'state'. The religious struggle for Muslims, therefore, has not been between the church and the state, but for the state; hence this identity of faith and power, religion and state, as well as the very strong appeal of an Islamic 'state' among Muslims.[6] Muslim power-mongers of both secular and religious varieties discovered in this appeal a powerful instrument for manipulation and mobilization of the Muslim masses which is so clearly revealed in contemporary Muslim politics in South Asia, as delineated below.

II

The question about Pakistan in relation to Islam is tautological. Islam is so integral to the origins of Pakistan as well as its subsequent development. The attainment of independence left the political leaders with the remaining major task of fulfilling the Islamic aspirations of the religious leadership and the masses of Muslims.[7] At the dawn of independence religious demands and expectations of the people naturally loomed large on the Pakistan horizon. The inability or unwillingness of the Pakistani rulers to rise up to this popular expectation, and more importantly, their cynical manipulation and exploitation of religious emotions and concerns of the Muslim masses, giving rise to unending social and political confusions and uncertainties have been the source of many a human tragedy of an epic proportion. A 'Muslim' state created for the Muslims was an immediate reality as early as its creation, but to call it 'Islamic' involved a great deal more. The story of Pakistan politics since its inception is one of a blatant pursuit of political self-interests by Pakistani ruling elites disguised in terms of a religious discourse. A probe into the changing social composition of the Pakistani ruling classes and the structure of state power in Pakistan is essential to understand the role and place of Islam in this politics of elite dominance.

The most salient and enduring feature of the political system and the power structure in Pakistan has been the dominance of the big and firmly entrenched landlord and the rising capitalist classes, buttressed by the military-bureaucratic oligarchy. Pakistan inherited a colonial state apparatus in the form of its army and bureaucracy virtually intact, a rather weak 'national' party in the Muslim League dominated by landlords, and a political culture totally inadequate to ensure the primacy of the political process and of representative government. Relative to the political institutions at the dawn of independence, the military-bureaucratic structure in Pakistan was, therefore, far more developed. This set the stage for a remarkable and almost perpetual dominance of the state apparatus and politics of Pakistan by the bureaucracy and the army. There have been some shifts, over the years, in the relative power and position of each of the partners in the military-bureaucracy entente but the complementarity between the two remained unassailed.[8] The close nexus of the military, landed, and capitalist interests was reinforced by some calculated measures taken by the successive military regimes. The officer corps were generally drawn from the land-owning class since the colonial times. General Ayub Khan's regime both strengthened and extended this integration of the military into the propertied class. He began to make land grants to senior army officers and thus created landed interests even among officers not belonging to land-owning families. Likewise, officer corps found their ways into the commercial and industrial establishments, being offered coveted positions in the boards after retirement, often as chairpersons in public corporations in the nationalized sector. This particular trend had accelerated even further under the regime of General Zia ul-Haq.[9]

The Pakistan economy was clearly geared to this political structure. The program of economic growth launched under the military regimes in the '1960s was designed to concentrate incomes in the hands of the industrial and landed magnates. The investment targets were to be achieved on the basis of the doctrine of 'functional inequality', involving transfer of incomes from the poorer to the high-income groups. We have discussed below how General Zia's 'profit and loss sharing' system, justified in terms of Islamic prohibition of *riba* (interest), made such transfer of incomes easier.[10] It is not surprising therefore that by the end of that decade, a small group of families with interlocking directorates dominated industry, banking, and insurance in Pakistan. Thus forty-three families represented 76.8 per cent of all manufacturing assets (including foreign and government assets). The major industrial families were a close-knit group. Often tied by kinship relations, they usually sat on each other's board of directors. About one-third of such seats in companies controlled by the forty-three families were occupied by members of other families within the forty-three.[11]

III

Islam was brought in to play a seminal role by the Pakistani governing elite in its politics of total dominance. This role is summed up, in broad and general terms, by a Pakistani scholar:

> Aware of the attachment of the masses to Islam, the ruling classes hope to secure a future for themselves by establishing an authoritarian and exploitative system, which they claim to be Islamic. It is with this aim in view that the so-called Islamisation of state and society has been undertaken in Pakistan.[12]

To perpetuate an inegalitarian system the strategy of the governing classes was to proclaim Pakistan an ideological state based on Islam, and not a democracy. They were also able to draw, on the basis of mutual interests, the support of the conservative ulama (scriptural scholars) who pressed medieval Islamic scholastic tradition to the service of the Pakistani rulers, defending the status quo and legitimizing authoritarian rule.

Islam is, however, amenable to other interpretations. The Muslim fundamentalist party, the Jamaat-i-Islami under Maulana Maududi, challenged the unholy alliance between the conservative ulama and the government, and projected their own model of the 'Islamic state'. President Ayub Khan banned the Jamaat-i-Islami and arrested its leaders, including Maulana Maududi, on the ground of its carrying on 'subversive activities against the state' and constituting 'a danger to the public peace'.[13]

The difficulties facing the Pakistani rulers stemmed from the fact that howsoever onerous was the undertaking of building an Islamic society, they could not evade it. No state can live in a vacuum. Islamic or not, some ideology was critical for Pakistan's sustenance. Compulsions of this nature forced, in the next decade, a dramatic reversal of the situation, when the Jamaat's persistent campaign and penetration of the military cadres brought about the overthrow of Zulfiqar Ali Bhutto's civilian government through a military coup by General Zia ul-Haq, who was a close relation of Mian Tufail, the chief of the Jamaat. By the late 1960s, significant changes in the social composition of the army had been occurring. Until then, the officers were 'predominantly from the landowning class' and brought up in the British military tradition. The new officer corps began to draw on the petite bourgeoisie in both the urban and rural areas. They were drawn largely from the economically depressed migrants from East Punjab—like Zia ul-Haq himself—and the unirrigated Potwar region of West Punjab. This new officer corps were 'less literate and more religious', 'socially more conservative', and susceptible to the Jamaat's puritanism.[14]

IV

The Zia regime unleashed, not unexpectedly, a process of unprecedented Islamization of the country's institutions. His series of reforms, labelled *Nizam-I Mustafa* (Rule of the Prophet), professedly designed to bring the country's laws into conformity with Islamic principles and values, covered three aspects of the Pakistani life: educational,

judicial-legal, and economic. The educational reforms laid down Arabic
as a compulsory foreign language requirement, made courses in the
Quranic and Islamic studies obligatory throughout the educational system,
and proposed segregation of sexes in educational institutions at the
upper level. With the promulgation of four *hudud* (sing. *hadd*, an offence
contrary to clear Quranic sanctions) ordinances, outlining Islamic punishments and standards of evidence for theft, adultery, consumption of
alcohol, and false imputation of immodesty to women, he provided for
harsh and inhumane physical punishments like amputation of hands and
stoning to death. New judicial institutions in the forms of Federal Sharia
Court (Islamic law court) and the Appellate Bench of the Supreme Court
were set in place to implement the new laws. There is an obvious
element of tokenism in such reforms coloured in Islamic hues in as
much as the jurisdiction of the sharia courts, largely stacked with
'Islamic moderates', excluded constitutional principles, fiscal matters,
and martial law regulations.[15]

It is the Zia regime's much-vaunted program of Islamizing Pakistan's
economy that has attracted wide attention. His economic program
consisted of three major reforms, claimed to have been Islamically
inspired. The first two are compulsory collection of *zakat* (a tax assessed against capital assets, popularly called 'poor tax') and *ushr*
(agricultural tax). Both of these taxes are traditional Islamic methods
of collecting and distributing welfare. Zakat is assessed at 2.5 per cent
of cash value of financial assets, and ushr at 5 per cent of the profits
from agricultural land. The collected taxes are made available to local
Zakat Committees for distribution to poor Muslims and to charities. The
third measure, relative to the Islamic injunction against collection of
riba, is officially labelled the Profit and Loss Sharing (PLS) system,
popular as interest-free banking. The measure, in essence, is one of
replacement of the principle of limited liability by a system of sharing
profit and loss.

If the objective of this innovative measure was to eliminate financial
extortion and exploitation, it seemed to have gone just the other way.
First, a fairly large proportion of deposits belonged to the lower middle
class, and the system discriminated against the poorer depositors. The
profit to be paid to the depositor was determined by the bank's operations, while the investor could receive loans from banks at zero interest
with a nominal service charge and thus make a large profit. A number
of cases were actually reported where a 'large number of interest-free
or low-interest loans earmarked for small farmers' had been 'advanced
to large and influential farmers with contacts with the ruling hierarchy.'[16] Secondly, the system led to widespread fraud, resulting from the

corrupt business people resorting to 'multiple account books'. Thirdly, the business community complained of undesirable interference by the bureaucrats of public-controlled nationalized banks with the manage- ment of individual projects, obviously prompted by the profit and loss considerations. Fourthly, leaving aside the issue of the application of the PLS system to the entire economy, a substantial proportion of the banking sector continued to operate under the interest-based system. It would appear from this that 'the purpose of the government is not so much to abolish the institution of interest as to make it appear to the public that interest has been eliminated from financial transactions.'[17] Finally, the exclusive concern with the elimination of interest from the organized financial sector appeared hypocritical in the light of wide prevalence in the rural sector, on one hand, of extortionate interest rates charged from small farmers and landless peasants by money- lender landlords, and on the other, of *muzara'a* (share-cropping, ground rent).

Zia's accidental death or assassination (as widely suspected) has shifted the focus of Pakistan politics away from Islamization and the Jamaat (cited as a possible motive under the assassination theory), but one would have to add, only for a while. Because, judging by the past events, one would be disinclined to overlook Islam in relation to Pakistan as yet.

V

Almost on the same note one is inclined to conclude about Islam in relation to Bangladesh and its politics. The dramatic events there, happening at a kaleidoscopic speed in the last few decades, leave no doubt that much of Bangladesh's problems can be attributed to the pressures of a dual identity of which Islam is one and vital; the other no less seminal is the local Bengali linguistic-cultural identity. The salience of Islam in Bangladesh, in a wider historical perspective, is posited in her participation in the Pakistan movement, leading to the Partition of 1947. The failures, inadequacies, and insincerities of the Pakistan rulers, repeatedly demonstrated in their dealings with Islam, caused a Bengali backlash in its vigorous and chauvinistic affirmation of the Bengali self to the point of almost undermining Islamic relevance to the Bangladeshis.[18]

On the morrow of the liberation, while Sheikh Mujeeb was still in the West Pakistan jail, many enthusiastic members of the caretaker government of Bangladesh tried to prevail upon and even pressurize schools and other institutions to drop 'Islam' or 'Muslim' from their names. Some Dhaka University academics and other members of the Bengali intelligentsia urged substitution of readings from the Quran, on the National Radio and Television, by 'Speaking the Truth' based on secular morality and ethics.[19] On his return Mujeeb banned all religion-based political parties and groups. The process was carried further with the promulgation of the new constitution whereby the People's Republic of Bangladesh adopted 'secularism' as one of the fundamental constitutional objectives. In a series of sweeping educational reforms, history books were purged of Pakistani heroes, religious instructions for minorities were introduced in schools, and on the basis of the recommendations contained in an Interim Report of the Education Commission (May 1973), religious instructions at schools from grades one to eight ceased, while it was made an elective subject from grades nine to twelve, and only for humanities. But the yawning gap between the social reality and the political idealism of the new leaders was soon revealed, as the secular ethos of the government's education policy was rejected by 75 per cent of the people included in a government-sponsored survey, comprising primarily educationists at the school, college, and university levels. They spoke in favour of a more balanced modern religious instruction. The revised education policy retained religious instruction at all levels of schools except for grades one to five.[20]

This presaged an orthodox Muslim backlash, very resentful of the secularizing policies of the Mujeeb government, especially its ban on religious parties. The religious emotion was further roused by Mujeeb's close economic and political relations with the 'godless' Russians and 'fanatical Hindu' Indians. Rampant smuggling across the Bangladesh-India borders gave the Islamists the opportunity of pointing their fingers at India's 'evil' designs on Bangladesh and its hegemonic ambition. The accommodation of differences with Pakistan and Pakistan's recognition of Bangladesh had also removed a major obstacle in the way of repairing the broken bridge of Muslim fraternity of the former united Pakistan. Mujeeb attempted to placate the 'Islamic' elements by way of enhanced Islamization of his speech and lifestyle, restoring the hitherto suspended Islamic Foundation to an Islamic Academy, and attending the first Islamic Conference (1974) held in Pakistan, being escorted from Bangladesh by two Arab heads of government. But it all came too late. Such religious issues, taken together with the gigantic failure of his government to deliver the economic and political goods, brought about his downfall with a military coup (1975).

Mujeeb's overthrow marked the beginning of a long period of blatant military rule, successively under Major General Zia ur-Rahman

(1976–81) and Lieutenant General Husain Muhammad Ershad (1982–91), sought to be redeemed at times by dubious attempts at civilianization. The authoritarian nature of the government persisted until the stepping down of Ershad under popular pressure and the return of parliamentary governments. Following in the footsteps of their Pakistani counterparts, these two strongmen of Bangladesh saw political merits in the use of Islamic religious-cultural symbols. While Zia ur-Rahman seemed to have brought some degree of discretion and restraint to bear on his Islamizing ardour, Ershad bared it all. All in all, Islam bounced back in the post-Mujeeb phase onto the Bangladesh scene. The constitution of 1973 was amended to replace 'secularism' with the solemn proclamation: 'Absolute trust and faith in the Almighty Allah shall be the basis of all action,' as well as to declare that 'solidarity with Muslim states' should become a fundamental objective of the state. Religious instructions from grade one to eight were made compulsory, and new textbook writing with appropriate religious contents was authorized. Islamic broadcasts and telecasts over the government-controlled media proliferated. From the mid-1970s there had been a profusion of religious literature, polemical, and didactic, published in Bangladesh at the initiatives of individuals, religious associations, and the government. The government made generous financial support to such projects, primarily through the Islamic Academy. The period also coincided with a phenomenal mushrooming of Islamic religious-cultural associations, the mosque societies, the Islamic missions, and so on.[21] Ershad became well-known for his public display of piety, repair, and beautification works on mosque, and posters and wall-hangings of excerpts from the Quran in government offices and public buildings. He set up a Department of Religious Affairs to supervise, inter alia, matters relating to the hajj-pilgrimage. He was also credited with the establishment of the Zakat Fund, nominating himself as the chairman. Finally, the ban on political parties based on religion was removed to bring a host of small and not-so-small parties into the political arena. The strongest Islamic party and the most inveterate opponent of secularism to resurface in Bangladesh politics was Jamaat-i-Islami, which had been growing steadily on a political platform of fundamentalism, the Islamic state, staunch pro-Pakistanism, and rabid anti-Indianism. This particular aspect of the legacy of military rule has very largely compromised the character, strength, and stability of the representative government in the post-military governance of Bangladesh. This is clearly reflected in the tempestuous history of the successive parliamentary governments. of a somewhat dynastic nature—initially of Begum Khalida Zia, the widow of Zia ur-Rahman, followed by that of Sheikh Hasina, daughter of

Sheikh Mujeeb, and the further return of Khalida Zia at the head of a coalition in which Jamaat-i Islami is a strong contender. The masses of people, deprived and suffering as they are, appear no better than tragic victims of cold and cruel manipulations by self-seeking political and religious leaders. The real tragedy of the masses of people, who voted for an Islamic El Dorado on the eve of independence and Partition, lies in their later discovery and realization of their lack of choice and freedom to find Islam its rightful place in their own lives and in the life of the country. Neither the people of Bangladesh nor that of Pakistan have ever had a fair chance to ask for what they want of their religion, and not be told by others of what to expect.

VI

How much of all this preoccupations with Islam in the Pakistan and Bangladesh politics that we have explored are real religious concerns? The question, to many, may seem totally unwarranted. To the extent that motivations underlying particular political behaviours and actions are inscrutable one may consider conceding the point. But no religious action in the political arena does have the right to go unchallenged, especially in a given circumstance where such an action is amenable to secular explanations as well. Much of what we perused above as politics might well have been Islamically inspired. But unless and until we are content to conclude on the basis of mere assumptions, we are obliged to raise reasonable questions and doubts to satisfy ourselves before we arrive at our conclusions. A religious concern expressed in the contexts of politics by a Muslim elite, whether religious or non-religious, assume a deeper and more intricate meaning when placed in the contexts of possible secular explanations for the same. Much of the religious discourses among political and religious elites of Pakistan and Bangladesh may not become entirely meaningful if totally divorced from vital secular considerations such as the need for legitimizing the authoritarian rule, mobilizing the masses, promoting national integration or suppressing ethnic subnationalism, targeting the petro-dollar and the profitable labour market of the Middle East, and so on. The attraction and attachment to puritanical or militant Islam for the believers in times of social and political challenges, changes, and dislocations are likewise concerns not wholly spiritual. In history and politics human motivations are largely a matter of conjecture, but it behoves us to remain most careful in informing and investing such conjectures with knowledge and reason.

Endnotes

1. *New York Times* (18 June 1978): 'The Moslem world rekindles its militancy'. The present article was written before the unprecedented spate of Muslim jihadi militant actions, including suicide bombings, especially since the dawn of the new millennium, which have virtually ensconced and universalized the popular notion of a 'fanatical and violent Muslim'.

2. Set in the context of the historic self-assertion of the Arab oil barons, the Arab world of Saudi Arabia, Egypt, Libya, Syria, Iraq, and Lebanon witnessed significant developments, widely perceived as flowing from a resurgent, and even revolutionary Islam. The most publicized case of the revolutionary Islam in action was, however, in the non-Arab world of Iran, providing the glaring example of a clerical order under Ayatollah Khomeini successfully bringing about the downfall of the world's oldest monarchy. About the same time the news media found, thanks to Moscow's intervention in Afghanistan, a new focus in the religious war of the Mujahideen against the 'godless communists' in that country.

3. My own studies in Islam in the regional context of Bengal: see A. Roy, *The Islamic Syncretistic Tradition of Bengal* (Princeton, 1983).

4. In July 1989, the South Asian Institute, University of Heidelberg, West Germany, organized a powerful international conference, claiming it as the first one on the 'Regional Varieties of Islam in Pre-modern South Asia'. The outcome of the conference is published in a thick volume, including my own contribution: Asim Roy, 'The Interface of Islamization, Regionalization and Syncretization: the Bengal Paradigm', in A.L. Dallapiccola and S.Z. Lallemant (eds), *Islam and Indian Regions* (Stuttgart, 1992), pp. 95–128.

5. E. Ahmed, 'Islam and politics', in M.A. Khan (ed.), *Islam, Politics and the State. The Pakistan Experience* (London, 1985), p. 13.

6. W.C. Smith, *Islam in Modern History* (Princeton, 1957), pp. 10ff, 211: n. 6.

7. Poignantly illustrative of this confusion in people's minds is the anecdote that Jinnah, the doyen of the 'Westernized' Muslims in the Indian subcontinent, was greeted by the rural folks of Sind with 'Long Live Mawlana, Muhammad 'Ali Jinnah'. Jinnah is said to have taken the trouble of making them able to distinguish between political and religious leadership; H. Bolitho, *Jinnah, Creator of Pakistan* (London, 1954), p. 213.

8. H. Alavi, 'The military in the state of Pakistan', paper presented at the Institute of Development Studies and Institute of Commonwealth Studies Conference, Sussex, England; cited in Khan (ed.), *Islam, Politics and the State*, p. 210.

9. A. Hussain, 'Pakistan: the crisis of the state', in Khan (ed.), ibid.; also Craig Baxter et. al., *Government and Politics in South Asia* (Boulder, USA, 2nd edn, 1991), p. 215.

10. See below, pp. 6–7.

11. L.J. White, *Industrial Concentration and Economic Power in Pakistan* (Princeton, 1972), pp. 81–5.

12. O.A. Khan, 'Political and Economic Aspects of Islamisation', in Khan (ed.), *Islam, Politics and the State*, p. 127.
13. *Pakistan Times* (18 June 1964).
14. Hussain, 'Pakistan: the crisis of the state', in Khan (ed.), *Islam, Politics and the State*, pp. 222–3.
15. *The Major Acts* (Lahore, Khyber Law Publishers, 1984), pp. 1-30; C.H. Kennedy, 'Islamisation in Pakistan: implementation of the hudood ordinances,' *Asian Survey*, Vol. 28, no. 3 (March 1988), pp. 307–16.
16. O.A. Khan, 'Political and Economic Aspects of Islamisation', in Khan (ed.), *Islam, Politics and the State*, p. 151.
17. Ibid.
18. In the anguished words of a Bangladeshi historian: 'To suppress the popular demands for basic rights and to serve the selfish individual, group, and party interests, the rulers exploited the name of Islam and the religious sentiments of the people. Any demand or even a small action from East Bengal for a rightful share in the administration of the country was termed as anti-Islam and anti-Pakistan and condemned in very strong terms as spreading "provincialism and subversion". The demand of East Bengal to recognize Bengali as one of the state languages of Pakistan culminated in the tragic events of 21 February 1952.' K.M. Mohsin, 'Trends of Islam in Bangladesh,' in R. Ahmed (ed), *Islam in Bangladesh. Society, Culture and Politics* (Dhaka, 1983), pp. 227–8.
19. T. Maniruzzaman, 'Bangladesh Politics: Secular and Islamic Trends', in Ahmed (ed.), ibid., p. 193.
20. Maniruzzaman, ibid., pp. 194–7.
21. Mohsin, 'Trends of Islam in Bangladesh', pp. 233ff.

Contributors

Javeed Alam is Professor at the Centre for European Studies, Central Institute of English and Foreign Languages, Osmania University, Hyderabad.

Kate Brittlebank is Lecturer at the School of History and Classics, University of Tasmania, Australia.

I.J. Catanach is Emeritus Professor at the School of History, University of Canterbury, New Zealand.

Ian Copland is Associate Professor at the School of Historical Studies, Monash University, Australia.

Adeel Khan is Lecturer in Health Sociology at the School of Health, University of New England, Australia.

Dominique-Sila Khan holds doctorates in Literature and Anthropology from the Sorbonne University in Paris. She is currently working as an independent researcher in Jaipur, associated with the Institute of Rajasthan Studies, specializing in hindu–muslim interactions in South Asia.

W.H. McLeod is Emeritus Professor at the Department of History, University of Otago, New Zealand.

Zawahir Moir is associated with the Research Program at the Institute of Ismaili Studies, London and also the School of Oriental and African Studies, London.

Asim Roy is Honorary Fellow at the School of History and Classics, University of Tasmania, Australia. Formerly, he was Director of the Asia Centre in the same University.

Francis Robinson is Professor of the History of South Asia, Royal Holloway, University of London, U.K.

Samina Yasmeen is Senior Lecturer in Political Science and International Relations and Director of the Centre for Muslim States and Societies at the School of Social and Cultural Studies, University of Western Australia, Australia.